SPIRITUAL
& DEMONIC
MAGIC

MAGIC IN HISTORY

SPIRITUAL & DEMONIC MAGIC

from Ficino to Campanella

D.P. WALKER

THE PENNSYLVANIA STATE UNIVERSITY PRESS
UNIVERSITY PARK, PENNSYLVANIA

Copyright © G. & G.T.V. Gush, 2000
Introduction © Brian P. Copenhaver, 2000

Published in 2000 in the United States of America and Canada
The Pennsylvania State University Press, University Park, PA 16802

Second printing, 2003

First published as volume 22 of Studies of the Warburg Institute,
The Warburg Institute, University of London, 1958

ISBN 978-0-271-02045-7

Library of Congress Cataloging in Publication Data
A CIP catalog record for the book is available from the Library of Congress

*Cover illustration: Saturn with the zodiac signs of Aquarius and Capricorn
(Bridgeman Art Library/Biblioteca Estense, Modena)*

Printed in the United States of America

CONTENTS

FOREWORD

The first chapter of this book consists largely of two articles of mine, "Ficino's Spiritus and Music", published in *Annales Musicologiques*, 1953, and "Le Chant Orphique de Marsile Ficin", published in *Musique et Poésie au XVIe siècle* (in the collection: *Le Choeur des Muses*), 1954; the publishers of these two volumes, the *Société de la Musique d'autrefois* and the *Centre National de la Recherche Scientifique*, have kindly given me permission to reproduce these two articles. The rest of the book was written during my time as a Fellow of the Warburg Institute. I wish to express my thanks to the members of this institute, and especially to Miss Frances Yates and Professor Bing, who have given me invaluable help and encouragement.

October 1956.   D. P. WALKER

INTRODUCTION

D.P. WALKER AND THE THEORY OF MAGIC IN THE RENAISSANCE

Aby Warburg, whose remarkable library in Hamburg became the core of the Warburg Institute of the University of London, shaped twentieth-century scholarship more than the small volume of his finished work might suggest. Warburg's influence on cultural history was especially profound, and – long before the study of magic had become fashionable or even reputable – he identified magic as a core problem in the development of Western culture. Thus, when Daniel Pickering Walker's *Spiritual and Demonic Magic* appeared in 1958 as volume 22 of the Studies of the Warburg Library, it advanced a program of research initiated by Warburg himself.

Walker had been a Senior Research Fellow at the Warburg in 1953 but was not elected to a permanent appointment there until 1961. He held the Warburg's Chair in the History of the Classical Tradition from 1975 until he retired in 1981, after which he remained active during the four years before his death in 1985. Before coming permanently to the Warburg, Walker's work at University College, London grew out of his student research at Oxford on musical humanism, mainly French, a topic on which he began to publish in the early 40s. This early musicological material has been collected by Penelope Gouk in *Music, Spirit and Language in the Renaissance* (London, Variorum, 1985). His first important study of magic, 'Orpheus the Theologian and Renaissance Platonists,' appeared in the *Journal of the Warburg and Courtauld Institutes* in 1953.

Five years later Walker finished *Spiritual and Demonic Magic from Ficino to Campanella*, a ground-breaking book that remains the basis of contemporary scholarly understanding of the theory of magic in post-medieval Europe. His previous career in musicology laid the foundations for its first chapter, on 'Ficino and Music.' Walker's technical and practical understanding of music enabled him to see how this art provided an important part of a physical theory of magic, and he had come to see that renaissance magicians, since they were pious Christians, needed such a theory if they were to make claims for a natural magic, as distinct from the demonic magic that all good Christians must renounce. His key insight about music was that its physical medium, air, resembled what the Stoics and other ancient thinkers had called *pneuma* in Greek, *spiritus* in Latin, and had often used as the conceptual link between lightly embodied spiritual substances (like the lower soul) and highly rarefied material substances (like the smoke of sacrifices). Since the strings of a lyre could be made to resonate with the cosmic tones of the planets and stars, the magus could communicate with these higher powers through this magical medium

Thus, long before 'theory' became a common calling of humanist scholars, Walker was able to show that belief in magic on the part of educated Europeans was not simply habitual or traditional; he identified and described its theoretical foundations. Walker's demonstration that there was such a thing as a theory of magic in renaissance Europe was critical for two reasons: first, magic had usually been treated as something 'primitive' and hence non-theoretical; second, the philosophical theory of magic reached one of its two high points in the period studied by Walker (the other having been in late antiquity). Warburg had been aware of both these facts – obsessed by them, in fact, because he feared that human culture oscillates perpetually between a primitive magical reflex and the refined theorizing that opposed but could never overcome it. Walker showed how very refined such theorizing became in the renaissance.

The title of Walker's book points to one of the main theoretical distinctions elaborated by students of magic in that period: he distinguishes 'spiritual' from 'demonic' magic where others have used the terminology of 'demonic' and 'natural,' but the polarity is the same. In some cases, when magicians cause strange effects by calling on the aid of non-human persons, the magic is 'demonic'; in others, when strange effects come from manipulating physical objects rather than conversing with persons, the magic is 'natural' or 'spiritual.' Walker chose the latter term because Marsilio Ficino's theory of magic, his starting point, depended on *spiritus*. He also saw that magic might qualify as non-demonic and hence natural (or spiritual) if the music were non-verbal; the musician who plays his lyre to a higher heavenly power without singing could not be accused of invoking a demon. Invocation is inverted prayer; both require the sending of verbal messages between persons. Walker also realized, however, that Ficino's magical music probably included words – the Orphic hymns – and that additional refinements of the theory would be needed to protect the Orphic songs.

These distinctions and others – natural/demonic, verbal/non-verbal, transitive/intransitive – are the elements of the theory that Walker discovered in the prominent early modern thinkers that he discusses, most of all Ficino. He explored Ficino's Neoplatonic sources, Plotinus especially, and also noted the importance of the 'god-making' passages of the Hermetic *Asclepius*. He related Ficino's magic to the ideas of his predecessors, contemporaries and disciples – Pletho, Giovanni Pico, Lazarelli, Diacetto – and also traced its influence through Agrippa, Campanella, Giorgi, Paolini, Paracelsus and other later figures. His comments on Pietro Pomponazzi and Thomas Erastus are especially important for the contrast that they offer to Ficino's theory. Although Ficino wanted a natural magic, he left himself prey to the demons through his Orphic singing. Pomponazzi's response, motivated by his fidelity to Aristotelian natural philosophy, was to exclude the demons entirely, as a matter of philosophical principle, leaving only the physical channels of *spiritus*, imagination and occult qualities to explain magical effects. If Pomponazzi's magic was entirely natural, Erasmus insisted that it was altogether demonic, removing astral influence from its usual role in producing occult qualities and replacing the stars with the God who created them.

Before Walker clarified all this in little more than two hundred pages of clear, simple, sometimes reticent prose, Anglophone readers curious about the history of magic depended mainly on the copious, learned but tendentious eight volumes of the *History of Magic and Experimental Science* by Lynn Thorndike. Thorndike's polemical chapters on Ficino, Pico and other figures studied by Walker are hostile to the concept of a renaissance in European history and contemptuous of that period's most eminent thinkers. Walker's approach is, on the one hand, fairer to the renaissance but, on the other hand, startlingly innovative in taking magic seriously as a feature of European high culture.

Guided by Warburg's approach to the transmission of classical high culture, Walker was well equipped to understand how Ficino, Pico and others had integrated their interest in magic into their humanist classicism, depending on the latter to legitimate the former. Although Eugenio Garin had long since established this for Italian scholars, in Anglo-American scholarship it was Walker who put magic on the same plane with other issues of central concern to renaissance humanists, thus preparing the way for Frances Yates's epochal work on *Giordano Bruno and the Hermetic Tradition* a few years later, in 1964. Because of what Walker and Yates wrote in the late 50s and early 60s, early modern occultism began to attract more and more attention and eventually emerged as a key problem in early modern European cultural history.

Because of its initial celebrity and the debate on the Hermetic tradition in literature and science that it kindled, more people know Yates's *Bruno* than Walker's *Magic*, but of the two it is Walker's book which has better stood the test of time and learned criticism. It has been and is to be treasured by scholars and students of cultural and intellectual history, history of science, history of philosophy, art history, literature, religious studies and other fields.

BRIAN P. COPENHAVER
UCLA
November 1999

BIBLIOGRAPHY

Copenhaver, Brian P., 'Scholastic Philosophy and Renaissance Magic in the *De vita* of Marsilio Ficino,' *Renaissance Quarterly*, 37 (1984)

——, 'Astrology and Magic,' in *The Cambridge History of Renaissance Philosophy*, ed. Charles Schmitt and Quentin Skinner (Cambridge, Cambridge University Press, 1987)

——, 'Hermes Trismegistus, Proclus and the Question of a Philosophy of Magic in the Renaissance,' in *Hermeticism and the Renaissance: Intellectual History and the Occult in Early Modern Europe*, eds. I. Merkel and A. Debus (Washington, D.C., Folger Books, 1988)

——, 'Natural Magic, Hermetism and Occultism in Early Modern Science,' in *Reappraisals of the Scientific Revolution*, eds. D. Lindberg and R. Westman (Cambridge, Cambridge University Press, 1990)

——, *Hermetica: The Greek Corpus Hermeticum and the Latin Asclepius in English Translation, with Notes and Introduction* (Cambridge, Cambridge University Press, 1995)

——, 'The Occultist Tradition and its Critics in Seventeenth Century Philosophy,' in *The Cambridge History of Seventeenth Century Philosophy*, eds. M. Ayers and D. Garber (Cambridge, Cambridge University Press, 1998)

Screech, Michael, 'Daniel Pickering Walker,' *Proceedings of the British Academy*, 72 (1986): 501–9

Walker, D.P., 'The Astral Body in Renaissance Medicine,' *Journal of the Warburg and Courtauld Institutes*, 1958: 119–33

——, *The Decline of Hell: Seventeenth Century Discussions of Eternal Torment* (Chicago, University of Chicago Press, 1964)

——, *The Ancient Theology: Studies in Christian Platonism from the Fifteenth to the Eighteenth Century* (London, Duckworth, 1972)

——, *Unclean Spirits: Possession and Exorcism in France and England in the Late Sixteenth and Early Seventeenth Centuries* (Philadelphia, University of Pennsylvania Press, 1981)

——, 'Valentine Greatrakes, the Irish Stroker, and the Question of Miracles,' in P.G. Castex, ed., *Mélanges sur la littérature de la renaissance à la mémoire de V.L. Saulnier* (Geneva, Droz, 1984), pp. 343–56

——, *Il concetto di spirito o anima in Henry More e Ralph Cudworth*, 'Lezioni della Scuola di Studi Superiori in Napoli, 5' (Naples, Bibliopolis, 1986)

PART I

CHAPTER I. FICINO AND MUSIC

(1) Ficino's Music-Spirit Theory

Of the three Books of Ficino's *De Triplici Vita*[1] the first deals with preserving the health of scholars, the second with prolonging their life, and the third with astral influences on them (*De Vita coelitùs comparanda*)[2]. Through all three, Ficino's attention is devoted not so much to man's soul or body as to his *spiritus*. What this term meant for him may, I hope, appear more fully later; for the moment it will do to quote the definition he gives near the beginning of his treatise. Soldiers, says Ficino, care for their arms, musicians for their instruments, hunters for their hounds,

> only the priests of the Muses, only the hunters after the supreme good and truth are so negligent (alas) and so unfortunate that they seem utterly to neglect that instrument by which they can, in a way, measure and grasp the whole world. An instrument of this sort is the spirit, which by the physicians is defined as a certain vapour of the blood, pure, subtle, hot and lucid. And, formed from the subtler blood by the heat of the heart, it flies to the brain, and there the soul assiduously employs it for the exercise of both the interior and exterior senses. Thus the blood serves the spirit, the spirit the senses, and finally the senses reason.[3]

---

[1] Florence, 1489; Ficino, *Opera Omnia*, Basileae, 1576, p. 493.

[2] This title might mean either "on obtaining life from the heavens", or "on instituting one's life celestially"; in view of Ficino's fondness for puns, it probably means both. Ficino, in the dedication of this Book (*Op. Omn.*, p. 529), says that it is a commentary on "librum Plotini de favore coelitùs hauriendo tractantem". Kristeller (*Supplementum Ficinianum*, Florence, 1937, I, lxxxiv) states that this "liber Plotini" is *Ennead*, IV, iii, 11, because in one ms. the *De Vita Coel. Comp.* appears among the commentaries on Plotinus in this place. It seems to me perhaps more likely that it is *Enn.*, IV, iv, of which c. 30-42 deal with astral influence in much greater detail.

[3] Ficino, *Op. Omn.*, p. 496 (*De Tr. V.*, I, ii): "Soli verò Musarum sacerdotes, soli summi boni veritatisque venatores, tam negligentes (proh nefas) tamque infortunati sunt, ut instrumentum illud, quo mundum universum metiri quodammodo

This seems to be a deliberate limitation of the meaning of *spiritus* to a normal, medical sense: it is a corporeal vapour, centred in the brain and flowing through the nervous system; it is the first instrument of the incorporeal soul, an instrument for sense-perception, imagination and motor-activity—the link between body and soul [1]. For now, then, let it remain something like the "esprits" of Descartes' *Traité des Passions* [2], with which most modern readers will be familiar.

The spirit of the studious is especially likely to need care, because their constant use of it in thinking and imagining consumes it. It has to be replaced from the subtler part of the blood, and this renders the remaining blood dense, dry and black [3]. In consequence such persons are always of a melancholy temperament [4]. The spirits which derive from a melancholy humour (black bile) are exceptionally fine, hot, agile and combustible, like brandy [5]. They are, therefore, liable to ignite and produce a temporary state of mania or exaltation, followed by extreme depression and lethargy, caused by the black smoke left after the fire. If, however, melancholy is properly tempered with a little phlegm and bile, and a lot of blood, then the spirits will glow, not burn [6], and make possible continuous study of the highest order. These extremes of madness and stupidity, or of contem-

& capere possunt, negligere penitus videntur. Instrumentum eiusmodi spiritus ipse est, qui apud medicos vapor quidam sanguinis, purus, subtilis, calidus & lucidus definitur. Atque ab ipso cordis calore, ex subtiliori sanguine procreatus volat ad cerebrum, ibique animus ad sensus tam interiores, quàm exteriores exercendos assiduè utitur. Quamobrem sanguis spiritui servit, spiritus sensibus, sensus denique rationi."

[1] I know of no modern work on mediaeval and Renaissance pneumatology. Good starting-points for the former would be Costa ben Luca's *De Animae & Spiritus discrimine* (usually attributed to Constantinus Africanus, *Opera*, Basileae, 1536, p. 308) and Albertus Magnus, *De Spiritu & Respiratione* (*Op. Omn.*, ed. Borgnet, Vol. IX, Paris, 1890, p. 213); for the latter, Fernel, *Physiologia* Lib. IV (*Medicina*, Paris, 1554, p. 102), and Bertacchi, *De Spiritibus*, Venetiis, 1584. For ancient sources, see G. Verbeke, *L'Évolution de la doctrine du Pneuma du Stoïcisme à S.Augustin*, Paris, 1945, pp. 206-212 & passim.

[2] Descartes, *Les Passions de l'Ame*, Paris, 1649, art. 8 seq.

[3] Ficino, *Op. Omn.*, p. 497 (*De Tr. V.*, I, iv).

[4] Ibid.; cf. Panofsky & Saxl, *Dürer's 'Melencolia I'*, Berlin, 1923 (*Studien der Bibl. Warburg*, II).

[5] Ficino, *Op. Omn.*, p. 498 (*De Tr. V.*, I, vi).

[6] Ibid., pp. 497-8 (I, v).

plative genius, are of course connected with the ambivalent influence of the planet Saturn, to which melancholics are subject [1]; hence, as we shall see, the importance for scholars of attracting the influence of the benign planets: the Sun, Jupiter, Venus and Mercury.

To preserve the health of the spirit and to avoid the perils of melancholy Ficino gives detailed advice on diet and régime [2]. For nourishing and purifying the spirit he concentrates on three types of things: wine and aromatic foods, odours and pure, sunny air, and music [3]. These are sometimes made to correspond to the threefold division of the spirits into natural, vital and animal [4]. But Ficino does not work out these distinctions in detail, nor employ them consistently. Of the three types of nourishment music seems to be considered the most important, and its action is said to be on either or both of the two higher kinds of spirit, vital or animal. After recommending the use of wine, incense, aromatic herbs and so forth, he writes:

finally, if the vapours exhaled by merely vegetable life are greatly beneficial to your life, how beneficial do you think will be aerial songs to the spirit which is indeed entirely aerial, harmonic songs to the harmonic spirit, warm and thus living to the living, endowed with sense to the sensitive, conceived by reason to the rational [5]?

[1] See Panofsky & Saxl, op. cit., pp. 3-14, 25 seq., 32-47, & App. IV.

[2] e.g. *Op. Omn.*, p. 499 (*De Tr. V.*, I, vii, "Quinque praecipuè studiosorum hostes: Pituita, Atra bilis, Coitus, Satietas, Matutinus Somnus"); 501 (I, x, list of foods); 505-8 (I, xviii-xxiii, recipes for remedies against melancholy).

[3] e.g. *Op. Omn.*, p. 502 (I, x): "Nihil autem adversus hanc pestem [sc. melancholiam] valentius est, quàm vinum leve, clarum, suave, odorum, ad spiritus prae ceteris perspicuos generandos aptissimum . . . Tenendus ore hyancinthus, qui animum vehementer exhilarat"; 525 (II, xviii): "cuius [sc. spiritus animalis] quidem qualitas maximi momenti est ingeniosis, eiusmodi spiritus plurimum laborantibus. Itaque ad nullos potius quàm ad eos attinet puri luminosique aëris, odorumque delectus, atque Musicae. Haec enim tria spiritus animalis fomenta praecipua judicantur"; 568 (III, xxiv).

[4] e.g. Ficino, *Op. Omn.*, p. 523 (*De Tr. V.*, II, xv), 546 (III, xi); cf. Avicenna, *De Medicinis Cordialibus*, Tract. I, c. i, 9, *Cantica*, lines 81-96 (Avicenna, *Liber Canonis*, Venetiis, 1582, fos 557 v, 560 r, 568 r); the first of these works, to which Ficino refers (ibid., p. 535, III, iv) gives similar directions for nourishing and comforting the *spiritus cordiales* (i.e. *vitales*), but does not mention music. On the origins of the triple *spiritus* see Verbeke, op. cit., pp. 77 (Chrysippus), 192 (Pneumatic School), 206 (Galen).

[5] Ficino, *Op. Omn.*, p. 523 (*De Tr. V.*, II, xv): "Denique si vapores exhalantes

That is to say, the peculiar power of music is due to a similarity between the material medium in which it is transmitted, air, and the human spirit, to the fact that both are living kinds of air, moving in an highly organized way, and that both, through the text of the song, can carry an intellectual content.

We can get a clearer picture of this connexion from other writings of Ficino; for it is a theory which he expounded many times, and which he must have considered of great importance, since he even inserted it into his version of Iamblichus' *De Mysteriis* [1] and into an unavowed borrowing from St. Augustine's *De Musica* [2]. For example, in a letter to Antonio Canisiano, who had asked why he combined musical and medical studies, Ficino justifies himself by citing examples of the therapeutic power of music (beginning with the Biblical archetype: Saul and David), and goes on:

> Nor is this surprising; for, since song and sound arise from the cogitation of the mind, the impetus of the phantasy [3], and the feeling of the heart, and, together with the air they have broken up and tempered, strike the aerial spirit of the hearer, which is the junction of the soul and body, they easily move the phantasy, affect the heart and penetrate into the deep recesses of the mind [4].

It is in fact not surprising that a song, being the product of mind, imagination and feeling, should, if transmitted, react on

ex vita duntaxat vegetali magnopere vitae vestrae prosunt, quantum profuturos existimatis cantus aerios, quidem spiritu [read: spiritui, as in ed. of 1489] prorsus aerio, harmonicos harmonico, calentes adhuc vivos, vivo, sensu praeditos sensuali, ratione conceptos rationali?"

[1] Ibid., p. 1885, corresponding to Iamblichus, *De Myst.*, III, ix, x.

[2] Ibid., p. 178 (*Theologia Platonica*, VII, vi), from "Videtur mihi . . ." is quoted verbatim from Augustine, *De Musica*, VI, v, 10 (Migne, *Pat. Lat.*, 32, col. 1169). Cf. infra p. 7.

[3] On Ficino's use of this term, see Kristeller, *The Philosophy of Marsilio Ficino*, New York, 1943, pp. 235, 369 seq.; when distinguished from imagination, it is a higher faculty, which forms "intentions" (v. infra p. 10, note 1).

[4] Ficino, *Op. Omn.*, p. 651: "Neque mirum id quidem: nam quum cantus sonusque ex cogitatione mentis, & impetu phantasiae, cordisque affectu proficiscatur, atque una cum aere facto [read: fracto, as in Ficino, *Epistolae*, Venetiis, 1495, fo 24 v] & temperato, aereum audientis spiritum pulset, qui animae corporisque nodus est, facile phantasiam movet, afficitque cor & intima mentis penetralia penetrat". Cf. a very similar exposition (also in a medical context) in another letter, *Op. Omn.*, p. 609.

these faculties, just as a book or a picture might. The point which Ficino always emphasizes is that music has a stronger effect than anything transmitted through the other senses, because its medium, air, is of the same kind as the spirit. This needs some explanation, since in most psychologies employing the concept of spirit, and often in Ficino's, *all* sensation is by means of the spirit, and the media of all sense-data are some kind of spirit [1]. It is easy enough to see why the three lower senses (taste, smell, touch) are inferior to hearing; they cannot transmit an intellectual content, which music can do, owing to its text. We are left then with sight. There are two possible reasons why Ficino considered that visual impressions had a less powerful effect on the spirit than auditive ones—less powerful, though not necessarily lower in the hierarchy of the senses; indeed, it is precisely because hearing is not the highest, most intellectual sense that it affects more stongly the whole of the man[2].

First, Ficino sometimes adopts a theory of sensation according to which the sense-organ is of the same substance as what is sensed. In this scheme the eye contains something luminous ("luminosum aliquid")[3], or, with Aristotle, water, which being transparent is potentially luminous [4]; whereas the ear contains air, set deep within it so that it is untroubled by ordinary aerial disturbances [5]. When Ficino is copying out Augustine's exposition of this theory, in which the term *spiritus* is not used, he identifies this air in the ear with the spirit, substituting "aereus auris

[1] Ficino, *Op. Omn.*, p. 177 (*Theol. Plat.*, VII, vi), 212 (ibid., IX, v); cf. Verbeke, op. cit., pp. 32, 74-5, 212, 310, 501; Heitzman, "L'Agostinismo Avicenizzante e il punto di partenza di M. Ficino", *Giornale Critico della Filosofia Italiana*, 1935, pp. 306-9.

[2] Cf. infra p. 21. On the supremacy of sight, cf. Ficino, *Op. Omn.*, p. 1336 (*Comm. in Convivium*, Orat., V, c. ii, where the senses are associated with the elements, in descending order: sight—fire, hearing—air, smell—vapour, taste—water, touch—earth); E. Gombrich, "Botticelli's Mythologies", *Journal of the Warburg and Courtauld Institutes*, 1945, VIII, 20.

[3] Ficino and Augustine, loc. cit. supra p. 6 note (2); cf. Galen, *Dogm. Hipp. et Plat.*, VII, v (ed. Kühn, V, 627); Posidonius apud Sextum Empiricum, quoted by Verbeke, op. cit., pp. 133-4.

[4] Aristotle, *De Anima*, 424 b-425 a; *De sensu*, 438 b-439 a.

[5] Aristotle, *De Anima*, 420 a: "ὁ [sc. ἀήρ] δ'ἐν τοῖς ὡσὶν ἐγκατῳκοδόμηται πρὸς τὸ ἀκίνητος εἶναι, ὅπως ἀκριβῶς αἰσθάνηται πάσας τὰς διαφορὰς τῆς κινήσεως". Ficino and Augustine, loc. cit. supra, p. 6 note (2).

spiritus" for Augustine's "id quod in eo membro [sc. auribus] simile est aeri" [1]. Thus, whereas visual impressions have no direct contact with the spirit, but have to be transmitted to it by a sense-organ of another nature, sounds, being moving, animated air [2], combine directly with the *spiritus aereus* in the ear, and, without changing their nature, are not only conveyed to the soul but also affect the whole spirit, dispersed throughout the body.

But even this does not quite satisfactorily account for the peculiar difference between sight and hearing. For the spirit, especially in its higher kinds, is often thought to be of a nature more akin to light, fire or the *quinta essentia* of the heavens, than to air; and, as we shall see when dealing with the *De Vita coelitùs comparanda*, Ficino did perhaps sometimes think the human spirit was of this kind [3]. In this case, it would be of the same nature as the medium of light.

The second, more fundamental reason why sound affects the spirit more strongly than sight is because it transmits movement and is itself moving; whereas sight is conceived as transmitting only static images. The following passage from Ficino's commentary on the *Timaeus* explains this quite fully, and may be taken as his own opinion, since it owes little or nothing to Plato [4]. He asks why Plato said the soul was similar to musical consonance [5], rather than to any harmoniously composed object perceived by other senses, and answers:

Musical consonance occurs in the element which is the mean of all

[1] Ibid.

[2] Cf. infra p. 10.

[3] Cf. infra p. 13 note 1, 38.

[4] The conception of the peculiar penetration of sound may, as Hutton ("Some English Poems in Praise of Music", *English Miscellany*, 2, ed. Mario Praz, Rome, 1951, p. 21) suggests, owe something to the short passage on hearing in the *Timaeus* (67 a): "Sound we may define in general terms as the stroke inflicted by air on the brain and blood through the ears and passed on to the soul; while the motion it causes, starting in the head and ending in the region of the liver, is hearing" (trans. F. M. Cornford, *Plato's Cosmology*, London, 1937, p. 275; cf. pp. 320 seq.), contrasted with the passage on sight (*Timaeus*, 45 b; Cornford, pp. 152 seq.). Cf. *Timaeus Locrus*, 101 a, passage corresponding to *Timaeus* 67 a, but ending: "ἐν αὖ τούτοις]sc. ὠσὶν] πνεῦμα, οὗ ἁ κίνασις ἀκουά ἐστί."

[5] Ficino is referring to the division of the *anima mundi* into harmonic intervals (*Timaeus*, 35 b-36 b).

[i.e. air], and reaches the ears through motion, spherical motion: so that it is not surprising that it should be fitting to the soul, which is both the mean of things [1], and the origin of circular motion [2]. In addition, musical sound, more than anything else perceived by the senses, conveys, as if animated, the emotions and thoughts of the singer's or player's soul to the listeners' souls; thus it preeminently corresponds with the soul. Moreover, as regards sight, although visual impressions are in a way pure, yet they lack the effectiveness of motion, and are usually perceived only as an image, without reality; normally therefore, they move the soul only slightly. Smell, taste and touch are entirely material, and rather titillate the sense-organs than penetrate the depths of the soul. But musical sound by the movement of the air moves the body: by purified air it excites the aerial spirit which is the bond of body and soul: by emotion it affects the senses and at the same time the soul: by meaning it works on the mind: finally, by the very movement of the subtle air it penetrates strongly: by its contemperation it flows smoothly: by the conformity of its quality it floods us with a wonderful pleasure: by its nature, both spiritual and material, it at once seizes, and claims as its own, man in his entirety [3].

Hearing, then, both puts us in more direct contact with external reality, since sound consists of aerial movements which can actually occur in our spirit, whereas sight merely reproduces

---

[1] This is a fundamental tenet in Ficino's (and other Renaissance Platonists') philosophy; cf. Kristeller, *Philos. of M. F.*, pp. 106 seq, 120.

[2] The circular motion of the soul may also come directly from the *Timaeus*, 36 b seq. (*anima mundi*), 43 a seq. (human soul).

[3] Ficino, *Op. Omn.*, p. 1453 (*Comm. in Tim.*, c. xxviii): "Respondetur ad haec: Musicam consonantiam in elemento fieri omnium medio, perque motum, & hunc quidem orbicularem ad aures provenire: ut non mirum sit eam animae convenire, tum mediae rerum, tum motionis principio in circuitu revolubili. Adde quod concentus potissimum inter illa quae sentiuntur quasi animatus, affectum sensuumque cogitationem animae, sive canentis, sive sonantis, perfert in animos audientes: ideoque in primis cum animo congruit. Praeterea quae ad visum quidem spectant, & si pura quodammodo sunt, tamen absque motionis efficacia, & per imaginem solam absque rei natura saepius apprehenduntur: ideo parum movere animos solent. Quae vero ad olfactum, gustum, tactum, quasi valde materialia, potius instrumenta sensuum titillant, quàm animi intima penetrent. Concentus autem per aeream naturam in motu positam movet corpus: per purificatum aerem concitat spiritum aereum animae corporisque nodum: per affectum, afficit sensum simul & animum: per significationem, agit in mentem: denique per ipsum subtilis aeris motum, penetrat vehementer: per contemperationem lambit suaviter: per conformem qualitatem mira quadam voluptate perfundit: per naturam, tàm spiritalem quàm materialem, totum simul rapit & sibi vindicat hominem." Cf. ibid., p. 1885 (Ficino's version of Iamblichus, *De Myst.*), where the same comparison between hearing and the other senses occurs.

surface-images of things; and it powerfully affects the whole of us—the musical sound by working on the spirit, which links body and soul, and the text by working on the mind or intellect. The power of this effect is due to sound being movement, whereas vision is static. Now man's whole moral and emotional life consists of actions of the body and motions of the spirit and soul, and these can be imitated in music and transmitted by it. Ficino writes in the *De Vita coelitùs comparanda*:

Remember that song is the most powerful imitator of all things. For it imitates the intentions [1] and affections of the soul, and speech, and also reproduces bodily gestures, human movements and moral characters, and imitates and acts everything so powerfully that it immediately provokes both the singer and hearer to imitate and perform the same things [2].

The matter of song, he continues, is "warm air, even breathing, and in a measure living, made up of articulated limbs, like an animal, not only bearing movement and emotion, but even signification, like a mind, so that it can be said to be, as it were, a kind of aerial and rational animal." Musically moved air is alive, like a disembodied human spirit [3], and therefore naturally has the most powerful effect possible on the hearer's spirit.

One likely source for this distinction between hearing and other senses is the Ps. Aristotle *Problems*, which Ficino was probably reading at this time, since one of them is the starting-point of the whole theory of melancholy in the *De Triplici*

---

[1] "Intentiones" probably in the scholastic sense of the first stage of universal-ization from sense-impressions; cf. Kristeller, *Phil. of M. F.*, p. 235.

[2] Ficino, *Op. Omn.*, p. 563 (*De Tr. V.*, III, xxi): "Momento verò cantum esse imitatorem omnium potentissimum. Hic enim intentiones affectionesque animi imitatur, & verba, refert quoque gestus motusque corporis, & actus hominum, atque mores, tamque vehementer omnia imitatur, & agit, ut ad eadem imitanda, vel agenda, tum cantantem, tum audientes subito provocet . . . materia ipsa concentus purior est admodum, coeloque similior, quam materia medicine. Est enim aer etiam hic quidem calens, sive tepens, spirans adhuc, & quodammodo vivens, suis quibus-dam articulis artubusque compositus, sicut animal, nec solum motum ferens, affect-umque praeferens, verùm etiam significatum efferens quasi mentem, ut animal quoddam aëreum & rationale quodammodo dici possit. Concentus igitur spiritu sensuqe plenus . . . virtutem . . . trajicit in cantantem, atque ex hoc in proximum audientem . . ."; cf. ibid., p. 234 (*Theol. Plat.*, X, vii).

[3] Ibid.: "Cantus . . . fermè nihil aliud est quàm spiritus alter".

Vita[1]. Two of the Problems 'on music discuss shortly the questions: "Why is hearing the only perception which affects the moral character?"; "Why are rhythms and melodies, which are sounds, similar to moral characters, while flavours, colours and scents are not?"[2]. The answer in both cases is that sound, alone of things sensed, has movements; movements and actions are of the same nature, and actions have a moral character (ἦθος) or are symptomatic of it[3].

[1] Ps. Aristotle, *Problems*, XXX, 1. Cf. Panofsky & Saxl, op. cit., pp. 33 seq., 93 seq. (where this Problem is quoted in full).

[2] Aristotle, *Problems*, XXX, 27, 29.

[3] Ibid., XIX, 29: "ἢ ὅτι κινησεις εἶσιν [sc. ῥυθμοὶ καὶ μέλη] ὥσπερ καὶ αἱ πράξεις; ἤδη δὲ μὲν ἐνέργεια ἠθικὸν καὶ ποεῖ ἦθος, οἱ δὲ χυμοὶ καὶ τὰ χρώματα οὐ ποιοῦσιν ὁμοίως". On other classical sources for the ethical power of music, see D. P. Walker, "Musical Humanism in the 16th and early 17th centuries", *Music Review*, 1941-2, II, pp. 9 seq.; Hermann Abert, *Die Lehre vom Ethos in der Griechischen Musik*, Leipzig ,1899, pp. 48-9 & passim.

(2) FICINO'S ASTROLOGICAL MUSIC

The last Book of the *De Triplici Vita*, *De Vita coelitùs comparanda*, deals with astrological matters, especially with methods of tempering the melancholic influence of Saturn by attracting the benign influences of Jupiter, Venus, Mercury and, above all, the Sun. In spite of Ficino's somewhat vacillating attitude toward astrology [1], it can be stated: first, that he believed earnestly in the reality and importance of astral influences; secondly, that as a Catholic he could not openly accept an astrological determinism which included the soul and mind [2]. On this view, the highest part of man which could be directly influenced by the stars was the spirit.

But in the *De Vita coelitùs comparandu* the concept of spirit is plainly widened far beyond the bounds of its technical medical meaning. Ficino here accepts a theory of astrological influence, ultimately Stoic in origin, which postulates a cosmic spirit (*spiritus mundi*), flowing through the whole of the sensible universe, and thus providing a channel of influence between the heavenly bodies and the sublunar world [3]. Since the world, as in Plato and Plotinus [4], is one animal, its soul, like ours, must have a "first instrument" which transmits its powers to its body. This mean between the *anima* and *corpus mundi*, though analogous to our spirit, is not, says Ficino, made like ours out of the four

---

[1] Cf. Kristeller, *Phil. of. M. F.*, pp. 310 seq.; E. Garin, "Recenti Interpretazioni di Marsilio Ficino", *Giorn. crit. d. fil. ital.*, 1940, pp. 315 seq.

[2] Cf. Ficino's unpublished *Disputatio contra Iudicium Astrologorum* (Kristeller, *Suppl. Fic.* II, ll seq.; written in 1477 (v. ibid., I, cxl)), which is mainly concerned with safe-guarding man's freedom.

[3] Cf. Panofsky & Saxl, op. cit., p. 41; Verbeke, op. cit., pp. 11 seq. (Chapter on Stoicism); more important sources for Ficino are probably Neoplatonic and Hermetic, cf. infra pp. 36 seq.

[4] Plato, *Timaeus*, 30 c-31 a; Plotinus, *Enn.*, IV, iv, 32.

humours (and ultimately the four elements) [1], but may properly be called the fifth element, *quinta essentia* [2], i.e. the Aristotelian substance of the heavens, incorruptible "aether"; but it also contains the powers of the lower four elements, so that it can and does enter into ordinary sub-lunar bodies. This cosmic spirit, says Ficino [3]:

is a very subtle body; as it were not body and almost soul. Or again, as it were not soul and almost body. Its power contains very little earthy nature, but more watery, still more aerial and the maximum of fiery and starry nature ... It vivifies everything everywhere and is the imme- diate cause of all generation and motion; of which he [Virgil] says: "Spiritus intus alit ..." [4].

This cosmic spirit, which is also that of the alchemists [5], is like enough to ours for us to be able to nourish and purify our own spirit by attracting and absorbing it. "Undoubtedly the world lives and breathes, and we may absorb its breath (*spiritus*)" by means of our spirit, especially if we render this even more similar than it already is by nature to the *spiritus mundi*, "that is, if it becomes as celestial as possible" [6]. There are various ways of doing this. You may consume things which contain an abund- ance of pure cosmic spirit, such as wine, very white sugar, gold, the scent of cinnamon or roses [7]. To attract the "spiritual"

---

[1] Ficino, *Op. Omn.*, p. 535 (*De Tr. V.*, III, iii). Ficino is somewhat inconsistent about the substance of the human spirit; elsewhere it appears to be made of something like the quintessence (cf. next note), or the aether of the Neoplatonic vehicle of the soul (v. infra p. 38). In the *Theol. Plat.* (VII, vi, *Op. Omn.*, p. 177) e.g. he describes it as "tenuissimum quoddam lucidissimumque corpusculum".

[2] Aristotle, *De Caelo*, I, 2, 3. For Aristotle this was also the nature of man's innate spirit (*De Gen. Anim.*, II, 3, 736 b).

[3] *Op. Omn.*, p. 535 (*De Tr. V.*, III, iii): "Ipse verò est corpus tenuissimum, quasi non corpus, & jam anima. Item quasi non anima, & quasi jam corpus. In eius virtute minimum est naturae terrenae, plus autem aquae, plus item aëriae, rursus igneae stellaris quamplurimum ... Ipse verò ubique viget in omnibus generationis omnis proximus author atque motus, de quo ille: Spiritus intus alit ..."

[4] Virgil, *Aeneid*, VI, 726; cf. Ficino, *Op. Omn.*, p. 612, where this passage is quoted as referring to the Orphic Jupiter, equated with the *anima mundi*, and infra pp. 128-9.

[5] See F. Sherwood Taylor, *The Alchemists*, London, 1951, p. 11 seq. & passim.

[6] Ficino, *Op. Omn.*, p. 534 (*De Tr. V.*, III, iii, entitled: "Quod inter animam mundi et corpus eius manifestum, sit spiritus eius, in cuius virtute sunt quatuor elementa. Et quod nos per spiritum nostrum hunc possimus haurire"), p. 535 (III, iv).

[7] Ibid., p. 532 (III, i).

influence of a particular planet you may use animals, plants, people, subject to that planet—as food, scents, acquaintances; Ficino gives lists of these for the Sun and Jupiter [1]. You may perhaps use talismans (*imagines*); he is extremely worried and hesitant about these, but devotes a great deal of space to them [2]. Finally, you must use music fitted to the planet. Here again, it is music which is recommended most strongly.

The effectiveness of music for capturing planetary or celestial spirit rests on two principles, which ultimately connect. The first is the ancient and persistent theory, deriving from Plato's *Timaeus* or the Pythagoreans before him, that both the universe and man, the macrocosm and microcosm, are constructed on the same harmonic proportions [3]; that there is a music of the spheres, *musica mundana*, of man's body, spirit and soul, *musica humana*, of voices and instruments, *musica instrumentalis* [4]. Thus the use of anything having the same numerical proportions as a certain heavenly body or sphere will make your spirit similarly proportioned and provoke the required influx of celestial spirit, just as a vibrating string will make another, tuned to the same or a consonant note, vibrate in sympathy [5]. Ficino, in the *De Vita coelitùs comparanda*, refers several times to this theory [6], and applies it not only to music, but also to foods, medicines, talismans, etc. For example, when discussing the figures engraved on talismans, he writes [7]:

---

[1] Ibid., pp. 352-3; but "quomodo verò virtus Veneris attrahatur turturibus, columbis & motacillis [water-wagtails], & reliquis, non permittit pudor ostendere".

[2] e.g. *Op. Omn.*, p. 530 (*Ad Lectorem* of *De Tr. V.*, III), pp. 548-561 (III, xiii-xx). Cf. infra p. 42-3, 53.

[3] This is a vast subject; some of the main sources used in the Renaissance will be found in Hutton, op cit.; cf. infra pp. 81, 115 seq.

[4] These terms seem to originate with Boetius (v. Hutton, op. cit., p. 17).

[5] Ficino, *Op. Omn.*, p. 555 (*De Tr. V.*, III, xvii), 563 (III, xxi); a normal image in any exposition of universal magic sympathy, cf. e.g. Plotinus, *Enn.*, IV, iv, 41; Synesius, *De Insomn.*, Migne, *Pat. Gr.*, 66, col. 1285 b (Ficino trans., *Op. Omn.*, p. 1969). Since Ficino says the *De V.c.c.* is a commentary on Plotinus (v. supra p. 3 note (2)), *Enn.*, IV, iv, 30-44 is probably one immediate source of this theory of planetary influence, though there is little mention of spirit in this Ennead.

[6] E.g. *Op. Omn.*, p. 546 (*De Tr. V.*, III, xii), 564 (III, xxii); cf. ibid., pp. 1455 seq. (*Comm. in Tim.*).

[7] Ficino, *Op. Omn.*, p. 555 (*De Tr. V.*, III, xvii): "Non ignoras concentus per

You know that musical sound, by its numbers and proportions, has a marvellous power to sustain, move and affect the spirit, soul and body. But these proportions, made up of numbers, are, as it were kinds of figures, which are made of points and lines, but in motion. Similarly, celestial figures act by their movement; for these, by their harmonic rays and motions, which penetrate everything, constantly affect the spirit secretly, just as music does openly, in the most powerful way.

But, when Ficino comes to working out on this theory practical precepts for planetarily effective music, he finds himself in difficulties. In the long chapter devoted to astrological music [1], he gives a list of seven things by which celestial influences can be attracted [2]; they are, in ascending order:

1. Stones, metals, etc.   which pertain to the Moon
2. Plants, fruits, animals,   „   „   „ Mercury
3. Powders, vapours, odours,   „   „   „ Venus
4. Words, songs, sounds,   „   „   „ the Sun (Apollo, the mean of the seven)
5. Emotion, imagination [3],   „   „   „ Mars
6. Discursive reason,   „   „   „ Jupiter
7. Intellectual contemplation, divine intuition,   „   „   „ Saturn

He then continues [4]:

numeros proportionesque suas, vim habere mirabilem ad spiritum & animum & corpus sistendum, movendum, & afficiendum. Proportiones autem ex numeris constitutae, quasi figurae quaedam sunt, vel ex punctis lineisque factae, sed in motu. Similiter motu suo se habent ad agendum figurae coelestes, hae namque harmonicis, tùm radijs, tùm motibus suis omnia penetrantibus spiritum indies ita clam afficiunt, ut Musica praepotens palam afficere consuevit." The "figurae coelestes" are, I think, Plotinus' σχήματα (Enn., IV, iv, 34 seq.), i.e. patterns traced by the planets and constellations (cf. Ficino, ibid., pp. 531-2 (III, i)). Cf. Plotinus, Enn., IV, iv, 40 (Ficino, Comm. in Plot., Op. Omn., p. 1747), for music effecting "palam" what the stars do "clam".

[1] Ibid., p. 562 (III, xxi).
[2] "Quum verò septem Planetarum numero, septem quoque sint gradus, per quos à superioribus ad inferiora sit attractus, voces medium gradum obtinent, & Apollini dedicantur."
[3] "Vehementes imaginationis conceptus, formae, motus, affectus".
[4] Ibid.: "Quorsum haec? ut intelligas quemadmodum ex certa herbarum vaporumque compositione confecta, per artem tùm Medicam, tùm Astronomicam, resultat communis quaedam forma, velut harmonia quaedam siderum dotata muneribus. Sic ex tonis primò quidem ad stellarum normam electis, deinde ad earundem congruitatem inter se compositis, communem quasi formam fieri, atque in ea coelestem aliquam suboriri virtutem. Difficillimum quidem est judicatu, quales potissimùm

What are these for? That you may understand how from a certain combination of herbs and vapours, made by medical and astronomical art, results a certain form, like a kind of harmony endowed with gifts of the stars. Thus, from tones chosen by the rule of the stars, and then combined in accordance with the stars' mutual correspondences, a sort of common form can be made, and in this a certain celestial virtue will arise. It is indeed very difficult to judge what kind of tones will best fit what kind of stars, and what combinations of tones agree best with what stars and their aspects. But, partly by our own diligence, partly by divine destiny, . . . we have been able to accomplish this.

The way Ficino does accomplish it is by having recourse to the second of the two principles mentioned on the previous page. This is one we have already discussed, namely, that music imitates emotions and moral attitudes (ἤθεα) and thus influences those of the singer and listener. Since the planets have the moral character of the gods whose names they bear, this character can be imitated in music; by performing such music we can make ourselves, especially our spirit, more Jovial, Solarian, Venereal, etc. . . . This mimetic theory of music connects with the world-harmony one outlined above, because such mimetic music *is* a living spirit and the heavens also *are* musical spirit:

This kind of musical spirit [i.e. morally and planetarily effective song] actually touches and acts on the spirit, which is the mean between body and soul, and wholly disposes both in accordance with its own disposition. You will indeed allow that there is marvellous power in lively, singing spirit, if you concede to the Pythagoreans and Platonists that the heavens are spirit, ordering everything with their movements and tones [1].

Ficino gives three rules for composing this astrological music, prefacing them with the cautionary remark that he is not speaking

toni, qualibus conveniant stellis, quales inter tonorum compositiones, qualibus praecipuè sideribus, aspectibusque consentiant. Sed partim diligentia nostra, partim divina quadam sorte . . . id assequi possumus."

[1] Ficino, *Op. Omn.*, p. 563 (*De Tr. V.*, III, xxi): ". . . spiritus eiusmodi musicus propriè tangit, agitque in spiritum inter corpus animamque medium, & utrumque affectione sua prorsus afficientem. Mirabilem verò in concitato canenteque spiritu vim esse concedes, si Pythagoricis Platonicisque concesseris, coelum esse spiritum, motibus tonisque suis omnia disponentem."

of worshipping stars, but rather of imitating them, and by imitation capturing their natural emanations [1]; they are [2]:

Rules for fitting songs to the heavenly bodies:
1. Find out what powers and effects any particular star has in itself, what positions and aspects, and what these remove and produce. And insert these into the meaning of the text, detesting what they remove, approving what they produce.
2. Consider which star chiefly rules which place and man. Then observe what modes (*tonis*) and songs these regions and persons generally use, so that you may apply similar ones, together with the meaning just mentioned, to the words which you wish to offer to these same stars.
3. The daily positions and aspects of the stars are to be noticed; then investigate to what speech, songs, movements, dances, moral behaviour and actions, most men are usually incited under these aspects, so that you may make every effort to imitate these in your songs, which will agree with the similar disposition of the heavens and enable you to receive a similar influx from them.

A little further on we are given descriptions of the music appropriate to each planet. The Sun, Jupiter, Venus and Mercury, the benign planets, each have their particular kind of music; but Saturn, Mars and the Moon have only "voices"—no music [3]. The characters of these planetary modes are [4]:

[1] Ibid., p. 562: "... ne putes nos in praesentia de stellis adorandis loqui, sed potius imitandis, & imitatione captandis. Neque rursus de donis agere credas, quae stellae sint electione daturae, sed influxu potius naturali."

[2] Ibid. pp. 562-3: "Regulae cantum sideribus accommodaturae ... exquirere quas in se vires, quosve ex se effectus stella quelibet, & situs [original: sidus] & aspectus habeant, quae auferant, quae ferant. Atque verborum nostrorum significationibus haec inserire, detestari quae auferant, probare quae ferunt ... Considerare quae stella, cui loco maximè, vel homini dominetur. Deinde observare qualibus communiter hae regiones, & personae tonis utantur, & cantibus, ut ipse similes quosdam unà cum significationibus modò dictis, adhibeas verbis, quae sideribus eisdem studes [original: stupes] exponere ... situs aspectusque stellarum quotidianos animadverteret, atque sub his explorare, ad quales potissimùm sermones, cantus, motus, saltus, mores, actus, incitari homines plerique soleant, ut talia quaedam tu pro viribus imiteris in cantibus, coelo cuidam simili placituris, similemque suscepturus influxum."

[3] Ficino, *Op. Omn.*, p. 563 (*De Tr. V.*, III, xxi); Saturn has "voces tardas, graves, raucas, querelas", Mars "veloces, acutas, asperas, minaces", Luna "medias".

[4] Ibid.: "Concentus autem Jovi [tribuimus] quidem graves, & intentos, dulcesque, & cum constantia laetos. Contrà Veneri cum lascivia & mollitie voluptuosos cantus adscribimus. Inter hos verò medios Soli tribuimus & mercurio. Si una cum gratia suavitateque sunt venerabiles, & simplices, & intenti, Apollinei judicantur. Si una

2

Jupiter: music which is grave, earnest, sweet, and joyful with stability.
Venus: music which is voluptuous with wantonness and softness.
Apollo (the Sun): music which is venerable, simple and earnest, united
  with grace and smoothness.
Mercury: music which is somewhat less serious (than the Apolline)
  because of its gaiety, yet vigorous and various.

If any one of these "harmoniae" is sung frequently and atten-
tively, the singer's spirit will take on this character, having, by
natural sympathy, attracted the appropriate planetary spirit.

Since all music pertains primarily to Apollo, as can be seen from
the list on page 15, music of any kind tends to capture the sun's
influence and render the musicians solarian; which is eminently
desirable [1]. This preoccupation with the sun is, of course, typical
of all Ficino's work [2]. In his commentary on Plotinus he tells us
that people once worshipped the planets because of the benefits
obtainable by exposing one's soul and spirit to their influence;
but, he says, most of the Platonic philosophers worshipped only
the sun [3]:

Julian and Iamblichus composed orations to the Sun. Plato called the
sun the visible off-spring and image of the supreme God; Socrates,
while greeting the rising sun, often fell into an ecstasy. The Pythagoreans
sang to the lyre hymns to the rising sun. Concerning the cult of the sun,
let them look to that; but undoubtedly "God has placed his tabernacle
in the sun".

cum jucunditate remissiores quodammodo sunt, strenui tamen, atque multiplices,
Mercuriales existunt." Cf. ibid., p. 534 (III, ii): "Musicam gravem quidem Jovis
Solisque esse, levem Veneris, mediam verò Mercurij"; p. 546 (III, xi): "Soni quine-
tiam cantusque grati, blandique ad gratias omnes spectant atque Mercurium. Minaces
autem admodum atque flebiles Martem praeferunt & Saturnum."

  [1] Man in general is thought to be primarily solarian, and to a lesser degree jovial
and mercurial (ibid., p. 535 (III, ii)).

  [2] See his *Orphica Comparatio Solis, Liber de Sole, Liber de Lumine* (*Op. Omn.*, pp.
825, 965, 976).

  [3] Ibid., p. 1745: "plurimi verò praesertim Platonici atque id genus Philosophi,
solum adorabant inter coelestia Solem. Orationem ad Solem composuit Julianus et
Iamblichus. Solem Plato filium et imaginem summi Dei visibilem appellavit: Solem
Socrates orientem salutans ecstasim saepe patiebatur: Orienti Soli Pythagorici
hymnos lyra canebant. De cultu quidem Solis illi viderint: Deus certè in Sole posuit
tabernaculum suum." Ficino's sources are: Julian, Εἰς τον βασιλεα Ἡλιον, (*Works
of the Emperor Julian*, ed. W. C. Wright, London, 1913, I, 352); Plato, *Respubl.*, VI,
508 b-c, *Sympos.*, 220 c-d; Iamblichus, *De Vita Pythag.*, c. 25, 35; Psalm, XVIII, 6.

One may take it then as highly probable that Ficino's astrological music was most often addressed to the sun.

There is little doubt that Ficino himself performed the astrological music described in the *De Vita coelitùs comparanda*. We know from his own and his contemporaries' writings that he was in the habit of singing while accompanying himself on an instrument which he calls his *lyra* or his *lyra orphica* [1]. One reason for calling it Orphic was that the instrument was adorned with a picture showing Orpheus charming the animals and rocks with his lyre [2]. Now in most Renaissance representations of Orpheus the instrument he is playing is clearly a *lira da braccio*, or, less often, a treble viol or violin [3]. It seems to me likely then that Ficino accompanied his planetary songs on the *lira da braccio*. Even much later musical humanists associated the modern *lire* with ancient music; Zarlino was inclined to believe that the ancient lyre was like a *lira tedesca* (i.e. hurdy-gurdy) [4], and Mersenne wrote of the modern *lira* [5]:

le son de la Lyre est fort languissant et propre pour exciter à la dévotion, et pour faire rentrer l'esprit dans soy-mesme; l'on en use pour accompagner la voix et les récits ... il n'y a peut estre nul instrument qui représente si bien la Musique d'Orphée et de l'antiquité ...

If this conjecture is correct, one might suppose that Ficino's music was like that of the "improvvisatori sulla lira", of which,

---

[1] Ficino, *Op. Omn.*, pp. 608, 651, 673, 725, 871, 944; Lorenzo de 'Medici, *Opere*, Firenze, 1825, II, 157 (*L'Altercazione*); cf. Della Torre, *Storia dell'Accademia Platonica di Firenze*, Florence, 1902, pp. 490, 788-90, 792 seq.; Kristeller, "Music and Learning in the Early Italian Renaissance", *Journal of Renaissance and Baroque Music*, 1947, pp. 269-272, *Philos. of M. F.*, pp. 307 seq., *Suppl. Ficin.*, II, 37, 230, 262.

[2] See Naldi's poem to Ficino, *De Orpheo in ejus cythara picto*, in Kristeller, *Suppl. Ficin.*, II, 37.

[3] See G. Kinsky, *Musikhistorisches Museum von Wilhelm Heyer in Cöln*, Leipzig & Cöln, 1910-16, II, 383 seq.; B. Disertori, "L'Arciviolata lira in un quadro del Secento", *Rivista Musicale*, XLIV, 1940, p. 199. Cf. Sylvestro Ganassi dal Fontego, *Regola Rubertina*, Venice, 1542, ed. Max Schneider, Leipzig, 1924, p. ix, c. viii, who bases his identification of the ancient lyre with the violin or *lira*, rather than with the lute, on "l'autorità cavata d'Orfeo".

[4] Zarlino, *Istitutioni Harmoniche*, Venezia, 1558, III, lxxix, p. 290; cf. D. P. Walker, "Musical Humanism", *Music Review*, 1941-2, III, 55.

[5] Mersenne, *Harmonie Universelle*, Paris, 1636 IV des Instr., x, p. 206.

unfortunately, we know very little [1]. The expression "recitare", which is often used of these improvisers, suggests a very simple kind of chant, half-way between song and speech, something like the performance of a young boy of whom Poliziano wrote to Pico della Mirandola [2]:

he proclaimed an heroic ode, which he himself had composed in honour of our Pietro de' Medici. His voice was neither like someone reading nor like someone singing, but such that you heard both, yet neither separately; it was varied, however, as the words demanded, either even or modulated, now punctuated, now flowing, now exalted, now subdued, now relaxed, now tense, now slow, now hastening, always pure, always clear, always sweet . . .

Perhaps Ficino's music was something like this, or perhaps it was based on plain-song, since, as I shall try to show, his astrological singing came near to being a religious rite. Apart from such vague conjectures [3], all that one can say about the purely musical side of Ficino's singing is that it was monodic and that he was aiming at the same ideal of expressive, effect-producing music as the later musical humanists. His directions for fitting songs to the *ethea* of planets conform strikingly with, for example, Galilei's advice to composers to observe and note the exact tones, accents, rhythm, of various types of character, in various situations [4].

About the text, however, of Ficino's singing we can be more

---

[1] See André Pirro, "Léon X et la Musique", *Mélanges offerts à Henri Hauvette*, Paris, 1934, pp. 221 seq.; A. Einstein, *Italian Madrigal*, Princeton, 1949, I, 18, 76-7, 89, 92.

[2] Politian, *Opera*, Basileae, 1553, p. 165: "pronunciavit . . . heroicum carmen, quod ipsemet nuper in Petri Medici nostri laudem composuerat . . . Vox ipsa nec quasi legentis, nec quasi canentis, sed, in qua tamen utrunque sentires, neutrum discerneres: variè tamen, prout locus posceret, aut aequalis, aut inflexa, nunc distincta, nunc perpetua, nunc sublata, nunc deducta, nunc remissa, nunc contenta, nunc lenta, nunc incitata, semper emendata, semper clara, semper dulcis . . ."

[3] The nearest we get to a practical example of Ficino's planetary music is when he briefly describes how in Apulia those bitten by the tarantula are cured by special music which makes them dance; he comments: "Sonum verò illum ex indicijs esse Phoebeum Jovialemque conijcio" (ibid., p. 564); presumably he had not heard a *tarantella*. Cf. H. E. Sigerist, "The Story of Tarantism", *Music and Medicine*, ed. Schullian & Schoen, New York, 1948.

[4] Galilei, *Dialogo della musica antica e moderna*, Firenza, 1581, p. 89; cf. Walker, "Musical Humanism", II, 291-2.

precise; and for him, as, again, for later musical humanists [1], the text was much more important than the music. A song works on body, mind, and on whatever intermediate faculties may be between; but it is the text alone which can carry an intellectual content and thus influence the mind. The music, abstracted from its text, can reach no higher than the spirit, i.e. sense and feeling, or at most, through the spirit, the lower parts of the soul, phantasy and imagination. The status of song is clearly shown in the hierarchical list quoted above [2]: Apollo is just above the odours and unguents of Venus, just below the vehement imaginings of Mars, and far below the intellectual contemplation of Saturn [3]. But music has here the important position of being the mean of all seven grades precisely because it is not separated from text; it does therefore affect the whole man, mind as well as spirit and body. A similar placing of music and poetry occurs in Ficino's doctrine of the four *furores* [4]. They are the first and lowest kind of *furor*, but they have the privileged position of accompanying the other three (those of religious rites, prophecy, love):

no man possessed by *furor* is content with ordinary speech. But he breaks forth into shouting and singing and songs. Wherefore any *furor*, either that of prophecy, or of mysteries, or of love, since it leads to singing and poetry, can rightly be said to find its completion in the poetic *furor* [5].

What, then, were the words of Ficino's astrological songs?

---

[1] See Walker, "Musical Humanism", II, 9, 226 seq.

[2] p. 15.

[3] Cf. Ficino's introduction (*Op. Omn.*, p. 1559) to Plotinus, *Enn.*, I, iii, of which the first two chapters deal with the ascent of the soul through philosophy, love, music. Having stated the Plotinian triad: *ipsum bonum, intellectus, anima,* Ficino gives three modes of ascent to this: by Mercury, through reason, to the *ipsum bonum*; by Venus, through sight, to the *intellectus*, "in quo prima pulchritudo [idearum corruscat"; by Phoebus, through hearing, to the *anima*, "ad quam potissimum pertinet harmonia", and which is "vita mundi, quasi divinae intelligentiae spiritus". These constitute a descending hierarchy, but may all lead up, through Saturn, "intelligentiae ducem", to the *ipsum bonum*.

[4] Ibid., p. 1282 (*Camm. in Ion.*), 1361 (*Comm. in Conviv.*).

[5] Ficino, *Op. Omn.*, p. 1365 (*Comm. in Phaedr.*): "Furens autem nullus est simplici sermone contentus. Sed in clamorem prorumpit ,& cantus & carmina. Quamobrem furor quilibet, sive fatidicus, sive mysterialis, seu amatorius, dum in cantus procedit & carmina, merito in furorem poeticum videtur absolvi."

The answer, I think, is to be found in his Orphic singing, in his revival of the "antiquus ad Orphicam lyram cantus", which he lists among the triumphs of the Florence of his time, together with the resurrection of Plato by the Academy at Careggi[1]. Ficino's *lyra* was Orphic not only because it bore a picture of Orpheus, but also because it accompanied his singing of the Orphic Hymns, and probably other Orphic fragments [2]. Although he does not mention it in the *De Vita coelitùs comparanda*, I am convinced that his Orphic singing is the same as the astrological music there described.

From the second of Pico's *Conclusiones Orphicae* we learn that the Orphic Hymns were sung in a special manner for magic purposes [3]:

In natural magic nothing is more efficacious than the Hymns of Orpheus, if there be applied to them the suitable music, and disposition of soul, and the other circumstances known to the wise.

In Ficino's commentary on Plotinus we learn what these magic purposes are and what are the "other circumstances known to the wise". Commenting on a chapter where Plotinus remarks that we can capture planetary influences by "prayers, either simple or sung with art" [4], Ficino says [5]:

[1]   Ibid., p. 944; cf. pp. 822, 871, 608.

[2]   See Della Torre, op. cit., p. 789 (from Corsi's biography of Ficino: "Orphei hymnos exposuit, miraque, ut ferunt, dulcidine ad lyram antiquo more cecinit").

[3]   Pico, *Op. Omn.*, Basileae, 1572, I, 106: "Nihil efficacius hymnis Orphei in naturali magia, si debita musica, animi intentio et caeterae circumstantiae, quas norunt sapientes, fuerint adhibitae." Pico, also, was in the habit of singing "ad lyram" Latin prayers of which he had composed the words and music (G. F. Pico's *Life* of him, in front of this edition of his works).

[4]   Plotinus, *Enn.*, IV, iv, 38: "οἷον εὐχαῖς ἢ ἁπλαῖς ἢ τέχνῃ ᾀδομέναις". This book of Plotinus (IV, iv) may be the one on which the *De Triplici Vita* is supposed to be a commentary (v. supra p. 3 note (2)).

[5]   Ficino, *Op. Omn.*, p. 1747: "Intellectualis anima mundi et sphaerae cuiuslibet atque stellae subiunctam habet vegetalem vitam suo infusam corpori: per quam non electione, sed naturaliter generantur, moventurque sequentia, et beneficia capacibus conferuntur ... Vegetalis vita nostra vitae superius dictae admodum est conformis, similiter spiritus noster radijs illius tam occultis, quam manifestis omnia pentrantibus. Evadit etiam longè cognatior, quando erga vitam illam vehementer afficimur, consentaneum illi beneficium exoptantes, atque ita spiritum nostrum in illius radios transferimus amore: praesertim si cantum et lumen adhibemus, odoremque numini consentaneum, quales Orpheus hymnos mundanis numinibus consecravit. Item coelo incensi thuris odorem, aetheri ferventem crocum, stellis aromata, Saturno et Jovi styracem .... Spiritus enim per affectum, cantum, odorem, lumen cognatior effectus numini, uberiorem haurit illius influxum."

Our spirit is consonant with the heavenly rays which, occult or manifest, penetrate everything. We can make it still more consonant, if we vehemently direct our affections towards the star from which we wish to receive a certain benefit . . . above all, if we apply the song and light suitable to the astral deity and also the odour, as in the hymns of Orpheus addressed to cosmic deities.

He then gives a list of planets and odours taken from the Orphic Hymns, whose titles all contain the indication of a fumigation, e.g. "Hymn of the Sun. Fumigation: frankincense"[1]. He continues:

For when our spirit is made more consonant to a planetary deity by means of our emotions, the song, the odour and the light, it breathes in more copiously the influx which comes from this deity.

Bearing in mind that throughout the *De Triplici Vita* the chief means of nourishing the spirit are odours and music, wine and light[2], we can have little doubt that this Orphic singing is identical with Ficino's astrological music. The Orphic Hymns would have seemed to him particularly suitable for a good kind of magic singing, because Orpheus was a *priscus theologus*[3]. In the series of ancient theologians which goes from Zoroaster, Hermes Trismegistus and Moses to Plato, and from Plato to Christianity, Orpheus has a conspicuous place, because he is the most ancient of the Greeks, the master of Pythagoras, and through him of Plato. He is also, of course, the symbol of the powerful, effect-producing singer; and he was a magician[4].

Apart from those Orphic Hymns which are addressed to planetary deities, Ficino would probably have sung other Orphic fragments[5], other ancient prayers to the sun[6], and the 18th

---

[1] *Orphica*, ed. Abel, Leipzig, 1885, p. 61.

[2] V. supra p. 5 note (3); cf. *Op. Omn.*, p. 568 (*De Tr. V.*, III, xxiv): as our body is nourished by the four elements, so is our spirit by its "tenua quaedam elementa" —wine (earth), odour of wine (water), song and sound (air), light (fire).

[3] See D. P. Walker, "Orpheus the Theologian and Renaissance Platonists", *Journal of the Warburg and Courtauld Institutes*, XVI, 1953, p. 100. Cf. ibid., p. 102, the story of Ficino's working some successsful magic by Orphic singing.

[4] V. infra pp. 131, 147.

[5] See article cited in preceding note. There are many Orphic fragments suitable for sun-worship, e.g. Kern, *Orphicorum Fragmenta*, Berlin, 1922, fr. 62, 236-8.

[6] E.g. Proclus' *Hymn to the Sun* (*Eudociae Augustae, Procli Lycii . . . carm. gr. rel.*, rec. H. Ludwich, Lipsiae, 1897, pp. 133 seq.).

psalm of David [1], the Jewish Orpheus [2] ("Deus certè in Sole posuit tabernaculum suum").

[1] When, a century later, Patrizi (*Nova de Universis Philosophia*, Venetijs, 1593, fos 107 v-111 v (1st ed. 1591)) used this psalm (and the Orphic Hymn of the Sun) in a sun-worshipping context, the inquisitor, Jacopo de Lugo, noted (ibid., fo 111 v) "id quod refert Augustinus contra Faustum, Manicheos, scilicet ex illo psalmi dicto: In sole posuit tabernaculum suum: excidisse in adorationem solis, quoniam cum Christus (ut aiunt ipsi) in caelum ascenderet, corpus suum reliquit in globo solis, inde vero solam animam secum supra coelos ad dexteram patris evexit".

[2] On David and Orpheus, see Walker, "Orpheus", p. 101.

(3) FICINO'S MUSIC AND LATER MUSICAL THEORISTS

Ficino's theory of the peculiar connection between music and spirit seems to be original, in the sense that, though most or all of the elements of this theory have a long history, his combination of them does produce something new and valuable [1]. We have the familiar ingredients of medical spirits, the ethical power of ancient music and its therapeutic use [2], and Aristotelian-Augustinian accounts of hearing and the nature of sound; out of these Ficino creates a very satisfactory explanation of the "effects" of music, an explanation which is not without permanent value: the conception of musical sound as a living, "spiritual" animal [3] is, as a poetic image, remarkably adequate and profound. Similarly, his astrological music has obvious origins in the ancient magical and theurgic uses of music, mediaeval astrology, and Pythagorean-Neoplatonic ideas of universal harmony. In this case, Ficino adds something in that he is not content to point out possible analogies between macrocosm and microcosm, between musical and celestial harmonies, but gives practical directions for making music which may usefully exploit these analogies.

There are two main resemblances between Ficino's musical theory and later musical humanism. First, he is the earliest

---

[1] This is a very rash statement; it may well be that I have overlooked some important source. There are, of course, earlier references to music and the *spiritus* (e.g. Augustine, *Confessions*, X, xxxiii (Migne, *Pat. Lat.*, 32, col. 800: "Omnes affectus spiritus nostri pro sui diversitate habent proprios modos in voce atque cantu, quorum nescio qua occulta familiaritate excitentur"; or Dante, *Convivio*, II, xiii, 20 seq.: "la Musica trae a sè li spiriti umani, che quasi sono principalmente vaporiu del cuore, sì che quasi cessano da ogni operazione: sì e l'anima intera, quando l'ode, e la virtù di tutti quasi corre a lo spirito sensibile che riceve lo suono"); but I have come across none which can be said to foreshadow Ficino's music-spirit theory.

[2] See e.g. E. R. Dodds, *The Greeks and the Irrational*, Univ. of California Press, 1951, pp. 78 seq., 99; Abert. *Lehre vom Ethos*, pp. 15-6 & *passim*; Panofsky & Saxl, op. cit., p. 21.

[3] V. supra p. 10.

Renaissance writer I know of to treat the effects of music seriously and practically, and not merely as a constituent of the rhetorical topic of the *laus musicae* [1]. By providing them with a rational explanation, he removes them from the status of more or less legendary marvels, makes them into exciting realities, and, by his astrological music, indicates ways of reviving them. Secondly, as I have already mentioned [2], Ficino's conception of the relative importance of music and text is the same as that of the majority of 16th century humanists, namely, that the text alone reaches the mind and must therefore dominate the music.

If I am right in supposing that this music-spirit theory is in some measure a creation of Ficino's, then one may assume that contemporary or later appearances of it probably derive from him, and one would expect it to be widely adopted, since it fits so well with fundamental trends of 16th century musical humanism. On the whole, the facts confirm the assumption, but do not fulfill the expectation.

In the chief of the earlier humanist writers on music, Gafori, Ramis de Pareja, Lefèvre d'Etaples, Glarean, I have found no traces of Ficino's music-spirit theory. The first two of these are, of course, contemporaries of Ficino's and are unlikely to derive anything from him; but their example shows that the music-spirit theory does not normally occur in 15th century musical humanism. They both have chapters on *musica humana*. Gafori writes that through "musical concord the spiritual nature is joined to the body and the rational is bound to the irrational by concord" [3]; but "spiritual" is certainly used here in the Christian (modern) sense. Ramis de Pareja has parallels between the modes, humours and planets [4], which have a long mediaeval history [5],

---

[1] See James Hutton, "Some English Poems in Praise of Music", in *English Miscellany*, 2, ed. Mario Praz, Rome, 1951.

[2] V. supra p. 21.

[3] Gafori, *Teoricum Opus*, Neapolis, 1480, I, iii: "per eam [sc. musicam concordantiam] enim spiritualis natura corpori coniungitur & rationalis cum irrationali concordia copulatur".

[4] Ramis de Pareja, *Musica Practica*, 1482, ed. J. Wolf, Leipzig, 1901, pp. 56-8.

[5] See Abert, *Die Musikanschauung des Mittelalters*, Halle, 1905, pp. 173-4, 181-2.

and to which Ficino may owe something, or more probably to one of their ancient sources such as Ptolemy [1].

Agrippa, as we shall see, gives a very full exposition of the theory, often quoting Ficino verbatim and without acknowledgment [2]; in Gregor Reisch's encyclopaedia, *Margarita Philosophica*, it appears as an open borrowing [3]—he names Ficino and quotes from his commentary on the *Timaeus* [4]. Both these should have given the theory a fairly wide diffusion. It may have been, as A.-M. Schmidt suggests [5], from the *Margarita* that Maurice Scève learnt of it. He introduces it into his *Microcosme* [6] briefly and with unficinian demons:

> Musique, accent des cieux, plaisante symfonie
> Par contraires aspects formant son harmonie:
> Don de Nature amie à soulager à maints
> Voire à tous, nos labeurs, et nos travaux humains.
> Qui par l'esprit de l'air, noeu du corps, et de l'ame,
> Le sens à soy ravit, et le courage enflamme:
> Et par son doux concent non seulement vocale,
> Mais les Demons encor appaise instrumentale . . .

Scève was a friend of Pontus de Tyard and helped him in his study of Greek notation [7]; therefore, since Tyard was anyway heavily influenced by Ficino [8], one would expect his *Solitaire Second* to contain this theory in a full and conspicuous form. But all we find are somewhat uncertain and certainly casual references to it. Tyard writes, for example [9], that in ancient cities

la Musique servoit d'exercice pour reduire l'ame en une parfaite temperie de bonnes, louables, vertueuses moeurs, emouvant & appaisant

---

[1] Ptolemy, *Harmonica*, III, ii-xvi.
[2] V. infra p. 92.
[3] *Margarita Philosophica*, Argentinae, 1512, Lib. V, Tract. I (Musicae speculativae), cap. i.
[4] Quoted above p. 9.
[5] A.-M. Schmidt, *La Poésie Scientifique en France au XVIe siècle*, Paris, 1938, pp. 139 seq.
[6] Scève, *Oeuvres Poétiques*, ed. Guégan, Paris, 1927, p. 244 (*Microcosme*, 1562).
[7] See Tyard, *Discours Philosophiques*, Paris, 1587, fo 51 vo.
[8] Cf. infra pp. 120-2.
[9] Tyard, *Solitaire Second*, 1555, in his *Discours Philosophiques*, Paris, 1587, fo 41 vo.

par une naifve puissance & secrette energie, les passions & affections,
ainsi que par l'oreille les sons estoient transportez aux parties spirituelles.

Here one cannot be certain of the meaning of "spirituel", but
a later definition of the voice as "un air esmeu de l'esprit poussé
hors de la bouche, portant la conception de l'entendement" [1]
suggests that he may be using it in a medical (i.e. Ficinian) sense.

Zarlino refers several times, in the *Istitutioni Harmoniche*, to a
connexion between the human spirit and the effects of music;
but Ficino's theory cannot be said to play a great part in his work,
and, moreover, he is evidently confused about the meaning of
the term "spirit". The following [2] is clearly Ficinian, and probably
a reminiscence of the *De Triplici Vita*:

bene hà ordinato la natura, che hauendo in noi, mediante lo spirito,
congiunto insieme (come vogliono i Platonici) il Corpo et l'Anima:
a ciascun di loro, essendo deboli et infermi, hà proueduto di opportuni
rimedij: imperoche essendo il Corpo languido et infermo si viene a
risanare co'rimedij, che li porge la Medicina; et lo Spirito afflitto et
debole da gli spiriti aerei et dalli suoni et canti, che gli sono proportionati
rimedij è recreato: ma l'Anima rinchiusa in questo corporeo carcere,
si consola per via de gli alti et diuini misterij della sacra Theologia.

But in a later chapter, on *musica humana* [3], we are told that body
and soul are joined together "non già con legami corporei: ma
(come uolgiono i Platonici) con lo Spirito, il quale è incorporeo".
A little further in the same chapter [4] the spirit has faded away
altogether, becoming, as in ordinary Christian or modern usage,
a synonym of "soul"—"natura spirituale" is plainly contrasted
with "natura corporale", and both are said to be linked by
"concordia harmonica". Later still, Zarlino uses the term in its
ordinary medical sense, as the instrument of the soul for sensation
and movement [5].

Although Zarlino, as a musical theorist, had great standing

---

[1]   Ibid., fo 105 vo.
[2]   Zarlino, *Istitutioni Harmoniche*, Venetia, 1573 (1st ed. 1558), I, iv, p. 12.
[3]   Ibid., I, vii, p. 22.
[4]   Ibid., p. 23.
[5]   Ibid., II, viii, pp. 87-8.

and influence, I have not found any version of the music-spirit theory in the musical humanists following him, such as Mei, Galilei, Bardi or Bottrigari, nor even in La Boderie, who, as we shall see, revived a form of Ficino's Orphic singing [1]. There are other stray mentions of this theory, as in Scaliger [2], for example, and it survived into the 17th century [3]; but in general Ficino's influence on 16th century musical theory seems to have been slight, and it is not until Campanella that the music-spirit theory, in a new guise, dominates anyone's conception of music. The reasons for its comparatively slight success were probably: first, its association with dangerous magic, which was evidently much more apparent to 16th century readers than to us; secondly, the confusions and contradictions involved in the concept of spirit, of which Zarlino has just given us an example.

---

[1] In the Statutes of Baif's Academy the phrase "reserrant ou desserrant, ou accroississant l'esprit" (repr. Yates, *French Acad.*, p. 320) may come from Zarlino (*Ist.*, II ,viii), and may indicate that the Academy held a music-spirit theory. For La Boderie, v. infra pp. 122 seq.

[2] J. C. Scaliger, *Exoticarum exercitationum Liber Quintus Decimus*, Paris, 1557, fo 381.

[3] E.g. Burton, *Anatomy of Melancholy*, Part. II, Sect. II, Mem. VI, Subs. 3; Kircher, *Musurgia Universalis*, Romae, 1650, pp. 551-2; cf. Hutton, op. cit., pp. 4-5, 20-1, 36, 49.

CHAPTER II. FICINO'S MAGIC

(1) DIACCETO

The *De Triplici Vita* is presented as a medical treatise, and the practices recommended in it might be taken merely as somewhat odd medical remedies and régimes—odd only because of the large place given to talismans and music; for there is, of course, nothing odd in a Renaissance medical treatise dealing with spirits and astrology. If, however, we try to picture Ficino nourishing his spirit and making it more celestial, we shall, I think, be convinced that this simple interpretation is inadequate; he is indeed giving medical advice, but he is suggesting something else as well. The picture is something like this:

He is playing a *lira da braccio* or a lute, decorated with a picture of Orpheus charming animals, trees and rocks; he is singing these words:

Κλῦθι μάκαρ, πανδερκὲς, ἔχών αἰώνιον ὄμμα,

Τιτὰν χρυσαυγὴς, Ὑπερίων, οὐρανίον φῶς.

i.e. the Orphic Hymn of the Sun; he is burning frankincense, and at times he drinks wine; perhaps he contemplates a talisman; in day-time he is in sunlight, and at night he "represents the sun by fire" [1]. He is, in fact, performing a religious or magical rite—"a sacrament profane in mystery of wine".

This conjectural interpretation of Ficino's treatise is strengthened by the 16th century reactions to it and Campanella's use of it, as we shall see, and is strikingly confirmed by Ficino's disciple, Francesco Cattani da Diacceto [2]. The description of astrological

---

[1] Ficino, *Op. Omn.*, p. 568 (*De Tr. V.*, III, xxiv): directions for making the spirit "Phoebeus" by exposing oneself to sunlight, "atque igne referentes in nocte Solem citharae cantusque interim non obliti".

[2] See P. O. Kristeller, "Francesco da Diacceto and Florentine Platonism in the sixteenth century", *Miscellanea Giovanni Mercati* Vol. IV, Vatican, 1946, p. 260.

magic given by Diacceto is a particularly valuable piece of evidence
because he proclaimed himself a follower of Ficino, had known him
personally [1], and, according to one of his biographers, Frosino
Lapini, he not only "drank in avidly" Ficino's Platonic teaching,
but also "expressed it all most exactly in his habits and life" [2].
He was, however, by no means a mere copier of his master. As
Kristeller points out [3], he diverged from him in several important
ways, especially with regard to the relation between Platonism
and Christianity. Diacceto makes no attempt to christianize
Plato or Plotinus, and does not usually even bother to note where
they are compatible or not with Christian doctrine [4]. One would,
therefore, expect him to be much less discreet, and hence more
informative, than Ficino on the subject of Neoplatonic magic
and astrology; this expectation is in fact borne out. He seems less
interested in the subject than Ficino, and I should doubt if he
practised astrological magic himself; but he gives us a much fuller
and less disguised picture of the rite. This occurs in his treatise
De Pulchro, which is evidently based on Plotinus, both in content
and style. Diacceto manages to be even more obscure than his
model; but, fortunately, being concerned only with his references
to magic and what they may tell us about Ficino, we need look
only at one chapter of this work [5]. The title of this chapter is [6]:

The twofold soul, first and second, and its cognition likewise twofold,
from which derives the appetite for beauty, and natural Magic: the nature
of which he shows and which he differentiates from superstitious magic.

Diacceto prefaces it by saying that, since this subject has been
most thoroughly treated by the ancients and recently by "our

---

[1]   From about 1492 until Ficino's death in 1499 (see Kristeller, op. cit., p. 271).
[2]   Euphrosynus Lapinius, *Commentarius de Vita Francisci Catanei*, in Diacceto,
Opera Omnia . . ., Basileae, 1563,: "factum est, ut diligentissimus hic Ficini auditor,
non solum Platonicae illius disciplinae omnia praecepta avidè combiberit, sed moribus
ac vita accuratissimè, et ad unguem cuncta expresserit, ut Platonicum verè, simulque
Marsilij Ficini discipulum possis agnoscere."
[3]   Op. cit., pp. 294-5.
[4]   But cf. infra p. 35 his letter to Ganay.
[5]   Diacceto, *De Pulchro*, II, iv, *Op. Omn.*, p. 42.
[6]   Ibid.: "Anima duplex, prima & secunda, eiusque cognitio itidem duplex, à
qua Pulchri provenit appetentia, & naturalis Magia: cuius naturam exponit, & à
superstitiosa differentem facit."

leader", Ficino, he will write, as the spirit moves him, of things
which may seem novel and paradoxical not only to those who
are already suspicious of Platonism, but even to the Platonists
themselves[1]. He then presents a Neoplatonic theory of astrological
and magical effects: the world as one animal, whose soul, by
means of the stars, imprints forms on the sub-lunar world; these
are conveyed by cosmic spirit[2], and, if the form has been im-
perfectly received owing to the inadequacy of the receiving
matter, this imperfection can be corrected by attracting more
spirit from the appropriate planet. Diacceto's theory also introduces demons attached to each planet, who help in conveying
planetary influences and can also be attracted.

The "diligent capturer of planetary light"[3] must observe what
plants, animals, odours, figures, harmonies, hymns and ceremonies,
correspond to each planet. Then he must choose the moment
when the heavenly bodies are in a position favourable to the
planet he has chosen (which Diacceto now calls a "god"):

If for example he wishes to acquire solarian gifts, first he sees that
the sun is ascending in Leo or Aries, on the day and in the hour of the
sun. Then, robed in a solarian mantle of a solarian colour, such as gold,
and crowned with a mitre of laurel, on the altar, itself made of solarian
material, he burns myrrh and frankincense, the sun's own fumigations,
having strewn the ground with heliotrope and suchlike flowers. Also
he has an image of the sun in gold or chrysolite or carbuncle, that is,
of the kind they think corresponds to each of the sun's gifts. If, for
example, he wishes to cure diseases, he has an image of the sun enthroned,
crowned, and wearing a saffron cloak, likewise a raven and the figure
of the sun, which are to be engraved on gold when the sun is ascending
in the first face of Leo. Then, anointed with unguents made, under
the same celestial aspect, from saffron, balsam, yellow honey and anything else of that kind, and not forgetting the cock and the goat, he

---

[1] Ibid., pp. 42-3: "At quoniam & ab antiquis, & nuper à duce nostro Marsilio
de his exquisitissimè actum est, cùm mea quidem sententia nec plura aut meliora
dici valeant, consilium est, quò me perunque genius libenter trahit, ea potius exequi,
non quae nostris hominibus, quibus pleraque Platonicorum dogmata suspecta sunt,
novitatis speciem afferrent, sed quae fortè etiam Platonicis paradoxa videri possint."
[2] By a typical elaboration Diacceto makes the planets suck spirit ("purissimum
animae vehiculum") from the firmament and pass it on downwards (ibid. p. 45).
[3] "sedulus erraticarum luminis captator" (ibid., p. 45).

sings the sun's own hymn, such as Orpheus thought should be sung. For here is the force, and as it were the life, of the conciliation of the planet's favour. He sings, I say, first to the divine Henad of the Sun, then he sings to the Mind, and lastly he sings to the Soul; since One, Mind, Soul, are the three principles of all things. Also he uses a threefold harmony, of voice, of cithara, and of the whole body, of the kind he has discovered belongs to the sun: not one which by too much complexity produces wantonness, or which constantly displays gravity, but one which is the mean between these two, which both is joyful by its simplicity and at times does not avoid a mood of gravity. To all these he adds what he believes to be the most important: a strongly emotional disposition of the imagination, by which, as with pregnant women, the spirit is stamped with this kind of imprint, and flying out through the channels of the body, especially through the eyes, ferments and solidifies, like rennet, the kindred power of the heavens [1].

This planetary rite plainly derives from Ficino and includes all the important features of our conjectural reconstruction of Ficino's magic (except for the wine) [2]; but it also adds several details which make the operation more obviously a religious ceremony. The altar, the solarian priestly dress ("pallium" and "mitra"), and the Neoplatonic triad are not in the *De Vita coelitùs comparanda*; Diacceto does not himself try to connect this triad

---

[1] Diacceto, *Op. Omn.*, pp. 45-6: "Ut si velit solaria munera reportare, primò quidem observat solem in Leone aut in Ariete ascendere die, & hora solis. Mox solari amictus pallio, solarisque coloris, cujusmodi aurei sunt omnes, super altare & ipsum de solari materia conditum, laurea mitra coronatus, myrrham thusque accendit, sua solis suffimenta, solsequijs & florum id genus huiusmodi perstrata humo. Adhęc simulachrum solis habet in auro vel chrysolitho carbunculove, quale cuique munerum putant convenire. Ut si optet morbos curare, Solem in solio coronatum croceo indutum amictu, item corvum solisque figuram in auro signata surgente cum sole prima Leonis facie [orig.: faciei]. Praeterea unguentis oblitus, de croco, balsamo, flavo melle, & si qua sunt id genus, eadem coeli facie confectis, non sine gallo & ariete, canit suum solis hymnum, qualem Orpheus canendum esse censuit. Siquidem hic totius vis conciliationis, & quasi vita est. Canit inquam primò divinae Solis Henadi, canit dein menti, postremò canit animae. Siquidem unum, mens, anima, tria rerum omnium principia sunt. Ad haec triplici utitur harmonia, vocis, cythara, totiusque corporis, qualem Soli competere exploratum habet: non quae nimia compositura lasciviam pariat, aut quae gravitatem ubique prae se ferat: sed quae harum media, & sua quidem sit simplicitate jucunda, & obiter à gravitatis ingenio non recedat. His omnibus addit, quod quidem plurimum valere putaret, vehementum imaginationis affectum, à quo more praegnantium spiritus huiusmodi signatus charactere cùm per meatus relinquumque corpus, tum maximè per oculos evolitans, quasi coagulum cognatam coeli vim fermentat & sistit."

[2] I came across it long after I had written, and published, this reconstruction.

with the Christian Trinity, but the early Fathers and Thomas
Aquinas had done so, and, from Bessarion and Ficino onwards,
such a connection was of course a constant theme of Renaissance
Platonism[1]. This description also confirms for us two points
that are not explicitly in Ficino: that the astrological music was
used together with the talismans, and that the words of the
former were Orphic.

There are, however, some ways in which Diacceto does not
complete and confirm our reconstruction of Ficino's magic,
but perhaps diverges from it. One example is his elaboration of
the "spiritual" mechanism by which planetary influences are
captured: the operator's spirit, suitably stamped by his imaginative participation in the rite, flows out through his eyes to meet
and precipitate the planetary spirit. This elaboration, an unnecessary addition to Ficino's theory, derives evidently from the
usual explanation of fascination as caused by an emission of
noxious spirit from the operator's eyes[2]. A more important
divergence is the function accorded by Diacceto to planetary
demons; these can impart, not merely the corporeal benefits that
come from the planets, but those "which come from free-will
and choice", i.e. knowledge, intellectual gifts, and a wise man
will consider it "not only pious, but necessary, to perform hymns
and ceremonies" to attract them[3]. The magic in the De V.C.C.
does not appear to involve planetary demons, but only cosmic
spirit, nor to aim at an effect on the rational soul, but only on
the spirit; how far Ficino really diverged from Diacceto on this
point will be discussed later. Diacceto identified these celestial
demons, and the planetary intelligences, with angels, and believed

---

[1] See D. P. Walker, "Orpheus the Theologian", *Journal of Warburg & Courtauld Inst.*, XVI, 1953, pp. 116-9, and "*Prisca Theologia* in France", ibid., XVII, 1954, pp. 243-251.

[2] Mentioned by Diacceto later in this chapter (*Op. Omn.*, p. 47).

[3] Diacceto, *Op. Omn.*, p. 46: "Unius igitur principis animae vires sphaerarum stellarumque plures animae inter se partitae sunt, quas innumeri dęmonum ordines consequuntur, pro suo quisque modo, ut par est, opificio providentes ... Haec quidem optimè callens cùm à coelo, praeter corporea bona, quae ex arbitrio quoque sunt electioneque, optet: non solùm pium ducit, sed necessarium, divinorum numerorum dispensatoribus hymnos cęremoniasque reddere."

this identification to be orthodox; in the very worried letter he wrote to Germain de Ganay about the possible unorthodoxies of his Platonism, he asserts firmly, on the authority of Dionysius the Areopagite, one of the very few Christian writers he ever quotes, that this is so [1]. It appears from this letter that he was genuinely anxious about the compatibility of Platonism with Christianity, but quite unable to deal with the question [2]—an even rudimentary knowledge of theology was something he had not acquired from Ficino [3].

In view of these divergences we must not read back the whole of Diacceto's planet-worship into Ficino. But he provides, nevertheless, very strong evidence in favour of our interpretation of Ficino's astrological practices as something approaching near to a religious rite.

[1]   Ibid., p. 334.

[2]   He begins the letter: "Ego verò, mi Germane, semper in divinis probavi non mediocriter anxiam quandam curam, & ferè dixerim morositatem, alioqui gravem & permolestam.", and expresses gratitude to Ganay and the Parisian theologians for any criticism and advice they can give him on the subject (ibid., p. 332); cf. Kristeller, art. cit., p. 289.

[3]   This would account for the cautious but obscure remarks at the end of this chapter (Diacceto, Op. Omn., p. 47). After describing maleficent planetary magic, Diacceto concludes: "Ego verò ab adorandis stellis cessandum penitus contendo, omnino enim viri philosophi non esse: vel saltem si qui id contenderint, periculosum planè duco. Aucupari autem bona corporea stellarum observatione, ut quidem quodammodo non improbo, sic quoque nec laudo. Multo autem praestare censuerim, siquis est, qui hoc amore teneatur, hunc totum ad ipsum bonum, separatasque substantias converti, hinc omnia pro voto uberrimè consequuturum." The separatae substantiae are presumably angels or saints.

(2) SOURCES OF FICINO'S MAGIC

This kind of magic had many sources. Perhaps the most important, though Ficino does not avow it, and may not even have been conscious of it, is the mass, with its music, words of consecration, incense, lights, wine and supreme magical effect—transubstantiation. This, I would suggest, is a fundamental influence on all mediaeval and Renaissance magic, and a fundamental reason for the Church's condemnation of all magical practices. The Church has her own magic; there is no room for any other. The effort to make a sharp distinction between Christian rites and any kind of secular magic is, as we shall see, apparent in many 16th century discussions of such subjects [1]. As one would expect, it is rare for anyone overtly to accept the connexion between magic and the eucharist. This is however done by Peter of Abano in his *Conciliator* [2], a work which Ficino cites several times in the *De V.C.C.* [3]; and Ficino himself gives, "si fas est", the formula of consecration as an example of the magical power of words [4].

Peter of Abano and other mediaeval writers on magic, such as Roger Bacon, Alkindi [5], Avicenna [6], and "Picatrix" [7], are probably important sources for Ficino's talismans, and would suggest invocations to planets. But far more important are certain Neoplatonic texts: Proclus' *De Sacrificiis et Magia*, Iamblichus' *De*

---

[1] Cf. infra p. 83-4.

[2] Petrus Aponensis, *Liber Conciliator*, Venetiis, 1521, fo 201 vo (*Differentia* 156): "... sciendum quod experientia potest demonstrari ... precantationem conferre ... ut aperte illud summum sacramentum cum alijs multis ostendit eucharistie. Nomina etiam id confirmant divina notorie artis."

[3] E.g. Ficino, *Op. Omn.*, pp. 552, 557, 558.

[4] Ficino, *Op. Omn.*, p. 1218 (*Comm. in Tim.*); cf. infra p. 151.

[5] Cf. infra pp. 149 seq.

[6] Cf. infra pp. 162-3.

[7] See Thorndike, *History of Magic and experimental Science*, New York, 1923-41, II, 813-824.

Mysteriis and *Vita Pythagorae*, Porphyry's *De Abstinentia*, the *Hermetica*, especially the *Asclepius*. Most of these Ficino translated or paraphrased [1].

There are several obvious connections between these Neoplatonists and Ficino's magic. Proclus' *De Sacr. et Mag.* gives a concise exposition of sympathetic astrological magic, and his examples are mainly solarian [2]. From Marinus' biography of Proclus [3] Ficino would have learnt that Proclus had zealously sung and studied Orphic hymns [4] and had used "methods of purification, both Orphic and Chaldaean" in his theurgy. Iamblichus' *Vita Pythagorae* would have suggested Orphic and musical theurgic practices [5]. Pythagoras is there presented as being very like Orpheus, and as having in fact derived his religious ideas and practices from Orpheus' disciples [6]. Like Orpheus he had studied in Egypt [7], founded a religious sect, and produced musical effects [8], even on animals [9]. He was another musical *priscus theologus*. In the training of his disciples music took a prime place [10]. It was used to cure diseases of both soul and body, but chiefly to expel evil and troublesome passions and bring the soul into a state of virtuous harmony. The disciples were sent to sleep and awoken with special songs. Pythagoras himself was able to hear the harmony of the spheres [11]; but, since he believed that no one else could, he made vocal and instrumental imitations of it, so that, indirectly,

---

[1] Ficino, *Op. Omn.*, pp. 1928 (Proclus), 1873 (Iamblichus, *De Myst.*), 1932 (Porphyry), 1836 (*Hermetica*).

[2] Proclus, *De Sacr. et Mag.*, tr. Ficino, *Op. Omn.*, pp. 1928-9; the only mention of music is to show that cocks are more solarian than lions because "gallus quasi quibusdam hymnis applaudit surgenti soli".

[3] Marinus, *Life of Proclus*, tr. L. J. Rosán (in his *The Philosophy of Proclus*, New York, 1949), pp. 23-4, 27-8.

[4] Probably not those now known as Orphic Hymns, which are quoted by no ancient writer.

[5] Cf. Ficino, *Op. Omn.*, p. 562 (*De Tr. V.*, III, xxi): "Pythagorici verbis & cantibus, atque sonis mirabilia quaedam Phoebi & Orphei more facere consueti".

[6] Iamblichus, *De Vita Pyth.*, ed. I. A. Theodoretus, Franckerae, 1598, c. xxviii.

[7] Ibid., c. iii.

[8] c. xxv.

[9] c. xiii.

[10] c. xv, xxv.

[11] c. xv.

his disciples might be influenced by this celestial harmony. The Pythagoreans worshipped the rising sun[1].

There was also, I think, another less evident, but more fundamental type of influence exerted by the Neoplatonists on Ficino's magic. The immense importance which Ficino attributes to astral influence on man's spirit and his acceptance of a cosmic or celestial spirit both suggest that, at least in the *De Vita coelitùs comparanda*, his conception of the former is not merely the orthodox medical one. I think that he has at the back of his mind the Neoplatonic astral body, that is, the aetheric vehicle (ὄχημα) which the soul acquires from the various stars and spheres it passes through during its descent into the earthly body[2]. On this earth the vehicle, which began by being fine, shining and star-like, becomes heavy, dark and damp, and, unless purified and rendered more aetheric, it will at death drag down the soul to hell or to some lower incarnation. This conception of spirit (for the vehicle is historically connected with the Aristotelian, medical and Stoic *pneumata*) would account for its being peculiarly subject to astral influences, since it derives from the stars, and for the great urgency of its purification, since it does not leave the soul at death, but can drag it down or, if light and dry enough, ascend with it[3]. It would, moreover, have a special affinity to the spheres and their harmony, since its proper shape, before entering the physical body, is spherical, and its proper motion is circular[4].

---

[1] c. xxxv.

[2] See Verbeke, op. cit., pp. 267 (Plutarch), 306 seq. (Plotinus, Porphyry), 368 seq. (Proclus, Hierocles), 374 (Iamblichus); Proclus, *The Elements of Theology*, ed. E. R. Dodds, Oxford, 1933, p. 313, App. II "The Astral Body in Neoplatonism"; Ralph Cudworth, *The True Intellectual System of the Universe*, 2nd ed., London, 1743, II, 781 seq.

[3] This is an over-simplified account; for there are often two vehicles, one aetheric and one aerial, or even more (cf. Dodds, ed. cit. of Proclus, pp. 319-20); but it represents roughly the doctrine of Synesius (v. infra p. 39 note (1)). Cf. Porphyry, *Sententiae*, xxxii, on the eschatology of the vehicle (quoted by Cudworth, op. cit., II, 784); Philoponus, *In Aristot. de Anim.*, (quoted ibid., II, 786-7) on the nourishment and purification of the spirit with vapours.

[4] Ficino mentions the vehicle's spherical shape: ". . . corpus animae proximum. Hoc vocant Magi vehiculum animae, aethereumque scilicet corpusculum, acceptum ab aethere, immortale animae indumentum, naturali quidem figura rotundum propter aetheris regionem, sed in humanam effigiem sese transferens, quando corpus

The astral body was for the Neoplatonists primarily a religious conception—an explanation, I think, or justification of theurgic practices, i.e. methods of approaching God and salvation which are non-intellectual, such as fasting, lustrations, the use of incense, incantations, etc. To all these practices the astral body corresponds exactly; being corporeal, it can be acted on by similar physical things (vapours, scents, sounds); being the seat of imagination, of the irrational soul, it can be affected by prayers and images; since it survives after death, its condition is of the utmost importance.

The supposition that Ficino's human spirit is in some measure this aetheric vehicle is strengthened by the fact that, just before he wrote the De Vita coelitùs comparanda, he translated Synesius' De Insomniis, a classic exposition of Neoplatonic pneumatology [1], and that into his version of Iamblichus De Mysteriis, which is also concerned with the purification of the vehicle [2], he inserted his own music-spirit theory [3]. On this supposition, one can explain Ficino's not using the term vehiculum, nor referring to its astral origin, by the obvious unorthodoxy of a doctrine which assumes pre-existence of the soul and metempsychosis [4]. Where

humanum ingreditur, atque in priorem se restituens, quum egreditur". (Op. Omn., p. 404, Theol. Plat., XVIII, iv). Cf. Proclus, El. Theol., ed. cit., p. 308 (prop. 209, 210); Origen, De Oratione, XXXI, 29 (Migne, Pat. Gr., 11, col. 552). Ficino would also have found the circular motion of the vehicle in Plotinus, Enn., II, II, 2 ("Ἴσως δὲ καὶ παρ' ἡμῖν τὸ πνεῦμα τὸ περὶ τὴν ψυχὴν τοῦτο ποιεῖ', i.e. moves circularly, like the soul and the heavenly bodies). Cf. Ficino, Op. Omn., p. 1607 (Comm. in Plot., on this passage), 134 (Theol. Plat., IV, ii).

[1] Ficino, Op. Omn., p. 1968, dedication dated April 1489; the De Vita coelitùs comparanda was written in the summer of that year (dedication July 1489; cf. Panofsky & Saxl, op. cit., p. 34). On Synesius, see R. C. Kissling, "The ὄχημα-πνεῦμα of the Neo-platonists and the De Insomniis of Synesius of Cyrene", American Journal of Philology, XLIII, 1922, p. 318. Another important source for Ficino's knowledge of the astral body was probably Macrobius, Comm. in Somn. Scip., I, xii (Macrobius, Opera, Lipsiae, 1774, p. 68), from which Ficino quotes in the Theol. Plat. (XVIII, v, Op. Omn., p. 406); he would also have found there (II, iii, ed. cit., p. 135) the suggestion of using hymns which imitate the music of the spheres.

[2] Ficino, Op. Omn., p. 1900; Iamblichus, De Myst., ed. Parthey, Berlin, 1857, p. 239.

[3] V. supra p. 6 note (1). He refers several times to Iamblichus and Synesius in the De Vita coel. comp., e.g. pp. 531, 538, 562.

[4] Discussions of the astral body by Renaissance Platonists are rare and usually very cautious. Bessarion (In Calumniatorem Platonis, ed. L. Mohler, Paderborn, 1927, p. 367) defended it against George of Trebizond by taking it as a fabulous version of the Catholic spiritual body, but was evidently aware of the unorthodoxy

he does expound the doctrine of the astral body, in the *Theologia Platonica*, he is careful to preface his exposition with a denial of the astral descent of the soul and such remarks as: "it is pleasant sometimes to play poetically with the ancients", and to end his chapter with a declaration of submission to Christian theologians [1].

Of the sources for his magic to which Ficino himself refers the most important are the *Asclepius* and, of course, Plotinus. The *Asclepius*, like the *Orphica*, had great authority for Ficino because it was a work of Hermes Trismegistus, a *priscus theologus* even more ancient than Orpheus, indeed contemporary with Moses [2]; Plotinus was merely a late interpreter of this antique Egyptian wisdom. There is one particular passage in the *Asclepius* with which we shall be much concerned:

(Hermes:) What has already been said about man, although marvellous, is less so than this: that man has been able to discover the divine nature and produce it, is admirable beyond all other marvels. Our first ancestors, then, when [3] they were in grave error concerning the gods, being incredulous and paying no attention to worship and religion, invented the art of making gods. Having done so, they added a virtue appropriate to it, taken from the world's nature, and mixed these; since they could not make souls, they evoked the souls of demons or angels, and put them into images with holy and divine rites, so that through these souls the idols might have the power of doing good and evil ... (Asclepius:) ... of what kind is the quality of these terrestrial gods? (Hermes:) It consists, O Asclepius, of herbs, stones and aromas, which have in them a natural divine power. And it is for the following reason that people delight them with frequent sacrifices, with hymns and praises and sweet sounds concerted like the harmony of the heavens:

it involved. Nicolas Leonicus prefaced and ended his *De Tribus Animorum Vehiculis* (in his *Dialogi*, Lugduni, 1542, p. 82 (1st ed. 1524)) by solemnly warning his readers against accepting any Platonic views on the soul which do not conform with Christian dogma.

[1] See particularly *Op. Omn.*, p. 404 (*Theol. Plat.*, XVIII, iv), 405 (XVIII, v); Diacceto, also, was very interested in the Neoplatonic vehicle, but, typically, does not bother about its orthodoxy (cf. Diacceto, *Op. Omn.*, pp. 95, 115, 129, 169-170, 326-7, 349-359).

[2] See Walker, "The *Prisca Theologia* in France", *Journal of the Warburg and Courtauld Inst*, 1954, p. 209.

[3] Reading "quando" for "quoniam" on the assumption that the original was "ἐπεί" or "ἐπειδή".

that this heavenly thing, which has been attracted into the idol by repeated heavenly rites, may bear joyously with men and stay with them long [1].

This is undoubtedly a capital source for Ficino's general theory of magically influencing the spirit so that it may become receptive to celestial influxes. In the summary of this theory, with which the *De Triplici Vita* ends [2], he presents a paraphrase of the above passage as the source of Plotinus' *Ennead* IV, iii, 11 [3], which, according to Kristeller, is the "liber Plotini" on which the whole *De Vita coelitùs comparanda* is supposed to be a commentary [4]. This chapter of Plotinus, as Ficino interprets it, states that one can attract into, and retain in, a material object "something vital from the soul of the world and the souls of the spheres and stars", that is, celestial spirit, if the object is of a material and form which reflects the celestial source of spirit in question. This passage and the *Asclepius* one fit in with, and connect together, Ficino's

---

[1]   *Asclepius*, c. xiii, *Corpus Hermeticum*, ed. A. D. Nock & A. J. Festugière, Paris, 1945, pp. 347-9: "minus enim miranda, etsi miranda sunt, quae de homine dicta sunt; omnium enim mirabilium vincit admirationem, quod homo divinam potuit invenire naturam eamque efficere. Quoniam ergo proavi nostri multum errabant circa deorum rationem increduli et non animadvertentes ad cultum religionemque divinam, invenerunt artem qua efficerent deos. Cui inventae adjunxerunt virtutem de mundi natura convenientem eamque miscentes, quoniam animas facere non poterant, evocantes animas daemonum vel angelorum eas indiderunt imaginibus sanctis divinisque mysteriis, per quas idola et bene faciendi et male vires habere potuissent ... Et horum, o Trismegiste, deorum, qui terreni habentur, cujusmodi est qualitas? Constat, o Asclepi, de herbis, de lapidibus, et de aromatibus divinitatis naturalem vim in se habentibus, et propter hanc causam sacrificiis frequentibus oblectantur, hymnis et laudibus et dulcissimis sonis in modum caelestis harmoniae concinentibus, ut illud, quod caeleste est, caelestius [var.: caelesti usu] et frequentatione inlectum in idola possit laetum, humanitatis patiens, longa durare per tempora." Cf. ibid. p. 325, on man-made gods.

[2]   *Op. Omn.*, pp. 570-2 (*De Tr. V.*, III, xxvi); he also cites the passage on pp. 548, 561 (III, xiii, xx).

[3]   Plotinus, *Ennéades*, ed. and tr. Bréhier, Paris, 1924-38, IV, 78: "Les anciens sages qui ont voulu se rendre les dieux présents en construisant des temples et des statues, me paraissent avoir bien vu la nature de l'univers; ils ont compris qu'il est toujours facile d'attirer l'âme universelle, mais qu'il est particulièrement aisé de la retenir, en construisant un objet disposé à subir son influence et à en recevoir la participation. Or la représentation imagée d'une chose est toujours disposée à subir l'influence de son modèle, elle est comme un miroir capable d'en saisir l'apparence." Then follows the sun as an example of a visible representation of an intelligible model.

[4]   V. supra p. 3 note (2).

astrological medicine, music and talismans; and he is plainly using them to reinforce his own theory. He cannot, however, quite pass over the fact that Hermes is talking about pagan idolatry and demons, and therefore goes on to a worried and muddled defence of his own magic. He admits that the Egyptians' magic was "illicit", because the demons in the statues were worshipped as gods; but implies that demons are all right if used as means and not worshipped as ends [1]. He then provides an alternative line of defence by citing Thomas Aquinas to show that purely astrological magic could not produce demon-inhabited images [2]; therefore, we are left to imply, his own talismans and Orphic singing have nothing to do with demons.

Elsewhere in the De Triplici Vita, and in his Apologia for it, Ficino shows evident anxiety about the orthodoxy of his astrological practices; he is worried chiefly about the talismans, but also about the music. On the former, for example, he writes in the Ad Lectorem of the De Vita coelitùs comparanda [3]:

If you do not approve of talismans, which were however invented to benefit men's health, but which I myself do not so much approve of as merely describe, then dismiss them, with my permission, even, if you wish, on my advice.

With regard to music, he wishes to assert that his astrological songs are not "cantiones", i.e. incantations used to summon

---

[1]   Ficino, Op. Omn., p. 571: "Addit [sc. Hermes] sapientes quondam Aegyptios, qui & sacerdotes erant, quum non possent rationibus persuadere populo esse deos, id est, spiritus aliquos super hominibus, excogitasse Magicum hoc illicitum, quo demones allicientes in statuas esse numina declararent [i.e. Ascl., xiii, ct. supra]. Sed Iamblichus damnat Aegyptios, quòd daemonas non solùm ut gradus quosdam ad superiores deos investigandos acceperint, sed plurimum adoraverint. Chaldaeos verò daemonibus non occupatos Aegyptiis anteponit." The reference must be to Iamblichus, De Myst., VI, vii, where, however, demons as "gradus" do not occur.

[2]   Ficino, ibid.: "Ego autem primò ex beati Thomae sententia puto, si modo statuas loquentes effecerint [referring to Ascl., viii, ed. cit., p. 326, on oracular idols], non simplicem ipsum stellarum influxum ibi formavisse verba, sed daemones. Deinde, si fortè contigerit, eos in eiusmodi statuas ingredi, non arbitror hos ibi per coelestem influxum fuisse devinctos, sed potius suis cultoribus obsequutos denique decepturos". Thomas, Contra Gentiles, III, civ-cvi.

[3]   Op. Omn., p. 530: "Si non probas imagines astronomicas alioquin pro valitudine mortalium adinventas, quas & ego non tam probo quam narro, has utique me concedente, ac etiam si vis consulente dimittito." Cf. ibid., pp. 552, 555, 558, 561.

demons and compel them to produce some magical effect. He mentions Hermes' use of music to attract spirits into idols (in the *Asclepius* passage just quoted), and other ancient magical uses of music, and then says [1]:

But I myself prefer to dismiss incantations. For even Psellus the Platonist disapproves of them and laughs at them.

When he is trying to defend his own magic, Ficino frequently cites Thomas Aquinas. Now Thomas' position with regard to magic is, in the genuine works [2], quite clear. Natural substances, such as herbs and gems, may have certain powers connected with their astrological affinities, and it is legitimate to use these in medicine; but, if letters or characters are engraved on the stones, or invocations and incantations used with the herbs, any resultant effect is the work of bad demons, and the operator has entered into an express or tacit pact with the Devil [3]. Thomas associates the *Asclepius* with magic, and quotes Augustine's emphatic condemnation of the passage on idols [4]. Thomas' view thus plainly condemns both Ficino's talismans and his astrological music, and Ficino makes his defence against this condemnation very weak by quoting the idolatrous *Asclepius* passage and connecting his own magic with it. He had, nevertheless, a possible line of defence. As Cardinal Caietano later pointed out [5], Thomas condemns astrological magic only because he believes it to involve commerce with demons; and the ground for this belief is that characters on talismans, or invocations and prayers, cannot directly produce a natural physical effect, and must therefore be addressed to intelligent beings who do produce the magical

---

[1] *Op. Omn.*, p. 549 (*De Tr. V.*, III, xiii): "Sed cantiones equidem libenter omitto. Nam & Psellus Platonicus eas improbat atque deridet" (referring perhaps to Psellus, *Expos. Orac. Chald.*, Migne, *Pat. Gr.*, 122, col. 1134). Cf. ibid., p. 562 (III, xxi). He never uses the words "cantio" or "carmen" for his own singing, but usually "cantus".

[2] V. infra p. 221.

[3] Thomas Aquinas, *Contra Gentiles*, III, civ-cvi; *Summa Theologica*, 2da 2dae, q. 96, a. ii; cf. infra p. 167.

[4] Thomas, *Contra Gent.*, III, civ; Augustine, *Civ. Dei*, VIII, xxiii.

[5] Tommaso de Vio Cardinal Caietano, *Comm. in Thom. Aq. Sum. Th.*, loc. cit. (Thomas, *Opera Omnia*, Romae, 1570, T. XI, Pars Altera, fos 241 ro-242 ro). Cf. infra p. 221.

effect, i.e. to demons. Since the main emphasis in the *De V.C.C.*
is on the conditioning of the operator's body, spirit and imagination, so that they are in a state peculiarly receptive to celestiainfluxes, Thomas' argument does not apply. Ficino could claim
that the characters and invocations were directed to the operator's
intelligence and imagination, not to an *intelligentia separata*, i.e.
an angel or demon; that when he sang a hymn to the sun, he did
not hope to make the sun do anything out of the ordinary, but
to make his own spirit more solarian, to make it more receptive
to the natural influxes from the sun. Adversaries of Ficinian
magic would argue that there was always the danger that a
deceiving demon might hear the hymn and produce some magical
effect or delusion; and this, as we shall see, is what many later
critics of Ficino thought.

(3) FICINO AND THE DEMONS

But are we anyway sure that the magic of the *De Vita coelitùs Comparanda*, including the Orphic singing, was not directed towards good demons or angels [1]? I think not. Demons are seldom mentioned in the *De V.C.C.*; and it is plain that in this work Ficino is anxious to avoid them. He is suggesting magical practices which are supposed to be non-demonic, to work by the influence of an impersonal planetary spirit on man's spirit and body, but no higher, and not by the influence of a personal "spirit" (i.e. demon), possessed of a soul, who could act directly on man's rational soul. But even here there are traces of a more dangerous magic. Saturn influences the intellect [2], and we are told that angels or *animae celestes* can directly influence our souls [3]. There is the idolatry in the *Asclepius* [4]. And from the chapter on familiar demons or *genii* it is clear that these are the same both as one's guardian angel and as one's dominant planet [5]. From Ficino's other works it is quite evident that he believed in demons, good and bad, associated with planets, and in their powerful and constant influence on man's body, spirit, and soul. Moreover the Neoplatonic sources of his magic were demonic, and the magic described by his disciple, Diacceto, is clearly demonic. And we know, on his own evidence, that at least twice,

[1] I am using these terms (good demon, angel) as synonyms, as they were for Ficino.

[2] Ficino, *Op. Omn.*, p. 564 (*De Tr. V.*, III, xxii): "Mens denique contemplatrix . . . Saturno se quodammodo exponit".

[3] Ibid., p. 566: "ubicunque dicimus coelestium ad nos dona descendere, intellige tum corporum coelestium dotes in corpora nostra venire per spiritum nostrum ritè paratum, tum eadem prius etiam per radios suos influere in spiritum naturaliter, vel quodammodocunque illis expositum. Tum etiam animarum coelestium bona, partim in eundem spiritum per radios prosilire, atque hinc in nostros animos redundare, partim ab animis eorum, vel ab angelis in animos hominum illis expositos, pervenire".

[4] V. supra p. 42.

[5] Ficino, *Op. Omn.*, pp. 566-8 (*De Tr. V.*, III, xxiii).

in 1494 and 1495, he succeeded in casting out bad Saturnian demons by astrological means[1].

The questions we must ask are: does Ficino anywhere advocate demonic magic, or describe it in a way that definitely connects it with the magic of the *De V.C.C.*, which he did recommend and almost certainly practised himself? In other words, are the apparently non-demonic, subjective, "spiritual" practices of the *De V.C.C.* merely a dishonest camouflage for a revival of Neoplatonic theurgy? The answers to these questions can be neither simple nor conclusive; but the questions themselves are important, in two ways. First, if Ficino's magic was addressed to angels and meant to influence the higher part of his soul, it was plainly a religion, a revival of ancient, pagan theurgy, a kind of astrological polytheism which even the most liberal Catholic could not admit. Secondly, even if it could be claimed that the planetary angels were generally accepted by theologians and their cult, within the same limits as prescribed for that of saints, was permissible[2], it would nevertheless be inexcusably reckless to direct any kind of prayer or rite to them other than those sanctioned by the tradition of the Church; the bad demons, who are eminently deceptive, are always lying in wait for the opportunity to delude those who try to make contact with good demons[3]. Any magic then, that is meant to be compatible with Christianity, must avoid demons, good or bad, and we would not expect a Christian openly to advocate any kind of demonic magic or admit that he practised it himself. We are looking for something that will probably be hidden.

From Ficino's numerous expositions of demonology the following general outline can be gathered[4]. Demons are primarily

---

[1] Ibid., pp. 1469-1470 (*Comm. in Tim.*, c. xxiv); cf. Giov. Corsi, *Marsilii Ficini Vita*, ed. Bandini, in Ph. Villani, *Liber de civitatis Florentiae famosis civibus . . .*, ed. G. C. Galletti, Florentiae, 1847, p. 191: "in Magia habitus est singularis, atque divinus pluribus e locis malis daemonibus, ac manibus fugatis . . .".

[2] For Thomas Aquinas on this v. infra p. 137.

[3] Cf. Campanella's experience, infra p. 228.

[4] Some of the main passages are: Ficino, *Op. Omn.*, pp. 209, 223, 289, 302, 339, 377-8, 482, 1342, 1381, 1437, 1465, 1528, 1708.

planetary, though there are also supercelestial and elemental ones.
They have souls and aetheric or aërial bodies, according to their
status [1]; these bodies are of a like nature to the human spirit [2].
Planetary demons, then, are like men without earthly bodies who
live in the heavenly spheres; they perform the function of transmitting celestial influences; they can, being both soul and spirit,
act both on man's spirit and his soul. The Neoplatonic hierarchy
of demons is identified with the Christian hierarchy of angels [3].
A guardian angel is the same as a familiar planetary demon [4].
There are bad demons, of a low status and with aërial bodies, who
trouble men's spirits and imagination.

Considered as mediums of planetary influence, demons are
exactly parallel to the Soul and Spirit of the World; the only,
but crucial, difference is that the former are individual, personal,
whereas the latter is general, impersonal. But it would be difficult
to believe simultaneously in both kinds of planetary influence;
the celestial spirits cannot be both personal and impersonal. Or
might it be possible to reconcile the two by supposing that the
impersonal spirit comes from the heavenly bodies and works on
man's body and spirit, but no higher, whereas the personal spirits,
the demons, who have souls, work primarily on man's soul and
mind? I think this may have been what Ficino did suppose; the
reconciliation is unsatisfactory logically, but people do not usually
think logically about magic, especially if they believe in it. It is
unsatisfactory because the demons have spiritual bodies closely
akin to human spirits on which they can and do act; this Ficino
tells us explicitly. The following passage from his *Commentary* on
the *Laws* shows clearly that demonic planetary influence completely
overlaps influence from the planets' bodies and includes in addition
the influence of a soul on a soul [5]:

[1] The supercelestial ones have no bodies.
[2] Cf. Ficino, *Op. Omn.*, pp. 876, 1293, 1503.
[3] The starting point of this is, of course, Ps. Dionysius; but the distribution of
the Dionysian angelic hierachies among the celestial spheres seems to begin with
Dante, cf. J. Hutton, op. cit., p. 23.
[4] Cf. Ficino, *Op. Omn.*, pp. 1387, 1515, 1636.
[5] Ficino, *Op. Omn.*, p. 1503: "Mitto in praesentia quantum ingeniorum discrimen

That the powers of the higher spirits, however it may be done, influence our spirits we cannot deny, since we clearly see that our bodies are moved by the higher bodies ... But if these spirits act on our spirits, they also act on our bodies. Indeed passions of the human body, whether induced by these higher spirits or higher bodies, overflow into the soul in so far as the soul, by acquired or natural affects, has sunk itself in the body. But there is this difference: that those [celestial] bodies move our souls through our bodies; the [celestial] spirits, on the other hand, both move the soul through the body, and directly move the soul, and move it through that [human] spirit which the Physicians often call the bond of the soul and body.

Any planetary effect, then, even if confined to the human body, might be caused by a demon. The only grounds for hoping that it was not would be that the means by which the effect was produced were not such as require a demon, that is, not prayers, figures, words, that could only be effective through being understood by another intelligent being. It would be just possible to argue that the practices of the *De V.C.C.* are of this kind, though the talismans and planetary music would need a lot of explaining; and Ficino did so argue in that work, in his *Apologia* for it, and in some of his other references to it. But if my conjecture about the Orphic singing is correct, then these arguments must appear weak and disingenuous. These hymns are clearly prayers addressed to *numina* of some kind; moreover, on several occasions, Ficino himself states that some of them are addressed to demons [1]. He does so in a most revealing passage of his *Commentary* on St. Paul's *Epistle to the Romans*, I, xxiii: "And (sc. the pagans "professing themselves to be wise") changed the glory of the uncor-

---

afferat familiarum cuiusque hominis varietas daemonum. Quòd autem spirituum superiorum vires, nostris quomodocunque ita fiat, spiritibus influant, negare non possumus, quando manifestè videmus corpora nostra corporibus superioribus agitari ... Quod si spiritus illi in nostros agunt spiritus, agunt insuper & in corpora. Passio verò corporum humanorum, sive à spiritibus illis, sive à corporibus superioribus inferatur, eatenus redundat in anima, quatenus tam comparato, quàm naturali affectu animus sese mergit in corpus. Verum hoc interest, quòd corpora illa per corpora nostra movent animas: spiritus autem tum animas per corpora movent, tum per animas, tum etiam per illum spiritum, quem Physici saepe nodum animae invicem, corporisque cognominant."

[1] Cf. Ficino, *Op. Omn.*, pp. 131, 383, 1715.

ruptible God into an image made like to corruptible man, and to birds, and four footed beasts, and creeping things". Ficino writes on this [1]:

But are we to suppose that the most learned high-priests of that religion worshipped such objects as if they were spirits (*numina*)? Certainly not; but rather that they gave occasion to the common people for such an absurd kind of worship. Indeed, as we show in the Commentaries on Plato and Plotinus and in the Third Book of the *De Vita*, the ancient sages arranged certain long series of mundane gods, as they call them, and of the demons and spirits (*numina*) who follow them in order; under each star certain demons, who dwell in that part of the heavens, and under them in the air various other demons, all endowed with the same quality and family-name as the superior ones—·Saturnian ones under Saturn, Jovial under Jupiter, and the Martial, Phoebean and others likewise; and also Saturnian and Jovial men under the

[1] Ficino, *Op. Omn.*, p. 440: "Sed nunquid existimandum est, doctissimos illius Religionis Antistites pro numinibus talia coluisse? Nequaquam. Imò tam absurdè adorationis ansas vulgo dedisse. Profectò quemadmodum in Commentarijs in Platonem atque Plotinum, & in tertio de vita tractamus, sapientes antiqui mundanorum, ut aiunt, Deorum daemonumque, & numinum gradatim inde sequentium, series quasdam longas disposuerunt. Sub qualibet stella certos ibi coelicolas, sub ijs in aëre alios deinceps, aliosque daemones, eadem scilicet proprietate cum superioribus cognomentoque praeditos. Saturnios sub Saturno, sub Jove Jovios, & Martios atque Phoebeos, caeterosque similiter. Praeterea sub Saturnijs, Iovijsque daemonibus Saturnios homines atque Jovios. Animalia rursus praeter hominem ad hunc, vel alium coelestem, vel coelicolam, vel daemonem pertinentia, nec animalia tantum, sed plantas etiam & metalla, & lapides quosdam superiorum proprietates saltem imaginarias habere putarunt. Et ut in praesentia mittam, quomodo Magi per inferiorum electionem compositionemque docuerint homines ad se superiora quaedam cum inferioribus congruentia oportunè deducere. Certè religionis illius Antistites, qui ijdem atque Magi fuerunt, ubi templa coelestibus & coelicolis coelicolisbusque dicaverunt, serie certa dispositas ibidem, & statuas hominum locaverunt, quos prae caeteris existimabant praecipuo quodam ejusmodi numinum influxu genitos, & munere praeditos. Saturnumque hominem appellabant, aut Jovem, sub Saturno, vel Jove coelesti, vel aërio constitutum. Adhibebant & animalia, & ligna, & metalla, & saxa characteresque simulachra eisdem numinibus congruentia. Forte verò animalia in primis quorum similitudines aliquis in coelo notaverant vel effinxerant. De his autem in tertio libro latiùs disputamus. Praeterea voluerunt, ut arbitror, nimium indulgere vulgo, & inferiorum bonorum cupido, & superstitionibus ejusmodi dedito. Qua quidem indulgentia caecum miserumque vulgus adorandis infimis subjecerunt. Mercurius ter maximus testis est religionis Aegyptiae patres statuas in templis arte magica fabricatas collocare consuevisse, & in eas daemones defunctorumque animas excitare. Iam verò Orpheus, magnus religionis illius author, hymnos quamplurimos non solum coelestibus, sed etiam daemonibus, daemonicisque hominibus consecravit, certasque certis subfumigationes adhibuit. Superstitiones autem multò etiam magis aniles & iniquas, & turpes introduxerunt Pontifices multi, civiles & Poëtae ... Jure itaque Varro, ubi tres Theologias enarrat, philosophicam & civilem atque poëticam, duas hic sequentes prima longè inferiores esse censet.

Saturnian and Jovial demons; and then, as well as men, animals pertaining to one or another celestial or other demon, and not only animals, for they thought that even plants and metals and certain stones had the properties of the higher beings, or at least images of them. For the present I will pass over how the *Magi* taught men, by selecting and putting together lower things, to draw down for their own benefit certain higher things corresponding to the lower ones. But undoubtedly the high-priests of that religion, who were the same as the *Magi*, when they dedicated temples to celestial [gods] and heaven-dwelling demons, also placed there, arranged in certain series, statues of men whom they considered to be born, more than others, under a special influx of such spirits (*numina*) and endowed with their gifts. They called a man Saturn or Jupiter, who was subject to the heavenly or aërial Saturn or Jupiter. They added animals, woods, metals, stones and characters, as images corresponding to the same spirits (*numina*); probably chiefly animals of which they had noted or invented likenesses to certain [figures] in the heavens. But these things we discuss more fully in the Third Book [of the *De Vita*]. Moreover, they were willing, I think, to yield too much to the common people, who are desirous of lower goods and given to such superstitions; by this indulgence they subjected the blind and wretched people to the worship of the basest objects. Hermes Trismegistus is a witness that the fathers of Egyptian religion were wont to place in their temples statues fashioned by magic art and to attract into them demons and the souls of the dead. Indeed, Orpheus, the great founder of that religion, devoted many of his hymns not only to celestial [gods], but also to demons and demonic men, and added particular fumigations for each. But much more foolish, wicked and abominable superstitions were introduced by many Priests, both civil and poetic ... Varro rightly, where he speaks of three theologies, philosophical, civil and poëtic, considers the latter two by far inferior to the first.

This certainly implies that the *De V.C.C.* is really about planetary demons, as described in the *Commentaries* on Plato and Plotinus, and about methods of obtaining benefits from them; and that these methods, which include using the series of planetary objects, as listed in the *De V.C.C.*, are connected with the Orphic Hymns. It also mentions two other dangerous themes of the *De V.C.C.*: the demonic, man-made gods of the *Asclepius* and the planetary guardian demons. We can see here, I think, the complexity, the conflicts and hesitations of Ficino's attitude. He begins by boldly defending pagan religion against St. Paul's contemptuous condemnation [1]—of course the learnèd ancients did not worship idols and animals—but at once admits that they may have led the ignorant into idolatry. Then follows the defence of good pagan religion explained as being astrological magic. The statues did not represent gods or demons, but men especially influenced by a certain planet; the animals and other objects were talismanic. The wise and learnèd priests were not worshipping these; they were just using them for magical operations, by which, presumably, they attracted good planetary demons. Then again he admits that these practices led astray the ignorant into idolatry and superstition. But finally even these superstitions are defended by introducing, from Augustine, Varro's three theologies [2]: natural (which Ficino calls philosophical), civil or political, and fabulous or poetic; according to Ficino, the really bad superstitions derived only from the latter two, not from the "philosophical" religion he has just described.

It is clear that Ficino is strongly attracted by this kind of magic or theurgy, that he considers it valuable, and also it is clear that he is aware that it is dangerous. His conclusion seems to be that its dangers might be avoided if it remained within a learnèd, philosophical circle, and were kept secret from the ignorant *vulgus*, who would distort it into idolatry and superstition.

Other references by Ficino to the *De V.C.C.* show the same uncertainty and hesitation. Sometimes, as in the passage just quoted, he openly connects it with planetary demons [3]; sometimes he contrasts demonic magic with the magic of the *De V.C.C.* and asserts that the latter is truly natural [4]. In a chapter of his *Commentary* on the *Timaeus*, having briefly expounded the theory that the heavens, as the spirit of the *anima mundi*, cause all elemental changes, especially through the moon, he remarks that he will

---

[1] Ficino repeats the beginning of this defence later in the same Commentary (p. 449), and again refers to the *De V.C.C.*

[2] Augustine, *Civ. Dei*, VI, v seq.

[3] E.g. Ficino, *Op. Omn.*, p. 1144 (*Comm. in Parmen.*, c. xx).

[4] E.g. Ibid., p. 1749 (*Comm. in Plot.*), quoted infra p. 166.

not now explain "how powers and images of the celestial [bodies] may be discovered in aquatic and terrestrial things", because he has already dealt with this subject adequately in the *De V.C.C.* [1]. He then goes on to give the derivation of planetary demons from the Ideas in the Intelligible World, without again mentioning the *De V.C.C.* This perhaps confirms my suggestion that Ficino supposed the *spiritus mundi* to act on the body and spirit, and demons primarily on the soul, and that the practices in the *De Vita coelitùs comparanda* were meant to appear to be confined to the former kind of influence.

The *Apologia* for the *De Triplici Vita* contains a formal denial that his magic is demonic [2]. But one can see from this document, dated 19th September 1489, that Ficino is expecting trouble, possibly that he has already been accused of dangerous magic. From various letters written between May and August 1490 [3] one gathers that he is worried about the effect of his book at Rome, is trying to gain the Pope's support, and has in some way been calumniated [4]. On August 1st Ermolao Barbaro, to whom he had first addressed himself, wrote to say that all was well, and that Innocent VIII was speaking most favourably of him. He had evidently been in some sort of danger, since he wrote to Rinaldo Orsini (Archbishop of Florence) [5]:

Lately you snatched your lamb Ficino from the voracious jaws of the wolves and to Saturn, who was dangerously attacking, you like Jupiter were in opposition.

[1] Ficino, *Op. Omn.*, p. 1463 (*Comm. in Tim.*, c. xl): "Mitto equidem nunc, quo modo vires imaginesque coelestium in rebus aquatilibus terrenisque deprehendantur. Hoc enim in libro de vita tertio satis diximus".

[2] Ibid., p. 573: (after a passage on the *Magi* at Christ's nativity) "duo sunt magiae genera. Unum quidem eorum, qui certo quodam cultu daemonas sibi conciliant, quorum opera freti fabricant saepe portenta. Hoc autem penitus explosum est, quando princeps hujus mundi ejectus est foras [*John*, XII, 31]. Alterum verò eorum, qui naturales materias opportunè causis subjiciunt naturalibus, mira quadam ratione formandas."

[3] Ibid., pp. 910-912; cf. Kristeller, *Suppl.*, I, lxxxv; Della Torre, *Storia dell'Acc. Fior.*, pp. 623-5.

[4] Ficino, *Op. Omn.*, p. 910, letter to Francesco Soderini.

[5] Ibid., p. 911: "tu nuper agnum tuum Ficinum piè admodum ex voracibus luporum faucibus eruisti, & Saturno iam nos graviter invadenti, tu quasi Juppiter es oppositus . . ."

He then goes on to say that Orsini has in fact a Jovial horoscope, and that, since with Orsini's help he has gained the Pope's favour, he wishes the Vicar of God a long life; he would therefore like to be informed of the Pope's illnesses, temperament and horoscope, so that he can invent some, presumably astrological, medicines for him. This letter shows that Ficino was not in the least worried about his ordinary astrological practices [1]; it was the talismans and planetary music that were dangerous.

From all this evidence I think the following conclusions can be drawn. The magic that Ficino practised, and which is partially described in the *De V.C.C.*, was addressed to good planetary demons. But in the *De Vita coelitùs Comparanda*, which is the only work where he recommends magic that he evidently practised himself, he put forward, with some lapses, a programme for a non-demonic magic, utilizing the *spiritus mundi* and reaching no higher than the human spirit. This magic, which from now on I shall call "spiritual magic", was the only one he could have openly recommended, both for reasons of personal safety, and because he truly believed that good demonic magic, if it went outside a small intellectual aristocracy, would be distorted by the ignorant into idolatry. His vacillations and hesitations when discussing demonic magic are due, I think, not only to prudence, but also to real doubts in his own mind; he was both attracted by it and afraid of it.

---

[1] Another of Ficino's letters (*Op. Omn.*, p. 911) about the same business, addressed to Marco Barbo, Cardinal of S. Marco, indicates the same attitude. He compares Barbo also to Jupiter, who has appeared to him after, in the *Apologia*, he had called on Hercules and Apollo, just as when Plotinus' *daimon* was summoned a god appeared (Porphyry, *Vita Plot.*, 10).

(4) FICINO AND GIOVANNI PICO

Ficino's later remarks on the *De Vita coelitùs comparanda*, in his letter to Poliziano[1] about Giovanni Pico's massive treatise against divinatory astrology[2], show the same uneasiness and vacillation: he was just collecting every remedy that *might* help, but not asserting that they all would—he was perhaps a little too free, and so forth. As Garin rightly concludes[3], there is no reason to doubt, on the grounds of this letter, that Ficino, with whatever hesitance and cautiousness, still had a strong belief in some sort of astrology. Nor does Pico's statement, in his *Adversus Astrologiam*, that Ficino encouraged him to write against astrology[4], carry any greater weight. For it all depends on what *kind* of astrology is being attacked. In Ficino's eyes, Pico was attacking not his own "good" astrology, but the "bad" astrology of those "plebeian" astrologgers[5], which he himself had criticized in his commentaries on Plotinus[6].

There was for everyone, without exception, a good and a bad astrology, just as, for nearly everyone, there was a good and a bad magic. There was general agreement on the criteria for distinguishing the magics: bad magic was to do with the devil and demons;

---

[1] Ficino, *Op. Omn.*, p. 968 (letter of August 1494).

[2] Giovanni Pico della Mirandola, *Disputationes adversus Astrologiam divinatricem*, a cura di E. Garin, Firenze, 1946, 2 Vols. (Latin text and Italian translation. The first edition is of 1496. The work was written in 1493-4).

[3] Garin, Introduction to his edition of Pico, *Adv. Astr.*, pp. 8-12, and his "Recenti Interpretazioni di Marsilio Ficino", *Giorn. crit. d. fil. ital.*, 1940, pp. 311 seq.

[4] Pico, ibid., p. 60: "noster Marsilius scripsit adversus eos aperte, Plotini vestigia secutus . . . [cf. infra note (6)] . . . quod si, valetudini consulens hominum, aliquando corrogat sibi de caelo quaedam etiam auxilia, optat ille potius ita fieri posse quam credat. Testari hominis mentem fidelissime possum, quo familiariter utor, nec habui ad detegendam istam fallaciam qui me saepius et efficacius adhortaretur, ne quotiens una facetiamus uberior nobis occasio segesque ridendi quam de vanitate astrologorum . . .".

[5] Ficino, *Op. Omn.*, p. 1609 (*Comm. in Plotinum*, Enn. II, lib. iii).

[6] Ficino, *Op. Omn.*, pp. 1609 seq.

good magic was "natural"—though one could of course argue endlessly about the proper application of these criteria and a few people thought that all magic was demonic. With astrology the situation was more varied and fluid; for here the criteria depended on religious convictions which were themselves neither stable nor universally held. One might be tempted to say that bad astrology limited or destroyed man's and God's freedom of will; but then, at least after the reformation, there were plenty of Christians who denied man's free-will [1], and at all times there have been Christians who have rejected a voluntaristic conception of God (i.e. a God whose decision makes something good, as opposed to a God who decides on what is already good). Nevertheless, it is, I think, generally true that astrology was accepted or rejected in so far as it safeguarded or infringed human responsability and divine providence.

Ficino and Pico would certainly have agreed on this criterion, and their conceptions of "good" astrology did not differ so much as the polemical tone of Pico's *Adversus Astrologiam* might lead one to suppose. In the Third Book of this treatise Pico states as his own a theory of astral influence which is almost identical with Ficino's [2]. The heavens are the universal cause of all motion and life in the sub-lunar world. They operate by means of a heat which is not elemental ,but which contains "in perfection and virtue" all the elemental qualities. This heat is borne by a "celestial spirit", which penetrates everywhere, nourishing, tempering, forming, vivifying. It is analogous to the spirit which, in men and animals, unites body and soul, "a very fine, invisible body, most closely akin to the light and heat of the stars" [3]. Moreover, animal spirits

[1] Calvin, in his *Advertissement contre l'Astrologie, qu'on appelle judiciaire* (*Recueil des Opuscules, C'est à dire, Petits traictez de M. Jean Calvin* . . ., Geneve, 1566, pp. 1118-1137), defends "l'astrologie naturelle", which assumes the astral determination of man's bodily disposition and even of large-scale calamities; the only danger is that we might claim our sins were astrologically caused or fail to believe that calamities are God's punishment for them.

[2] Pico, *Adv. Astr.*, III, iv, ed. cit., pp. 194 seq.

[3] Pico, ibid., p. 206: "in omnibus etiam viventibus, inter hoc quod videtur crassius habitaculum et animam, vitae fontem, medius est quem spiritum appellamus,

are not capable of generating or preserving bodies, of performing the functions of sense-perception, unless they have the help of celestial spirit, which, being more mobile, pure, efficacious and therefore closer to life, strengthens the infirmity of the inferior [i.e. animal] spirit and, by its intercourse with it, makes it more akin to the soul [1].

Pico insists elsewhere on this close and beneficial connection of celestial to animal spirits [2]. It is clear that he could not possibly have disapproved of Ficino's general intention, in the *De Vita coelitùs comparanda*, of making man's spirit more celestial; but he would have considered that the means Ficino suggests for so doing were mistaken. Pico insists that celestial influences are only a universal cause of sublunar phenomena; all specific differences of quality or motion are due to differences inherent in the receiving matter or soul. One could not, therefore, on his view, say that any particular herb, sound or food was more solarian or venereal than any other, nor use it to transform one's own spirit, as Ficino proposed; nor could one consider oneself as specially subject to the influence of any one planet.

At the time of writing the *Adversus Astrologiam* (1493-4), then, Pico would have considered Ficino's treatise mistaken; but he would not have thought that it contained the "bad" astrology which he was attacking, for Ficino is careful to safeguard human and divine liberty. I am inclined to think that a few years earlier, even when the *De Vita coelitùs comparanda* was published (1489), he may have wholly approved of it.

tenuissimum corpus et invisible, luci calorique sidereo maxime cognatum, cui vita praecipue adest perque eum suas in hoc visibile atque retrorsum vires explicat atque diffundit."

[1] Pico, ibid., p. 208: "Non sunt autem, vel gignendis corporibus, vel servandis, vel muneribus sensuum obeundis, utiles isti spiritus, si caelestis spiritus, hoc est caloris quem diximus, ope destituantur, qui mobilior, purior, efficacior, proptereaque proximior vitae, roborat infirmitatem spiritus inferioris et suo commertio reddit animae cognatiorem."

[2] Pico, ibid., III, vi, p. 218: "cum inter sublunaria corpora materiem reperit [sc. calor caelestis] sibi cognatam, et beneficus semper et vivifice tantum calorificus invenitur. Etenim nulla potius talis quam spiritus, et praesertim humanus, qui sanguineus vapor, tenuis, clarus, mobilis, coelo, quemadmodum scribunt Aristoteles et Avicenna, proportione respondet. Hunc caeli calor ita semper fovet et roborat, et fere sit illi quod ad crassius corpus ipse spiritus est . . .".

First, the chapters in the *Adversus Astrologiam* on celestial and human spirit are so close to Ficino's thought that it seems highly probable they derive from him. Secondly, we have the testimony of Gian-Francesco Pico, who was certainly not inclined to exaggerate his uncle's belief in astrology, that at the time of Pico's *Apologia* for his *Conclusiones* (i.e. 1486-7)[1] he still believed in divinatory astrology[2]. Thirdly, as I have already suggested[3], there may be a connection between Ficino's magic and some of Pico's Orphic *Conclusiones*; these undoubtedly propose a magical use of Orphic hymns, and the only "good", non-demonic, use I can think of would be an astrological one.

When Tommaso Buoninsegni, a Dominican professor of theology at the University of Florence, published in 1581 his Latin translation of Savonarola's Italian treatise against divinatory astrology[4], a popular, compendious version of Pico's, he prefaced it with a long *apologia* for Pico's and Savonarola's anti-astrological writings. This *apologia* is more like a plea for leniency than a defence. Opponents of their works, we are told, claim that they have proved nothing against sober and prudent astrologers, who are strictly orthodox, do not pretend to foretell particular events, and are careful to subject all their predictions to the inscrutable will of God. Moreover, these defenders of good astrology have the authority of Thomas Aquinas on their side, who "in innumerable places" teaches that even man's mind and will are indirectly influenced by the stars, through their effect on his body[5].

---

[1] The *Conclusiones* were published in Dec. 1486; the *Apologia* in May 1487.

[2] G. F. Pico, *Op. Omn.*, 1573, p. 631 (*De Rerum Praenotione*, VII, ii). In the *Heptaplus* (written at Florence 1588-9) Pico attacks "genethliaci", i.e. divinatory astrology (*Heptaplus*, V, iv, ed. Garin, Florence, 1942, pp. 296-8), but clearly accepts the influence of particular planets (ibid., II, iii, p. 232-6). After a warning against excessive subjection to the stars (II, vii, p. 242-4; we are brothers not slaves of the celestial souls), he writes "neque stellarum imagines in metallis, sed illius, idest Verbi Dei imaginem in nostris animis reformemus". This might be a reference to Ficino's talismans.

[3] V. supra p. 22. Cf. *Heptaplus*, II, vi, p. 242, where Pico connects the Orphic hymns with the intelligences that move the heavens.

[4] Savonarola, *Opus eximium adversus divinatricem astronomian ... Interprete F. Thoma Boninsignio ...*, Florentiae, 1581.

[5] Cf. infra pp. 214-5 on Thomas and astrology.

Buoninsegni then, instead of answering these critics, says [1]:

Indeed, to speak freely my opinion in so grave a matter, I have never been able to convince myself, nor be led to believe that Pico, Savonarola and other excellent men wished to condemn true and legitimate astrology.

Good astrologers, like Ptolemy himself [2], take care to safeguard free-will and providence. It was against the bad astrologers, who subject man's will entirely to the heavens and who derive religions from planetary conjunctions, that Pico and Savonarola were writing. If sometimes, carried away by their just anger against this bad, superstitious astrology, they went too far and also attacked good astrology, Buoninsegni begs the reader to forgive them; they were merely over-zealous, and perhaps inevitably so, since in correcting an abuse one is almost bound to fall into the opposite error, as one has to bend a curved stick too far the other way in order to straighten it, or as Augustine, when attacking the Manicheans, verged towards Pelagianism.

Not content with this curious *apologia* for Pico and Savonarola, Buoninsegni does his best to transform the latter's treatise into a work in favour of astrology by means of copious annotation. The authorities he uses in this are mainly Thomas Aquinas and his pro-astrological commentator, Cardinal Caietano [3]; but he even goes so far as to quote Pico's adversary Bellantius in order to defend horoscopes [4].

I would not deny that Buoninsegni was distorting Pico's and

---

[1]   Buoninsegni, in Savonarola, op. cit., p. 7: "Verum, ut quod in re tam gravi sentiam, libere dicam. Ego persuadere mihi nunquam potui, neque in eam cogitationem adduci, ut credam Picum, Savonarolam, caeterosque summos viros veram atque legitimam astrologiam damnare voluisse."

[2]   Ibid., pp. 8-9. He quotes from the Proemium of the *Tetrabiblos* (see Ptolemy, *De Praedictionibus Astronomicis cui titulum fecerunt Quadripartitum, Grecè & Latinè, Libri iiii. Philippo Melanthone interprete*, Basileae, n.d. (Ded. dated 1553), pp. 21 seq.).

[3]   Cf. infra pp. 214, 222.

[4]   Savonarola, *Adv. Astr.*, ed. Buoninsegni, pp. 104-5; cf. ibid., pp. 58-9, 88.

Bellantius (*De Astrologica veritate Liber Quaestionum. Astrologiae Defensio contra Ioannem Picum Mirandulanum* ..., Basileae, 1554, p. 171 (first ed. 1502)) wrote on Ficino: "Marsilius Ficinus Platonicus cuidam amico meo ejus inspecta genitura quaedam futura affirmavit, nihilque adversus astrologiam scripsisse audivimus, at sepe intentum legimus in libro de triplici vita quem jam plures sunt anni edidit pro astrologica facultate, ubi non modo de astrologia sed magica, quod majus est, diffuse tractat." This is a reply to Pico's statement about Ficino and astrology.

Savonarola's intentions. Nevertheless, his example shows us that it was possible to take their treatises as attacks only on "bad", irreligious astrology; and if, like Ficino, one knew one was a "good" astrologer, one could applaud their attacks whilst still believing in one's own astrology.

CHAPTER III. PLETHO, LAZARELLI AND FICINO

(1) PLETHO

There are reasons for thinking that Gemistus Pletho practised a kind of hymn-singing similar to Ficino's and even for conjecturing that Ficino's Orphic singing derives in some measure from Pletho. Although Pletho does not in his surviving works quote any *Orphica*, his religious ideas and interpretation of Plato were largely founded on the *prisca theologia*, particularly the *Oracula Chaldaica* [1], and he wrote out a copy of fourteen of the Orphic Hymns [2]. It seems likely that these have some connexion with the hymns that figure so prominently in the surviving fragments of his *Nomoi*, with the elaborate directions for singing them, for musical modes, postures, days and times of day [3]. Like the Orphic Hymns they are written in dactylic hexameters; their music seems to have been a combination of what Pletho knew about ancient Greek music [4] with Byzantine liturgical music [5]. They were addressed to Pletho's numerous gods, who bear the names of Greek pagan deities; the higher classes of gods are, as Pletho explicitly says [6], metaphysical or natural principles; the lower ones are planetary and stellar deities. Among the latter Pletho's devotion was given chiefly to the sun [7]; George of Trebizond wrote of him indignantly [8]:

[1] See Milton V. Anastos, "Pletho's Calendar and Liturgy", *Dumbarton Oaks Papers*, No. 4, Harvard U.P., 1948, pp. 279 seq.; Walker, "Orpheus", pp. 107-9.

[2] See J. Motellius, *Bibliothecae regiae Divi Marci Venetiatum ... Bibliotheca manuscripta Graeca et Latina*, I, Bassani, 1802, p. 269.

[3] Pletho, *Traité des Loix*, ed. C. Alexandre, tr. A. Pellisier, Paris, 1858, pp. 202 seq., 230 seq.; cf. Anastos, op. cit., pp. 255, 267 ("In both matter and style, Pletho's hymns ... closely resemble the pedantic hymns of Proclus and the pseudo-Orpheus"), 268.

[4] See Anastos, op. cit., p. 268; Pletho's short treatise on music, printed in his *Loix*, ed. cit., p. 458.

[5] See Anastos, op. cit., p. 268.

[6] Pletho, op. cit., ed. cit., pp. 2, 130, 202; cf. ibid., *Notice Préliminaire*, p. lix.

[7] Cf. François Masai, *Pléthon et le Platonisme de Mistra*, Paris, 1956, pp. 222 seq., 305.

[8] George of Trebizond, *Comparationes Phylosophorum Aristotelis et Platonis*,

I have seen, I myself have seen, I have seen and I have read prayers of his to the sun, hymns in which he extolled and adored the sun as creator of all things . . .

All that survive of these solar hymns are an altered version of Proclus' Hymn to the Sun [1], and the 9th hymn in the *Nomoi*, which begins [2]:

ὦ τοῦδ' οὐρανοῦ ἄναξ "Ηλιε, ἵλαος εἴης,

—the Sun is ruler of the other planets, and with them governs all terrestrial things. The latter hymn is quoted on a manuscript of Julian's *Oratio ad Solem* written by Demetrius Rhalles, who collected together the fragments of Pletho's *Nomoi* [3]. The theory of prayer with which Pletho introduces his hymns is remarkably like the theory of magic behind Ficino's astrological music; Pletho addresses his gods thus [4]:

May we carry out these rites in your honour in the most fitting manner, knowing that you have no need of anything whatever from us. But we are moulding and stamping our own imagination and that part of us which is most akin to the divine, allowing it both to enjoy the godly and the beautiful and making our imagination tractable and obedient to that which is divine in us.

Pletho's hymns and rites, like Ficino's [5], do not aim at any objective effect on the deity addressed, but only at a subjective transformation of the worshipper, particularly his imagination.

What historical connexion might there be between Pletho and Ficino? Pletho died in 1452, and the only time he was in Italy was for the Council of Florence in 1438-9; most of his *Nomoi* was

Venice, 1523, quoted by Anastos, op. cit., p. 211: "Vidi, vidi ego, vidi et legi preces in solem eius [sc. Plethonis], quibus, sicut creatorem totius, hymnis extollit atque adorat . . .".

[1] V. supra p. 23, note (6).
[2] Pletho, op. cit., ed. cit., p. 210; cf. ibid. p. 218 (Hymn XIX), and pp. 164-6, 174-8, on the predominant place of the Sun.
[3] See Anastos, op. cit., p. 211.
[4] Pletho, *Loix*, ed. cit., p. 150: "ἀγιστείας τὰς πρὸς ὑμᾶς, ὡς χρή τε καὶ μάλιστα τελῶμεν, ὡς ὑμᾶς μὲν οὐδέν τι τούτων τῶν παρ' ἡμῶν δεομένους εἰδότες. ἡμῶν δ'αὐτῶν τὸ φανταστικόν τε καὶ τῷ θειοτάτῳ ἡμῶν προσεχέστατον πλάττοντές τε καὶ τυποῦντες, καὶ ἅμα μὲν καὶ αὐτῷ τοῦ θείου τέ τι καλοῦ ἀπολαύειν διδόντες, ἅμα δ'ἡμῶν τῷ θεοτάτῳ εὐήνιόν τε παρασκευάζοντες καὶ εὐπειθές". Cf. ibid., p. 186.
[5] V. supra p. 44.

burnt and none of it was printed. Ficino finished his *De Vita coelitùs comparanda* in 1489; but his interest in the Orphic Hymns began as early as 1462, when he translated them [1], and there is one well-known document which may indicate, I think, that Ficino had Pletho's hymns in mind when he was inventing his astrological, Orphic singing. This document is Ficino's preface to his translation of and commentary on Plotinus [2], which he completed in August 1490 [3].

He begins this preface by asserting that Cosimo de' Medici conceived the project of resuscitating Plato after listening with enthusiasm to Pletho talking on Platonism during the Council of Florence. Over twenty years later he provided Ficino with the Greek texts of Plato and Plotinus, and in 1462 told him to produce translations of the *Hermetica* and Plato's works. Ficino finished the former in a few months. The Plato was not finished until 1477 and not published until 1484 [4]. Just as it was coming out of the press, Pico, who had been born in the year that Ficino began his Platonic studies (1463), arrived in Florence, and, inspired by the departed soul of Cosimo, incited Ficino to translate and comment on Plotinus. This was an example of divine providence working for the preservation of pure religion; just as it had worked by creating and maintaining the tradition of the *prisci theologi*—Hermes, Moses, Orpheus, Pythagoras, Plato . . .

We are here concerned not so much with the historical truth of these statements as with what they tell us about the state of mind of their writer. We have the following network of related facts which may have been present to Ficino when he wrote this preface. The *De Vita coelitùs comparanda* was part of the commentary on Plotinus; this commentary gives the key to Ficino's Orphic singing by connecting it with the astrological music of the *De Vita coelitùs comparanda*; Pico, who encouraged him to write it, had invented a magic use of the Orphic Hymns; Ficino, in intro-

---

[1] See Kristeller, *Suppl. Fic.*, I, cxliv-v; Della Torre, op cit., p. 537.
[2] Ficino, *Op. Omn.*, p. 1537.
[3] See Della Torre, op. cit., p. 625.
[4] V. ibid., pp. 606-7, 615.

ducing his Plotinus, recalls the inception of his Platonic studies in 1462 and connects this with Cosimo and Pletho; in 1462 Ficino translated the Orphic hymns and was already singing them— indeed, in a letter of September 1462, he ascribes Cosimo's patronage of his Platonic studies to the magical effect of his singing the Orphic "Hymnum ad Cosmum" [1]. If we add to this network of facts the supposition that Ficino knew about Pletho's hymn-singing—perhaps far more than we know now, it seems likely that when writing this preface he was thinking, amongst other things, of his astrological music and connecting it with Pico's magic, with his first interest in the Orphic Hymns and *Hermetica* in 1462, and with Pletho's hymns. The transmission need not necessarily have been through any writing of Pletho's, but may have been through Cosimo and other Florentines who listened to Pletho during the Council of Florence.

Against the supposition of this connexion between Ficino and Pletho we must weigh the following fact. Pletho was, at least in what we now have of the *Nomoi*, an overtly anti-christian writer [2], and philosophically he was a rigid determinist [3]. On both counts he would have been anathema to Ficino. But this objection is by no means conclusive; for I am suggesting not that Ficino was deeply or generally influenced by Pletho, but only that Pletho's kind of hymn-singing and his theory of prayer were one starting-point for Ficino's Orphic singing.

---

[1] Kristeller, *Suppl. Fic.*, II, 87; Della Torre, op. cit., p. 537; cf. Walker, "Orpheus" p. 102.

[2] See Pletho, *Loix*, ed. cit., p. 258; cf. Kieszkowski, *Studi sul Platonismo del Rinascimento in Italia*, Florence, 1936, p. 15.

[3] Pletho, ibid., p. 64 seq. (II, vi, περὶ εἱμαρμένης).

(2) Lazarelli

Between Lodovico Lazarelli and Ficino the only certain connexion is by way of the *Hermetica*. Lazarelli, in the dedication of a manuscript containing Ficino's translation of the *Pimander*, the *Asclepius*, and his own translation of the *Definitiones Asclepii*[1], mentions with strong approval Ficino's eulogistic preface to the *Pimander*[2]. Lazarelli's dialogue, the *Crater Hermetis*, culminates in a mystery, revealed in a hymn, which is based on the man-made gods in the *Asclepius*, i.e. on the passage (quoted above)[3] which was one of the main sources of the magic in the *De Vita coelitùs comparanda*. It is, then, certain that Lazarelli knew and approved of Ficino's *Pimander*, and at least probable that he was acquainted with the *De Triplici Vita*. Even if the latter statement is wrong and even if Lazarelli's *Crater Hermetis* owes nothing to the *De Vita coelitùs comparanda*, it nevertheless provides interesting comparative material; for we have here two nearly contemporary works both advocating magical or theurgic practices which are based largely on the same Hermetic source.

The *Crater Hermetis*, published in Lefèvre d'Étaples' edition of the *Pimander* and *Asclepius* of 1505[4], was written sometime not long before 1494. The speakers in the dialogue are Lazarelli and King Ferdinand of Aragon, who is represented as very old and retired from the world, and to whom the work is dedicated; Ferdinand died in 1494[5]. The king throughout plays the part

---

[1] See Kristeller, "Marsilio Ficino e Lodovico Lazarelli", *Annali della R. Scuola noramle sup. di Pisa*, Ser. II, Vol. VII, 1938, p. 243, 258.

[2] Lazarelli, first pref. of ms., Bibl. Comm. Viterbo, II D I 4, reprinted in Kristeller, art. cit., p. 258: "Ibi multa de Hermete nostro recte eleganter concinne et copiose dicta esse comperui quae me erga Marsilium operis interpretem mirum in modum amore affecerunt . . ."

[3] V. supra p. 40.

[4] *Contenta in hoc Volumine. Pimander. . . . Crater Hermetis A Lazarelo Septempedano . . .*, Parisiis, 1505, fo 60 vo.

[5] See Kristeller, art. cit., p. 251. There is a ms. version of the dialogue in which

of a docile disciple who is about to be initiated into a mystery which is both Christian and Hermetic—early in the dialogue Lazarelli tells him: "Christianus ego sum o Rex: et Hermeticum simul esse non pudet" [1]. The proceedings begin with a hymn, and after a time the king is passionately exhorted to listen with all possible attention to another hymn, which is to prepare him for the final revelation of the mystery [2]:

Apply here all the strength of your soul. Beseech, admire, praise, contemplate the divinity. For thus you will be properly disposed for the great secret god-making mystery which, if God help me, I am going to reveal; and in these things (as Hermes says) heaven and all heavenly beings delight . . . attend then with the whole emotional force of your mind, while I sing this hymn of contemplation . . .

This preparatory hymn begins:

> Eia mens mea cogita/
> Nunc miracula maxima:
> Quis fecit nichilo omnia?
> Solus sermo dei patris.
> Sit benedictus:
> Sermo parentis.
> Omnia laudes
> Dicite verbo.
> Quis celo rutilas faces/
> Eternis vicibus dedit;
> Ut rerum variant vices?
> Mens sola exoriens deo.
> Ergo pimander:
> Sit benedictus.
> Mentis imago:
> Mens cane mentem.

there are three speakers, the third being Pontano. Long extracts from this version (including the *Divinae Generationis Hymnus*) are given in *Testi Umanistici su l'Ermetismo, Testi di Ludovico Lazzarelli, F. Giorgio Veneto, Cornelio Agrippa di Nettesheim, a cura di E. Garin, M. Brini, C. Vasoli, C. Zambelli*, Roma, 1955, pp. 51 seq.

[1] *Crater Hermetis*, fo 61 vo.

[2] Ibid. fo 73 ro-vo: ". . . tui ingenij huc robur applica. obsecra / admirare / lauda / contemplare divinitatem. hoc enim pacto ad maximum et deificum mysterij arcanum: quod (modo deus assit) prompturus sum / commode disponeris. his quoque rebus (ut ait Hermes) celum celestesque delectantur omnes . . . Adesto itaque toto mentis affectu; dum contemplationis hunc hymnum concino."

Quis solem hunc nitidum sacre/
Fecit lucis imaginem
Scrutandi statuens gradus?
Lux sola ex patre defluens.
. . . .

It then goes on to the creation of man, who is redeemed by Christ and transformed by the Holy Ghost into a god:

Quis cum compleat omnia/
Ipsum solum hominem elevat:
Sorbet vertit et in deum?
Noster spiritifer deus.
Sit benedictus:
Spiritus almus.

The "effects" of this hymn on the king are all that could be desired [1]:

King: By this hymn of yours I am inflamed with an immense love toward God, by this hymn which extols man with such praises. And not only am I afire with love; but indeed I am almost stunned with wonder, as happens to those who by chance touch a torpedo-fish. For your hymn seemed of a kind that must derive not from the inspiration of the Muses but from the Word of God; what wonder then if it inflames the mind, draws it forth and snatches it away?

The king being now in a fit state to hear the revelation, Lazarelli begins a long preamble to it, so long that at one point the king interrupts [2]:

There is no need, Lazarelli, for you to strain my patience with such talking round and about. For, like a jar full of new wine without an air-hole, I am nearly bursting with expectation. Please relate more quickly what you have begun.

[1] *Cr. Herm.*, fo 75 vo: "ingenti amore erga deum / hoc tuo hymno inflammatus sum: qui tantis hominem preconijs extulit. et non solum amore incendor: verum etiam extra me stupore pene positus sum. quemadmodum accidere solet ijs: qui forte in torpedinem piscem inciderunt. talis enim tuus apparuit hymnus: non qui musarum ut aiunt inspiratione / sed verbi dei numine prodierit. quid mirum igitur: si mentem inflammat / si evocat / extraque rapit?"

[2] Ibid. fo 77 vo: "non opus est lazarele: ut tanta verborum circuitione / meam mentem intendas. Nam instar dolij musto pleni / quod spiramen non habet: pre nimia pene intentione disrumpor. digerere ocyus quod committis."

But for us this preamble is important. In it Lazarelli explains that, as the mind of God creates by His Word, so man by his mind and speech can procreate immortal progeny. By this he does not mean the creations of the arts and sciences; these are like equivocal progeny, i.e. the products of spontaneous generation, whereas Lazarelli means a creation analogous to univocal generation, in which the progeny is of the same species as the procreator. This mystery, then, will tell us how man's mind by means of words can procreate another being of the same kind. This mystery, which Hermes revealed to Asclepius, will show us "the kingdom of Israel (which poets call the Golden Age), for which Jesus Christ taught his disciples to pray"; it will give us the rest of the Sabbath after the six days' labour [1]. Then the *Divinae Generationis Hymnus* begins [2].

"The new novelty of novelties, greater than all marvels" is that "man has discovered the nature of God, and that the wise

---

[1] *Cr. Herm.*, fo 78 ro: "En israel regnum (quod poete auream vocant etatem) pro quo christus IHESVS docuit orare discipulos: nobis ante oculos proponitur. Sex operum laborumque dies transierunt: sabbati illusit requies . . ."

[2] Ibid. (beginning at line 36 of the hymn):

En nunc incipio. muta silentijs /
Pronis cuncta meos auribus audiant:
Divino gravidos eloquio sonos.
En tango digitis lyram.
Hec certe novitatum novitas nova /
Et mirabilibus maius id omnibus:
Naturam quod homo dei reppererit /
Quodque ipsam sapiens facit.
Nam sicut dominus vel genitor deus
Celestes generans procreat angelos:
Qui rerum species / qui capita omnium
Exemplaria / primaque.
Divas sic animas verus homo facit:
Quos terre vocat Athlantiades deos.
Qui gaudent homini vivere proximi
Letanturque hominis bono.
Hi dant somnia presaga / feruntque opem
Erumnis hominum dantque mala impijs.
Dant preclara pijs premia / sic dei
Complent imperium patris.
Hi sunt discipuli / hi sunt famuli dei /
Quos mundi figulus fecit apostolos
In tellure deos / quos nimis extulit:
Sensu de super indito.

(Cf. slightly different version in *Testi Umanistici*, ed. Garin, etc., pp. 66-7.).

man creates it". As God created the celestial angels who contain
the exemplary forms of all things, "so the true man makes divine
souls which he calls Atlantiad [1] gods of the earth. These are
pleased to live close to man and rejoice at his good fortune. They
give prophetic dreams and bring aid to the cares of men and bad
fortune to the impious. They give illustrious rewards to the pioụs
and so fulfill the rule of God the Father. These are the disciples,
these are the servants of God, whom the potter of the world
made apostles, whom as gods on earth he mightily exalted,
putting sense into them from above."

Evidently, this is closely modelled on the god-making passage
in the *Asclepius* [2]; indeed we are more or less told so. The king
is thrown into an even deeper ecstasy, and Lazarelli says that this
is only to be expected since this mystery has hardly ever before
been even hinted at; Hermes referred obscurely to it in all his
dialogues, but "recounted it much more openly" in the *Asclepius* [3];
otherwise it has only been indicated in the words and actions of
Christ and in the Cabala. With regard to Christ we are given
nothing more than the hint in the hymn about apostles [4]. From
the Cabala Lazarelli quotes an allegory which he says is in the
Sepher Yezira [5]; this, when interpreted, states that a new man
can be formed from the mind of a wise man and be vivified "by
the mystic disposition of letters through his limbs; for divine
generation is accomplished by the mystic utterance of words
which are made up of letters as elements" [6]. This is again the

---

[1]   Meaning, I think, Hermetic (Mercury the grandson of Atlas, cf. Ovid, *Metam.*,
2, 704; 2, 834; 8, 627).

[2]   V. supra p. 40.

[3]   *Cr. Herm.*, fo 78(bis) vo: "imprimis quidem Hermes: per omnes suos ...
dialogos / de hac re occulte precipit. sed in dialogo ad Asclepium ... multo apertius
narrat."

[4]   V. infra p. 71 note (5).

[5]   *Cr. Herm.*, fos 78(bis) vo-79 ro: "Abraham quoque in libro ... Zepher izira
... docet sic novos formari homines. eundem videlicet esse in desertum montem
ubi jumenta non pascant: e cujus medio adamam id est terram rubram et virgineam
esse eruendam / deinceps ex ea formandum esse hominem / et per membra / rite
litterarum elementa fore disponenda." The *Sepher Yezira* (*Liber Creationis*) was
traditionally ascribed to the patriarch Abraham. This allegory is not in any version
of it I have seen.

[6]   Ibid.: "Quod sic mea sententia est intelligendum. montes deserti: sunt divini

analogy with the divine creation through the Word, but in the cabalistic version according to which God created the universe through the 22 letters of the Hebrew alphabet [1]. It confirms what was already apparent from the preamble to the hymn—that Lazarelli holds a magical theory of language, that he believes that words have a real, not conventional connexion with things and can exert power over them [2].

This mystery is something which Lazarelli has not only learnt from the above authorities, but has known by his own experience [3]. When the king asks in what manner this work (*opus*, the proper word for a magical or alchemical operation) is done, Lazarelli replies that there is not time enough, for the sun is already setting and this work requires the observance of many conditions—it had better be put off to another time and performed in a more hidden and solitary place [4].

Kristeller discusses this mystery in his admirable article on Lazarelli and Ficino [5], and suggests that it consists of the rebirth which a religious teacher achieves in his converted disciple. This suggestion is strengthened by Lazarelli's statement that he had experienced the mystery himself. Now Lazarelli was a disciple of a certain Joannes Mercurius de Corigio, and in the dedicatory pieces of the above mentioned manuscript of the *Hermetica* [6] he

sapientes. qui ideo deserti. nam vulgo despiciuntur." The cattle are "corporei sensus". Adam, the red earth, is "ipsa sapientum mens". "Ex hac igitur terra / novus formatus homo: mystica litterarum per membra dispositione vivificatur. Nam divina generatio: mystica verborum prolatione / que litterarum componuntur elementis / sacratissime consumatur."

[1] V. e.g. *Abrahami Patriarchae Liber Iezirah, sive Formationis Mundi, ... vertebat ex Hebraeis, & commentariis illustrabat ... Gulielmus Postellus ...*, Parisiis, 1552; J. Pistorius, *Artis Caballisticae ...*, T. I, Basileae, 1587, p. 869, *Liber de Creatione* [i.e. *Sepher Yerzira*].

[2] Cf. infra p. 80.

[3] *Cr. Herm.*, fo 78(bis) ro: "arcanum arcanorum ... quod non tantum mihi est et auctoritate sapientum et rationibus persuasum; sed certe est et experientia cognitum."

[4] Ibid. fo 79 vo: "sed jam o rex ad hesperium sol inclinat oceanum / et in eo quod postulas / plurime observentur conditiones oportet ... differamus igitur in aliud tempus / in abditiorem et magis solitarium locum / sapientes Hebreorum imitantes".

[5] Art. cit. supra p. 64 note (1), pp. 253 seq. This interpretation is also accepted by M. Brini (*Testi Umanistici su l'Ermetismo*, ed. Garin etc., p. 29).

[6] V. supra p. 64 note 2.

speaks of his regeneration by Joannes, calls him his father, and says that he has begotten him again "aethereo semine" [1]. I think Kristeller's interpretation of the mystery is certainly right as far as it goes. But he himself admits that the Hymn in itself seems to be about demons—these created gods give prophetic dreams, they reward and punish—and it seems incredible that, if Lazarelli was talking only about ordinary Christian regeneration, he should not have said so and should not have cited John iii, 3-8 [2], since he does say that Christ indicated the mystery and he does quote from the Gospel of St. John [3]. Moreover, that Lazarelli was closely associated with Joannes Mercurius would lead one to suppose that the "novitatum novitas nova" was something more than the familiar regeneration of conversion, even though it might include it. For Joannes Mercurius was very odd indeed [4]. He appeared in Rome in 1484 wearing a crown of thorns bearing an inscription "Hic est puer meus Pimander quem ego elegi", preaching and distributing leaflets; at Lyons, in 1501, wearing the same garb, he performed miracles by natural magic, and promised Louis XII a son and twenty years' extra life. He was a wonder-working *magus*, who had himself, as Lazarelli tells us [5], been regenerated by Hermes Trismegistus.

I would suggest tentatively the following extension of Kristeller's interpretation of the mystery; it will, I think cover more completely the evidence we have. It was a magical operation by which the master provided his disciple with a good demon. The operation consisted mainly of words sung in some special manner. These sounds themselves became the demon; it is easy to under-

---

[1]   See Kristeller, art. cit., pp. 253. 259.

[2]   Beginning: "'Αμὴν, ἀμὴν λέγω σοι, ἐὰν μή τις γεννηθῇ ἄνωθεν, οὐ δύναται ἰδεῖν τὴν βασιλείαν τοῦ θεοῦ." Lazarelli may well have had this passage in mind; but his mystery was something more.

[3]   *Cr. Herm.*, fo 79 vo; *John*, x, 16. Cf. infra p. 72.

[4]   Kristeller, art. cit., pp. 246 seq.; Kurt Ohly, "Johannes Mercurius Corrigiensis", *Beiträge zur Inkunabelkunde*, Neue Folge, II, Leipzig, 1938, p. 133; *Testi Umanistici su l'Ermetismo*, p. 46 (and the references there given).

[5]   Kristeller, art. cit., p. 259:

Hic [sc. Hermes] te progenuit, tu me pater ecce reformas,
Tu pater, ille mihi est ergo vocandus avus.

stand how, if we take literally Ficino's probably metaphorical description of the matter of song:[1] "warm air, even breathing, and in a measure living, made up of articulated limbs, like an animal, not only bearing movement and emotion, but even signification, like a mind, so that it can be said to be, as it were, a kind of aerial and rational animal." Most demons have aerial bodies, and they have, of course, souls[2]. Lazarelli was not summoning demons; he was making them. These man-made demons were, I think, conceived of as separated bits of the Holy Spirit or the spirit of Christ; that is why the mystery is so extraordinary and momentous.

This interpretation fits every hint that Lazarelli gives us. Just before the Hymn Lazarelli, who had himself undergone this operation, says that he is inspired "not by a Socratic demon, but by the spirit of Jesus Christ which dwells in his worshippers"[3]. The operation is of the same kind as God's creation; for this too was accomplished by words, made up of Hebrew letters. It is of the same kind as the gift of the Holy Ghost to the apostles, the gift bestowed by Christ, the Word made flesh, of the Comforter which was to give them special knowledge and power[4]; for we know from the Hymn itself, and from a comment of Lefèvre d'Étaples on the *Asclepius*[5], that Lazarelli interpreted Hermes' attraction of demons into idols as being identical with Christ's inspiration of the apostles, "sensu de super indito". The mystery will be accomplished by the power of words and, I think, music; the old king is going to be initiated, and throughout the dialogue he is gradually being prepared by increasingly powerful hymns, producing more and more shattering effects, for the final ceremony,

[1] V. supra p. 20.
[2] Cf. supra pp. 46-7. For a good collection of demon-lore, see Ronsard, *Hymne des Daimons*, ed. critique et commentaire par A.-M. Schmidt, Paris, n. d.
[3] *Cr. Herm.*, fo 77 vo: "non a socratico demone percitus / sed a spiritu IHESV Christi / qui in suis cultoribus habitat."
[4] *John*, xiv, 26, xvi, 13.
[5] Lefèvre, ed. of *Hermetica*, 1505, fo 52 vo (commenting on *Ascl.*, viii & ix, where the man-made gods are first mentioned): "Lazarelus hunc locum ad Analogiam trahit quasi idola apostoli sint; fictor homo, Christus; virtus desuper inditus, spiritus sanctus". Cf. Walker, "*Prisca Theol.* in France", p. 241.

which is to take place in some "more hidden and solitary place". The mystery is being now revealed more openly than ever before, in order that the whole of mankind may be converted, that the "rest of the Sabbath", the millenium may begin, and Christ's words be fulfilled: "And other sheep I have, which are not of this fold: them also I must bring, and they shall hear my voice; and there shall be one fold, and one shepherd" [1].

I am not sure whether, as I have suggested, Lazarelli's magic derives in some measure from Ficino's music-spirit theory, and from the magic in the *De Vita coelitùs comparanda*; it seems probable, but there is certainly no conclusive evidence. In any case the two magics have interesting similarities and differences. They are both interpretations of the same Hermetic text on the magical insertion of demons into idols, interpretations which the authors think will fit in with their Christian beliefs; they both make great use of the "effects" of music, of non-liturgical hymns. And Lazarelli's magic, like Ficino's, is, I think, connected at a deep level with the mass—the obvious example of man's "making the divine nature". The main differences between them are: first, that Lazarelli's magic is not astrological—though of this I would not be certain, for when God's creation is used as an analogy to the mystery it is the creation of the heavenly bodies and their souls that is mentioned. Secondly that Ficino's magic does not involve eschatological hopes of universal conversion and the millenium, as Lazarelli's does. Finally, Lazarelli's magic is much more dangerous. It is overtly proclaimed as being of great religious importance and is plainly in competition with orthodox theurgic practices; whereas Ficino' magic could at least be presented and defended as a kind of astrological psycho-therapy.

---

[1] *Cr. Herm.*, fo 79 vo: "pre ceteris ... Christus IHESVS hoc arcanum revelavit. Sed prope est: ut quadam temporis plenitudine / apertius manifestet / ut impleatur quod ipse dixit. habeo alias oves: que non sunt ex hoc ovili / quas oportet me adducere. et tunc fiet unum ovile / et unus pastor." (*John*, x, 16).

PART II

In the rest of this book I shall be dealing with several kinds of magic and magical theory, and with various arguments for and against them. I shall be trying to trace the history of a tradition of Neoplatonic magic, exemplified by Ficino, of its connexions with other kinds of magic and with other related activities, and of the reactions against it. I shall discuss only a very few works from the vast literature on the subject of magic; but they will, I hope, be enough to show the main outlines of this history.

This tradition, as Ficino left it, comprised two kinds of magic, the natural, spiritual magic of the *De V.C.C.*, and the demonic magic, only hinted at in that work, but quite easily discoverable from his other writings. The tradition, therefore, was likely to grow in two divergent directions; which it did. The demonic magic, combined with mediaeval planetary magic, led to the overtly demonic, recklessly unorthodox magic of Agrippa and Paracelsus. The spiritual magic tended to dissolve into something else: music and poetry, as with La Boderie; orthodox Christianity, as with Giorgi; unorthodox Christianity, as with Persio. At the end of the 16th century the two strands of the tradition come together again in the planetary oratory of Paolini and the magic practised by Campanella.

Since the logical structure of theories of magic, as presented in 16th century writings, is both loose and obscure, I want here to suggest a scheme that will fit the theories we shall be dealing with; it will, I hope, help to clarify the relationship between the various topics that occur in most writings on magic.

The activities designated by the term natural magic all had a strong tendency to become indistinguishable from some other activity more properly called by another name; magic was always on the point of turning into art, science, practical psychology, or, above all, religion. I am not talking here merely about a vagueness or breadth in the use of the term—*magia naturalis* was indeed sometimes the exact equivalent of *philosophia naturalis*, as, for example in most of Porta's magic [1]—but about a real overlapping of the fields of all these activities, an overlapping which made the position of the concept of natural magic very insecure and resulted in its eventual disappearance. I shall try to explain the way in which magic overlaps with these other activities by means of this diagram, which is meant to indicate the relationship between the main themes of the theory of natural magic.

The planetary influence may act directly on the imagination of the operator, or indirectly through any or all of the forces. Effects can be produced by any one of the forces or their sub-divisions, or by any combination of them; but the *vis imaginativa* is nearly always present, for it is the fundamental, central force, and the others are usually used only as aids to heightening it or ways of communicating it. The most usual medium of trans-mission in the whole process is the spirit, cosmic and human The effects may be either on an animate being, or on an inanimate one (or directly on the body); the planets, considered sometimes as the former and sometimes as the latter (i.e. only their bodies), can produce a ricochetting effect back on to the operator's spirit and imagination. If the effect is on an animate being, it may be either subjective, remaining within the operator(s), or transitive, directed at some other person(s); in both cases it may be either purely psychological, remaining within the imagination or soul, or psychosomatic, affecting the body through the imagination.

This scheme is for a natural, non-demonic magic; but it could be altered to fit demonic magic by substituting angels or demons for the impersonal, "spiritual", planetary influences. The demons would be attracted or compelled by the various forces and would then accomplish the effects, acting not only on the body and spirit but also on the higher parts of the soul. In the present

[1] Cf. infra p. 158.

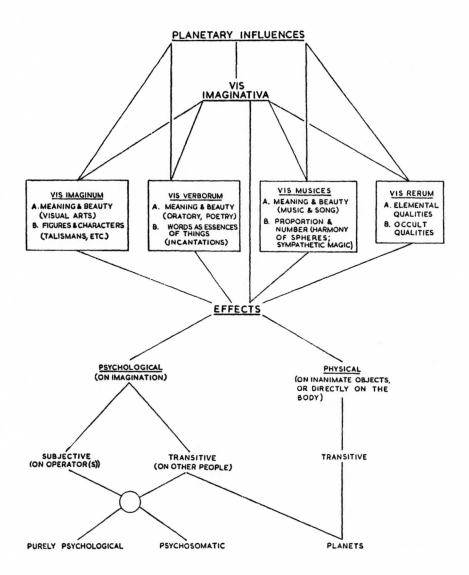

scheme, that is, of natural magic, the planets and the operator are not supposed to act directly on anything higher than the spirit, which is the vehicle of the imagination[1]. The effects produced on inanimate things or directly on bodies (unless by the *vis rerum*) are more difficult to explain without assuming a supernatural agent (angelic, demonic or divine) than the purely psychological ones; the same is true of the more odd or abnormal psychosomatic ones, for example, stigmatization or nervous diseases, as opposed to blushing or sleep. There is therefore a strong tendency for the effects of natural magic to be confined to the purely psychological, and the more ordinary psychosomatic ones. The more miraculous effects could be explained as natural, but only by assuming a power in the human spirit which was not generally admitted.

The A and B divisions of the *vires imaginum, verborum, musices, rerum*, do not all represent the same distinction, but they have this in common: the A forces of all these things are the ordinary, universally accepted ones, and, though they can be used for magical purposes, they can also and normally do produce effects which no one considered magical; whereas the B forces, though not all necessarily magical, are not universally admitted as real or legitimate, and their use is at least suspect of being magical. Any transitive effect produced by the *vis imaginativa* alone (e.g. telepathy) is obviously magical. The A and B kinds of the same or different forces may be combined in the same operation. The A kinds of the *vires imaginum, musices, verborum*, can produce aesthetic, affective or intellectual effects by the ordinary means of, respectively, painting (or any other visual art), music or song, oratory or poetry; the A kind of the *vis rerum* can produce ordinary effects on bodies through the elemental qualities of the things applied, as in any ordinary craft (e.g. cooking, or non-astrological medicine). Uses of these A forces are liable to be considered magical only if planetary influences are combined with them,

---

[1]   Natural magicians are neither consistent nor disingenuous on this point; they use the A kinds of the *vires imaginum & verborum*, which plainly have intellectual effects.

that is, if they are astrological painting, music, etc. Painting, music and oratory can be given astrological force by making them expressive of the character, the ἦθος, of a particular planet; it can be given to an elemental process by using the traditional correspondences between the planets and elemental qualities [1].

The B kinds of forces are more diverse and must be examined separately.

The B division of the *vis rerum* produces effects through the occult qualities of things, that is, their forces or virtues other than elemental ones; these qualities are usually thought to be caused by the planets, to correspond to a certain planet's character, and they are used to induce or reinforce the required planetary influence. The simple use of them, without the imagination of operator or patient being involved, is not necessarily magical, as, for example, the use of astrologically prepared medicines having their effects only on the body, or the use of a magnet to extract metal from a wound. But the classification of these cases is very doubtful, since it is seldom, if ever, that the imagination can be certainly excluded. In medicine the credulity or faith of the patient in the remedy is always of crucial importance. Even the magnet may be considered, as it was by Gilbert [2], to act like a soul, or, more precisely, as a fragment of the Soul of the Earth [3]. Plainly magical uses of the B kind of *vis rerum* occur when it is directed, usually in combination with other forces, at the operator's or patient's imagination, as when, for example, in Ficinian magic, groups of solarian, jovial or venereal plants, foods, animals, odours, are used in conjunction with planetary music and talismans. The main magical importance of occult qualities is in the resultant planetary grouping of objects, which can then be used by the other forces; one can, for example, make a picture, song or oration solarian by representing solarian objects (heliotrope, honey, cocks, etc.), or one could just sit and imagine them—in

---

[1] Cf. e.g., Frances Yates, "The Art of Ramon Lull", *Warburg Journal*, 1954.

[2] Gilbert, *De Magnete* . . ., Londini, 1600, II, iv, V, xii, V, i, pp. 68, 208 seq., 211 seq.

[3] Gilbert (ibid., pp. 208-9) explicitly connects this with the Platonic *anima mundi*.

both cases one's imagination would become more solarian. These groups of objects may also comprise human beings, who can be used in the same way.

The B division of the *vis imaginum* produces effects by means of such things as talismans, celestially activated statues, the *ars notoria*. The distinction between the A and B kinds of this force is, like all the others I am making, far from being hard and clear; but there is this difference between the two. The A force of an image is in proportion to its successful, beautiful representation or expression of its subject, even if this is astrological and meant to serve a magical purpose. The force of a B image lies solely in its astrological affinites; its shapes are often not representative at all (e.g. *ars notoria* signs, Paracelsan amulets), and, even if they are, the adequacy or beauty of the representation does not contribute to its efficacy [1]. The other forces, of the imagination, words, music, things, are often applied during its manufacture or use to reinforce the image's astrological power [2].

Since talismans usually bore words, letters or characters, as well as figures, they connect with the *vis verborum* and share with it the liability to accusations of demonic magic. The words or letters, not being representative, that is, having no one-to-one correspondence with a planet or planetary object, can only be effective through the medium of an intelligent being who understands their significance, namely, a human being, a planetary angel or a deceiving demon. One way out of this accusation is to confine the effects to the operator or to human patients who also see the talisman, whose signs can then be understood by them and become effective through their intelligences; this excludes effects on inanimate things, on the body, or at a distance. The other way out is by means of the B division of the *vis verborum*. This kind of verbal force rests on a theory of language according to which there is a real, not conventional, connection between words and what they denote; moreover the word is not merely like a quality

---

[1] Cf. Trithemius' directions for making a talisman. infra p. 87, and cf. pp. 179-181.
[2] Cf. passage quoted from the *Asclepius*, supra p. 40.

of the thing it designates, such as its colour or weight; it is, or exactly represents, its essence or substance [1]. A formula of words, therefore, may not only be an adequate substitute for the things denoted, but may even be more powerful. Instead of collecting together groups of planetary objects, we can, by naming them correctly by their real, ancient names, obtain an even greater celestial force. Here again, though this use of words obviously lends itself to magic, it is not necessarily magical; and, though it is distinct from ordinary operative uses of language, such as affective oratory or poetry, it may be combined with them in a magical operation—a poem, for example, might be both an expressive work of art and also an incantation, as, say, a hymn which both expressed the character of a god or planet and contained his true, ancient names.

The B division of the *vis musices* remained, as far as I know, purely theoretical. It is a theory that proposes the production of effects by means of the mathematical or numerical correspondence between the movements, distances or positions of the heavenly bodies and the proportions of consonant intervals in music. That this correspondence could be physically operative was explained by the analogy of the sympathetic vibration of strings. This theory is part of a wider cosmological theory, which supposes that the whole universe is constructed on these musical proportions, and which provides the most usual theoretical basis for sympathetic magic. One reason why this theory did not lead to practical music is that the musical representation of any given state of the heavens would provide only one chord and would suggest no particular melody or mode. Magical practices involving music, such as Ficino's, had therefore recourse to the A *vis musices*, which, through the text of the song or hymn, was combined with the A and B *vis verborum*.

We have now dealt with the means of producing effects.

---

[1] Cf. Walker, "*Prisca Theologia* in France", *Warburg Journal*, 1954, pp. 230 seq.; E. H. Gombrich, "*Icones Symbolicae*, The Visual Image in Neoplatonic Thought", *Warburg Journal*, XI, 1948, pp. 163 seq.

Ficinian magic, in terms of this scheme, uses the *vis imaginativa* combined with the *vires imaginum* B, *verborum* A & B, *musices* A, and *rerum* B. The effects it aims at are psychological and subjective. This description applies both to the spiritual magic of the *De V.C.C.*, and to his demonic magic. In the latter case the demons would be attracted by the several *vires*.

"Subjective", it will be remembered, means such effects as remain within the operator or those taking part in the operation, that is, either individually or collectively subjective, as opposed to transitive operations by which the operator imposes an effect on someone else without undergoing it himself. This distinction between subjective and transitive effects is important in two ways. First, if the effects are subjective, there is much less danger of the magic being demonic, since there is no transmission involved other than normal sense-perception—of the images, words, music or things used in the operation; whereas for many transitive effects the operation is not perceivable by the patient or the effect is on an inanimate object. It is still possible to claim that a subjective effect is accomplished by demons, but it is at least easily explicable without them. Secondly, it is only transitive operations that can be socially important; subjective magic may be good or bad from the point of view of morals or religion, but, since it does not affect other people, is not an instrument of power for social, political or proselytizing religious ends, such as were aimed at, for example, by Bruno or Campanella. Subjective magic, therefore, is much less likely than transitive to arouse fear and persecution. The use of transitive magic directed at animate beings constitutes an overlap with practical psychology; such magic is meant to control and direct other people's emotions by altering their imagination in a specific and permanent way. There is a marked tendency for such magical techniques to be centred on sexual feelings, both because they were probably recognized to be especially powerful and fundamental, and because they are in fact more closely linked with the imagination than other natural appetites. Treatises on witchcraft came near to being a pornographic *genre*; and Bruno made a remarkable attempt to outline a technique for controlling all emotions which is explicitly based on sexual attraction [1]. Subjective magic too can overlap with psychology, the only difference being that the techniques are applied to oneself, as in Ficinian magic; the sexual bias is not here apparent. These overlaps with psychology do not lead to the absorption of magic into another activity, since applied psychology did not exist in the 16th century as a separate discipline; in so far as it was consciously systematized, it was a part of religion, and this is one of the ways, perhaps the most important, in which magic overlaps with religion.

The production of effects by applied psychology or magic differs from many religious practices only in that no divine cause is assumed [2]. Natural, non-demonic magic is therefore an obvious threat to religion, since it claims to produce the same effects without any supernatural agent; its logical consequence is atheism or deism. Demonic or angelic magic avoids this danger, but is more evidently unacceptable to a Christian because it is a rival religion; the Christian revelation is unique and exclusive, and there is no room for any other religion. Prudent and wary Christians, therefore, prefer to consider all magic as demonic and to condemn it absolutely. Imprudent but well-meaning magicians attempt to achieve a non-demonic magic, in order to escape both the Devil and the obvious unorthodoxy of practising a rival religion. But their natural, subjective, purely psychological magic could explain all the effects of a subjective, psychological religion without assuming God. Ordinary Catholicism had some defence against this destructive explanation because many of its practices were of a miraculous kind which could not easily be so explained; they produced effects on inanimate things (bells, bread, crops), psychosomatic effects of a surprising kind (stigmata, cures of diseases), and employed techniques closely associated with magic, the *vis*

---

[1] Bruno, *Opera Latine Conscripta*, Florentiae, 1891, III, 637 seq. (*De Vinculis in Genere*).

[2] Cf. William James, *Varieties of Religious Experience*, London, 1902, pp. 508 seq.

imaginum and the *vis verborum*. But there still remained for Catholics the impossible task of demonstrating that these practices differed essentially from magical operations producing similar quasi-miraculous effects by similar means. Some evangelical Catholics and some Protestants attempted to remove or explain away such practices, and to condemn any but purely psychological religious effects as demonic magic. But since they had to accept the miracles in the New Testament, their position was not logically tenable, and, without the miracles, they were in danger of reducing their religion to a godless psychological technique, identical with natural psychological magic. The overlap of magic and religion produced then this dilemma: either a miraculous but plainly magical religion, or a purely psychological religion without a god. This dilemma was not of course explicitly stated, but it is clear that several anti-magical writers were aware of it and unable to find a way out. A very few pro-magicians, such as Pomponazzi, explained all religious effects, including miraculous ones, by natural (psychological and astrological) causes; and some very liberal Catholic magicians had no objection to identifying religious and magical practices. The historical importance of these connexions between magic and religion is, I think, that they led people to ask questions about religious practices and experiences which would not otherwise have occurred to them; and, by approaching religious problems through magic, which was at least partially identical with, or exactly analogous to religion, but which could be treated without reverence or devotion, they were able sometimes to suggest answers which, whether true or not, were new and fruitful.

CHAPTER IV. FICINO'S MAGIC IN THE 16TH CENTURY
I. WRITERS FAVOURABLE TO MAGIC AND ASTROLOGY

In discussing the reactions to Ficino's magic in the 16th century, I shall deal in this chapter with groups of thinkers whose religious and philosophical positions are such that they might be favourable to it—might either mention it sympathetically, or incorporate it into their own theory or practice. By no means all of them did so. On the whole Ficino's magic was not a success. In the next chapter I shall examine some of those writers whom one would expect, judging from their religious convictions, to condemn it outright, and who in fact did so.

(1) TRITHEMIUS. AGRIPPA. PARACELSUS & GOHORY

I have grouped these four magicians together, first because they are closely connected historically, and secondly because they represent a tradition of astrological magic which has close resemblances to Ficino's, but which is, I think, distinct from it. Aprippa's *De Occulta Philosophia* appeared with the blessing of Trithemius [1]; Paracelsus had plainly learnt much from it [2], and Jacques Gohory, commenting on Paracelsus, regarded him as Trithemius' disciple [3], which perhaps he was [4]. This kind of magic differs from Ficino's in being much more overtly demonic, and hence more obviously incompatible with Christianity. It is a continuation of the mediaeval magic, such as one finds in Avicenna, Roger Bacon, the

---

[1] Cornelius Agrippa, *De Occulta Philosophia Libri Tres*, n. p., 1533, sig. aa iij, letter to him from Trithemius, dated April 1510, expressing enthusiastic approval of the book.

[2] See W. E. Peuckert, *Theophrastus Paracelsus*, Berlin, 1943, pp. 36 seq.

[3] Leo Suavius (pseudonym for Gohory), *Theophrasti Paracelsi Philosophiae et Medicinae utriusque universae, Compendium, Ex optimis quibusque eius libris: Cum scholijs in libros IIII. eiusdem De Vita Longa, Plenos mysteriorum, parabolum, aenigmatum*, Basileae, 1568, pp. 160, 169.

[4] See Peuckert, op. cit., pp. 22, 410.

Picatrix, Arnaldus of Villanova, or Peter of Abano, in which operations are directed to the angels or spirits of planets, with the purpose of compelling them to do something extraordinary. Ficino enters the tradition with Agrippa's *De Occ. Phil.*, where the magic of the *De V.C.C.* is fully expounded, but in a context that robs it of any pretence of being natural and spiritual; the demons have come out into the open and dominate the scene. The effects aimed at are mainly transitive and not subjective, as with Ficino; this too is a step in a dangerous direction.

Trithemius

It cannot be proved with absolute certainty that Trithemius was in the habit of performing magical operations with the help of planetary angels, but it is highly probable. The main evidence for supposing so is in his *Steganographia*, which was not printed until 1606 [1], but was quite widely known in manuscript; Bovillus, Agrippa, Wier [2] and Gohory [3] had all read it. This book, as its title implies, has something to do with cryptography, a subject which he also treated in a published work, his *Polygraphia* [4]; it also appears to have something to do with invoking angels or spirits for some useful purpose—he also published a treatise, not containing invocations, on planetary angels, his *De Septem Secundadeis* [5], which sets forth a planetarily determined scheme of world history. Trithemius' adversaries, such as Bovillus, Wier or Del Rio [6], took the *Steganographia* as a manual of dangerous demonic magic, and made no attempt to interpret it as a crypto-

---

[1] Joannes Trithemius, *Steganographia, hoc est, ars per occultam scripturam animi sui voluntatem absentibus aperiendi certa* . . ., Darmstadii, 1606. Trithemius died in 1516.

[2] See Joannes Wier, *De Praestigiis Daemonum, & incantationibus, ac Veneficiis Libri sex, postrema editione sexta aucti & recogniti* . . ., Basileae, 1583, II, vi, col. 166 seq., where he quotes Bovillus' shocked letter to Germain de Ganay about the *Stegan.*, and states that he himself had read and copied it whilst living with Agrippa.

[3] Suavius, op. cit., p. 161, where he states that he owns a copy; he also quotes the Bovillus letter (ibid., p. 160).

[4] Trithemius, *Polygraphiae Libri Sex* . . ., n. p., 1518.

[5] Trithemius, *De Septem Secundadeis* . . ., Nurnberge, 1522.

[6] Wier, loc. cit.; Del Rio, *Disquisitionum Magicarum Libri Sex* . . ., Coloniae Agrippinae, 1679, II, q. iii, p. 111.

graphic treatise. Trithemius himself, in his preface to the work, in his letters and in an *Apologia* for it directed against Bovillus [1], carefully and emphatically denied that his book dealt with demonic magic, or with anything incompatible with Christian piety, and claimed that the invocations were only a disguise assumed to preserve its important secrets from the vulgar. Trithemius' defenders, both in the 16th and 17th centuries, assert that the book deals with nothing but ciphers or other innocent ways of secretly transmitting messages.

There is little doubt that the first two Books of the *Steganographia* do treat of cryptography, and that the angels and spirits in them can be satisfactorily explained as descriptions of the methods of encipherment. This is clearly and copiously demonstrated in a 17th century defence of Trithemius by a German cryptographer, W. E. Heidel [2]. But the Third Book, which is unfinished, does not, like the other two, contain any examples of enciphered messages; one is told to say the message over the picture of a planetary angel at a moment determined by complicated astrological calculations. It seems most unlikely that these could be disguised directions for encipherment or any kind of secret writing. The image of the angel is exactly described [3] and we are told that it need not be beautifully drawn as long as it is recognizable as a human figure. There is a short invocation, ending "In nomine patris & filii & spiritus sancti. Amen." The image is to be wrapped up together with an image of the recipient and buried under a threshhold. The message will be conveyed to the desired recipient within 24 hours, without the use of words, writing or messenger. By the same means you may also learn anything you wish to know about the recipient, "and everything

---

[1] See Wolfgang Ernst Heidel, *Joannis Trithemii . . . Steganographia . . . Vindicata Reserata et Illustrata* . . ., Norimbergae, 1721, pp. 72-8, where the relevant passages from Trithemius are quoted.

[2] Heidel, op. cit. (the dedication is dated 1676); this work resumes most of the earlier criticisms and interpretations of the *Stegan.*.

[3] Trithemius, *Stegan.*, III, apud Heidel, op. cit., p. 310: "fac imaginem ex cera vel pinge in chartam novam figuram Orifielis in modum viri barbati & nudi, stantis super taurum varii coloris, habentis in dextra librum & in sinistra calamum . . ."

that is happening in the world, you may learn, the constellation having been observed, by this art"[1].

Two later defenders of Trithemius' innocence of all magical practices, Gaspar Schott and Heidel, are nevertheless unable to suggest a cryptographic interpretation of the 3rd Book of the *Steganographia*[2], and do believe, I think rightly, that it describes a method of conveying messages mentioned by Agrippa, who had spent some time with Trithemius in his monastery discussing occult sciences and whose *De Occulta Philosophia* had been so warmly praised by him[3]. In a chapter of the *De Occ. Phil.* on air, to which he ascribes most of the properties usually given to spirit, Aprippa writes[4]:

The forms of things, although by their own nature they are conveyed to the senses of men and animals, can however, while they are in the air, receive a certain impression from the heavens, by means of which, as also by the fitness deriving from the recipient's disposition, they may be transmitted to the senses of one recipient rather than another. And hence it is possible, naturally, without any kind of superstition, and through the mediation of no other spirit, for a man to convey his thoughts to someone else in a very short time, however far apart they may be from each other; and, though the time in which this is done cannot be exactly measured, it will inevitably happen within twenty-four hours. And I know how to do this and have often done it. Abbot Trithemius also knew how to do it and used to do it.

---

[1]   Trithemius, ibid., p. 312: "Et omnia, quae fiunt in mundo, constellatione observata, per hanc artem scire poteris."

[2]   Heidel, op. cit., pp. 354-6; Schott, *Schola Steganographica* ..., Norimbergae, 1680, pp. 244-6. Heidel (p. 122) claims that he has discovered the "Key" to the 3rd Book, but he gives it in a cipher which I have not been able to break.

[3]   See letters between Agrippa and Trithemius at the beginning of Agrippa, *De Occ. Phil.*, n.p., 1533, sig. iij-iiij.

[4]   Agrippa, *De Occ. Phil.*, I, vi, p. ix: "Ipsae nanque rerum species, licet ex propria natura deferantur ad sensus hominum et animalium, possunt tamen a coelo, dum sunt in aere, acquirere aliquam impressionem, ex qua una cum aptitudine, a dispositione recipientis magis ferantur ad sensum unius, quam alterius. Atque hinc possibile est naturaliter, & procul omni superstitione, nullo alio spiritu mediante, hominem homini ad quamcunque, longissimam etiam vel incognitam distantiam & mansionem, brevissimo tempore posse nunciare mentis suae conceptum: etsi tempus in quo istud fit, non possit praecise mensurari, tamen inter uiginti quatuor horas id fieri omnino necesse est: et ego id facere novi, & saepius feci. Novit idem etiam, fecitque quondam abbas Tritemius."

It was a common belief that telepathic communication could be achieved by means of the human spirit conveyed in the air [1]; here the spirit, imprinted with the sender's thoughts, is precisely directed to one recipient by means of some astrological operation. Agrippa, it is true, denies that "any other spirit" is involved as a medium; this, however, may well mean that the message is not actually conveyed by a planetary spirit, but that it receives only its directive impression from the heavens, and the operation by which this impression is given might nevertheless require the help of a planetary angel.

I believe, then, that Trithemius' *Steganographia* is partly a treatise on cryptography in which the methods of encipherment are disguised as demonic magic, and partly a treatise on demonic magic. It is highly improbable, if Trithemius had merely wished to prevent a treatise on ciphers being too widely understood, that he would, being anyway suspected of black magic [2], have chosen such a dangerous disguise. On the other hand, if he wished to describe operations involving planetary angels, the cryptographic part of his book provided him with a convincing alibi. His protestations that he was not advocating invocations to demons or anything contrary to Christian piety were not perhaps downright lies. We must remember, first, that, as with astrology, my magic is always good and pious—only other people's is ever bad and diabolic; secondly, that there is nothing necessarily unorthodox in addressing prayers to angels, planetary or otherwise—for this the authority of Thomas Aquinas could be invoked [3], nor in hoping that they might do something to help you; it is merely perilous, because, as we shall see, it is difficult to distinguish good angels from deceiving demons. It should also be noted that Trithemius' astrological magic is not only a kind of telepathy; it is also a means of acquiring universal knowledge, "of everything that is happening in the world". We are back

---

[1]   V. infra pp. 159-160.
[2]   See letter of Trithemius quoted in Heidel, op. cit., p. 75.
[3]   V. infra p. 137.

again at Peter of Abano's prayer to Jupiter, which so greatly accelerated his scientific progress[1].

Agrippa

Any discussion of Agrippa's views on magic is made somewhat uncertain and complicated by the following facts. He did not publish his *De Occulta Philosophia*, which had been completed by 1510[2], until 1533, several years after the publication of his *De Vanitate Scientiarum* (1530), which contains a retraction of the former work and several discussions of various kinds of magic[3]. Agrippa reprinted these at the end of the *De Occ. Phil.*; in his preface he refers the reader to them and uses Ficino's feeble words to excuse h:mself for printing a book he had publicly renounced: "I am merely recounting these things, not approving of them"[4]. He also says that he has made considerable additions to it.

Before giving any weight to this retraction, we must remember, first, that the *De Vanitate* is a *Declamatio Invectiva*, that is, a rhetorical set-piece, and that therefore, though much of it is seriously evangelical, by no means all of its destructive scepticism is meant to be taken in earnest[5]; secondly that, though it contains one formal retraction of the *De Occ. Phil.*, this is limited to magic involving bad demons[6], and that the other discussions of magic, though far more cautious and less favourable than the *De Occ. Phil.*, do contain a defence of natural magic and even of theurgy, by which he means the obtaining of benefits by operations directed towards angels, including planetary ones[7]. There is,

---

[1] Petrus Aponensis, *Conciliator*, Venetiis, 1521, Dif. 113, 156, fos 158 vo, 202 ro; cf. Thorndike, op. cit., II, 900.

[2] This appears from Trithemius' letter at the beginning of the *De Occ. Phil.*

[3] Cornelius Agrippa, *De Incertitudine & vanitate scientiarum declamatio invectiva . . .*, n.p., 1539, c. xlviii (retraction), c. xli-xlvii (on magic).

[4] Agrippa, *De Occ. Phil.*, *Ad Lectorem*, sig. aaij: "Quod si qua reperitis, quae vobis non placeant, mittite illa, nec utimini: nam & ego vobis illa non probo, sed narro"; cf. Ficino, *Op. Omn.*, p. 530 (*Ad Lect.* of *De V.c.c.*).

[5] This is clear from Agrippa's *Apologia* for the *De Vanitate*; see M. A. Screech, "Rabelais, De Billon and Erasmus", *Bibl. d'Hum. & Ren.*, XIII, 1951, p. 246.

[6] Agrippa, *De Van.*, c. xlviii; note the final sentence, condemning magic "secundum operationem malorum spirituum".

[7] Agrippa, ibid., c. xlvi.

however, a real difference of attitude between the two books which indicates an unresolved conflict in Agrippa's mind. In the *De Vanitate*, and perhaps in later additions to the *De Occ. Phil.*, he is an earnest Evangelical, who is harsh on what he regards as superstitious abuses in the Catholic Church, and who is obviously wanting a Christianity as free of magic as possible. On the other hand, the chapters on magic in the *De Vanitate*, the fact of his publishing the *De Occ. Phil.*, and other evidence collected by Thorndike [1], show clearly that he continued to believe in the value of magic, even of the most dangerous kind.

Agrippa is the only writer I know of earlier than Paolini and Campanella to give a full exposition of the theory of Ficino's astrological magic, including the details of his planetary music. This exposition is taken, often *verbatim*, from the *De Triplici Vita*, and is combined with an Orphic *Conclusio* of Pico and an interpretation of the Orphic Hymns as astrological invocations; but it is dispersed and embedded in Agrippa's vast survey of magic, and therefore closely associated, one might say contaminated, with quite different kinds of magic. Though the *De Occ. Phil.* is predominantly Neoplatonic in its terminology and underlying metaphysical scheme, it includes many strands of magical theory, some of them hopelessly unorthodox; Agrippa has no cautious timidity about angels or demons, let alone talismans and incantations.

How Ficino's spiritual magic is transformed by appearing in the rich and varied context of Agrippa's magic can best be shown by a few examples. In all of these it must be remembered that Agrippa never openly cites modern writers, but frequently quotes from them; he is skilful at doing this, so that fragments of Ficino and Pico merge smoothly into the flow of his argument and seem to become part of it.

Early in his treatise Agrippa writes a chapter on the *spiritus mundi*, largely taken from Ficino, where he explains how planetary influences are conveyed by this spirit, which is analogous to

[1]   Thorndike, op. cit., V, 128 seq.

man's [1]. This is followed by fairly harmless chapters listing the various things which, containing an abundance of spirit and subject to various planets, are to be used for acquiring celestial benefits [2]. But then come directions for obtaining, not only celestial, "but even intellectual and divine" benefits, and this is accomplished by using these planetary things, herbs, incense, lights, sounds, to attract good demons or angels into statues, as in our familiar *Asclepius* passage, to which Agrippa refers. These directions are given without a word of caution, and more-over are said to be exactly parallel to the attraction of evil demons by obscene rites [3].

Part of Ficino's rules for planetary music, combined with the Pico *Conclusio* on the use of Orphic Hymns in magic, appear in a chapter on incantations [4]. These are to be directed towards the "numina" of stars, and the planetary angels are to be given their proper names. The operator's spirit, instead of being conditioned by the music into a suitably receptive state for planetary influence, as in the *De V.C.C.*, is here an active instrument, which is projected "into the enchanted thing in order to constrain or direct it" [5]. Ficino's musically transformed spirit appears here, "warm, breathing, living, bearing movement, emotion and meaning with it, articulated, endowed with sense, and conceived by reason" [6],

---

[1] Agrippa, *De Occ. Phil.*, I, xiv, p. xix; Ficino, *Op. Omn.*, p. 534 (*De Tr. V.*, III, iii).

[2] Agrippa, ibid., I, xv-xxxvii, pp. xx-xliv.

[3] Agrippa, ibid., I, xxxviii, xxxix, pp. xliv-xlv.

[4] Agrippa, ibid., I, lxxi, pp. xci-xcii: "In componendis itaque carminibus & orationibus pro attrahenda stellę aut numinis alicujus virtute, oportet diligenter considerare quas in se quaelibet stella continet virtutes, effectus & operationes atque haec carminibus inserere laudando, extollendo, ampliando, exornando, quae solet stella hujusmodi afferre & influere, deprimendo & improbando quae solet destruere & impedire ..." (for Ficino v. supra p. 17); cf. ibid., II, xxvi, p. clviii (planetary music), II, lix, p. ccvi (Orphic Hymns and astrology), and infra p. 174.

[5] Agrippa, *De Occ. Phil.*, I, lxxi, p. xcii: "Eiusmodi itaque carmina apte atque rite ad stellarum normam composita, intellectu sensuque plenissima, ... atque per imaginationis impetum vim maximam conspirant in incantante, atque subinde traijciunt in rem incantatam ad illam ligandam aut dirigendam, quorsum affectus sermonesque incantantis intenduntur."

[6] Agrippa, ibid., "Instrumentum vero ipsum incantantium est spiritus quidam purissimus harmonicus, calens, spirans, vivens, motum, affectum, significatum secum ferens, suis articulis compositus, praeditus sensu, ratione denique conceptus"; for Ficino v. supra p. 10.

but in Agrippa's hands it has become a means of enchanting, compelling, directing planetary angels.

Even where Agrippa is closely following Neoplatonic sources, he differs strikingly from Ficino and most later syncretists in that he makes no effort to force them into a Christian framework, or to warn the reader against the unorthodox religious ideas they contain. But he does not, like Diacceto, for example, merely omit such considerations and give what could be taken as an uncommented, historical account of Neoplatonic magical theories; he frequently, especially in the 3rd Book, discusses Christian prayers and ceremonies in relation to magic and pagan religions, and plainly regards them all as examples of the same basic activity. Magic and religion, Christian or pagan, are for him of the same nature; the *prisca theologia* is also a *prisca magia* and is accepted in a quite exceptionally "liberal" way. It was, of course, generally held that most of the *prisci theologi* were also *magi*; astrology and magic, for those who approved of them, were part of the ancient, extra-Christian revelation. The invention of these arts is regularly ascribed to Zoroaster [1]; we have already seen the importance of Hermes Trismegistus for Ficino's magic, and of Orpheus and the Neoplatonists.

Agrippa's remarkably thorough-going syncretism can be clearly seen even in the unusually careful chapter entitled: "On the two props of ceremonial magic, religon and superstition" [2]. Here we are told that all creatures, in their own several ways, worship their creator;

But the rites and ceremonies of religion vary with different times and places; and each religion has something good, which is directed towards

---

[1] There are many genealogies of *prisci magi* in the works of those writing both for and against magic, e.g. (pro) Giov. Pico, *De Hominis Dignitate* . . ., ed. Garin, Firenze, 1942, p. 148 (same passage also in his *Apologia* for the *Concl.*, *Op. Omn.*, Basileae, 1572, pp. 120-1); Gabriel Pirovanus, *De Astronomiae veritate Dialogus*, in Bellantius, *De Astrol. Verit.*, Basileae, 1554, pp. 269 seq. (first ed. 1506); (contra) Wier, *De Praest. Daem.*, Basileae, 1583, II, iii, cols. 146-150; Benedictus Pererius, *Adversus Fallaces et Superstitiosas Artes*, Ingolstadii, 1591, p. 92; cf. infra p. 146-7.

[2] Agrippa, *De Occ. Phil.*, III, iv, pp. ccxv-ccxvii, "De duobus ceremonialis Magiae adminiculis, religione & superstitione".

God Himself the Creator; and although God approves of only the
Christian religion, nevertheless He does not wholly reject other cults,
practised for His sake; and does not leave them unrewarded, if not
eternally, at least temporally ... [1].

God's anger is directed towards the irreligious, not towards
those who worship Him in a mistaken way. In so far as these
other religions differ from the true religion (i.e. Christianity),
they are superstitious, but they all contain some spark of the truth:

For no religion, as Lactantius tells us, is so mistaken that it does not
contain some wisdom; wherefore those may find forgiveness who
fulfilled man's highest office, if not in reality, at least in intention [2].

Moreover, even superstition is not wholly to be rejected. It is
tolerated by the Church in many cases, and can, if believed in
with sufficient force, produce by this credulity miraculous effects,
just as true religion does by faith. Examples of this are the excommunication of locusts in order to save crops, and the baptism
of bells so that they may repel devils and storms [3]. But, Agrippa
goes on, we must remember that the *prisci magi* were idolaters,
and not let their errors infect our Catholic religion. It is difficult
here to tell whether Agrippa the Evangelical is having a shot at
Catholic practices he thinks are superstitions, or whether Agrippa
the Magician is using them to justify his own magical practices.
The caution about the *prisci magi* is quite exceptional, and I
strongly suspect it is one of the later additions he mentions in
his preface.

Elsewhere Agrippa makes no attempt to distinguish between
true religion and superstition or magic. In a series of chapters

---

[1] Agrippa, *De Occ. Phil.*, III, iv, p. ccxvi: "Religionis autem ritus, ceremoniaeque,
pro temporum regionumque varietate, diversi sunt: & unaquaeque religio boni
aliquid habet, quod ad deum ipsum creatorem dirigitur: et licet unam solam Christia-
nam religionem deus approbet, caeteros tamen eius gratia susceptos cultus, non
penitus reprobat: & si non eterno, temporaneo tamen praemio irremuneratos non
relinquit ..."

[2] Agrippa, ibid., "Nulla enim religio (teste Lactantio) tam erronea, quae non
aliquid sapientiae contineat: qua veniam illi habere possunt, qui summum hominis
officium, si non re ipsa, tamen proposito tenuerunt."; Lactantius, *Div. Inst.*, II, iii
(Migne, *Pat. Lat.*, VI, col. 266).

[3] Cf. Wier on this subject (infra p. 155).

towards the end of the 3rd Book on prayers, sacraments and other religious rites [1], he constantly places Christian examples side by side, and on a level, with pagan or magical ones. In the chapter on prayer, for example, we are told, first, that if we are praying to God for, say, the destruction of our enemies, we should recall in our prayer the Flood, Sodom and Gomorrah, etc., and use those names of God that are expressive of anger and vengeance; secondly, that we should also address an "invocation" to the angel, star or saint, whose particular job it is to do this kind of work. The invocation is to be composed

in accordance with the rules given when we treated of the composition of incantations. For there is no difference between them, unless it be that they are incantations in so far as they affect our soul, and dispose its passions in conformity with certain spirits (*numina*), and are prayers in so far as they are addressed to a certain spirit in honour and veneration of it . . . [2].

Agrippa also thinks that prayers and purifications will be more effective on days and at times that are astrologically favourable—it was not "without cause that our Saviour said 'Are there not twelve hours in the day?'" [3]. In this part of his book ceremonies such as the baptism of bells are not said to be superstitious; they are effective "sacred incantations", used by the "primitive Church" [4].

One can see from all this that, although Agrippa's exposition

---

[1] Agrippa, *De Occ. Phil.*, III, lviii-lxiv, pp. cccxxix-cccxli.

[2] Agrippa, *De Occ. Phil.*, III, lxi, p. cccxxxvi: "Porro postulamus nobis eius quod optamus desiderij executorem suum angelum aliquem, sive stellam, sive unum ex heroibus, cui id officij incumbit, ad quem similiter sua dirigatur invocatio, quae & ipsa fabricanda est debito numero, pondere & mensura, juxta regulas traditas ubi de incantamentis componendis tractavimus. Nihil enim interest, nisi quia incantamenta sunt, quatenus animum nostrum afficiunt, eiusque passiones disponunt certis numinibus conformes: orationes autem sunt, quatenus alicui numini pro cultu ac veneratione exhibentur . . ."

[3] Agrippa, ibid., III, lxiv, p. cccxliii: "Horas etiam & dies pro operibus tuis elige, neque enim sine causa dixit salvator: Nonne duodecim sunt horae diei? & quae sequuntur. Tempora enim rebus nostris certam fortunam praestare posse docuerunt Astrologi, observarunt magi" (*John*, XI, 9); cf. ibid., III, lxiii, p. cccxl; and cf. Campanella on this subject, infra p. 218.

[4] Agrippa, ibid., III, lxiii, pp. cccxl-i: "Et ecclesia primitiva utebatur sacris quibusdam incantamentis, contra morbos, & tempestates . . ."

of Ficino's spiritual magic certainly gave it a wide diffusion, it may also have frightened people away from it. He exposes what Ficino, rather feebly, had tried to conceal: that his magic was really demonic. He also mixes it up with magic that aims at transitive, thaumaturgic effects, whereas Ficino's effects were subjective and psychological. Finally, and most importantly, by treating magic, pagan religion and Christianity as activities and beliefs of exactly the same kind, he demonstrates strikingly how dangerous Neoplatonic magic was from a Christian point of view. It is also relevant to this point that the spurious 4th Book of the *De Occ. Phil.*, where the magic is evidently black, was sometimes later believed to be by Agrippa [1], in spite of Wier's well-founded denials [2], which also did not prevent belief in the sinister stories about Agrippa's black dog [3]. Ficino has got into bad company.

Paracelsus and Jacques Gohory.

In dealing with Paracelsus' relation to Ficino's magic, I shall say as little as possible about Paracelsus's theories, and shall concentrate on one of his early commentators, Jacques Gohory, a Parisian who wrote under the name of Leo Suavius. There are several reasons for this. I doubt whether Paracelsus' philosophical writings are in fact intelligible, that is, whether they contain any coherent patterns of thought. To many 16th century readers it seemed evident that they did not, and even his early commentators either, like Gerard Dorn [4], add nothing to the text or, like Gohory, admit that they are not at all sure what it is about, let alone what it says. It is however possible to note some kinds of magic he mentions and apparently approves of, and even sometimes to guess that some battered fragment of an idea originally came

---

[1] Eg. g. Bodin, v. infra p. 174: cf. Thorndike, op cit., V, 136.
[2] Wier, *De Praest. Daem.*, 1583, II, v, cols. 161 seq.
[3] E.g. Ricardus Argentinus, *De Praestigiis et Incantationibus Daemonum* ..., Basileae, 1568, p. 46; cf. Thorndike, op. cit., V, 136-7.
[4] See Paracelsus, *Libri V De Vita longa, brevi, & sana. Deq. Triplici corpore. Iamdudum ab ipso authore obscurè editi, nunc verò opera & studio Gerardi Dornei Commentarijs illustrati*, Francofurti, 1583; cf. Dorn's translation of Paracelsus, *De Summis Naturae mysteriis Commentarii tres*, Basileae, 1584.

from Ficino, Agrippa, Trithemius, or some mediaeval source. Gohory, on the other hand, has for us the advantage of frequently talking about Ficino and comparing him with Paracelsus. Also, though he is by no means a lucid or hard-thinking writer, he does attempt to relate Paracelsus' utterances to other magical and philosophical theories. Gohory, moreover, had a wide circle of friends which included many of the most important scientific and literary figures of his time and country. His criticism of Ficinian magic and his championship of the magical tradition or Trithemius, Agrippa and Paracelsus may therefore have had considerable diffusion and influence by means of personal discussion.

Gohory was an advocate at the Parlement of Paris, and travelled abroad on several diplomatic missions—he was in Rome, with the French Ambassador Odet de Selve, from 1554 to 1556, where he knew Joachim Du Bellay and Olivier de Magny [1]; but most of his life was spent in Paris studying and writing. His publications show a very wide range of interests, which are however centred on the occult sciences, especially alchemy. He produced French translations of Machiavelli's *Discorsi* and *Il Principe* [2], of an anonymous Spanish account of Peru [3], of Lemnius' *De Occultis Naturae Miraculis* [4] and of three Books of the *Amadis de Gaule* [5]. This part of his literary works represents perhaps his contribution to the "illustration de la langue française". For he knew not only Du Bellay and Magny but also many other members and friends of the Pléiade: Dorat, Belleau, Baïf, Jodelle, M. A. Muret,

---

[1] See E. T. Hamy, "Un Précurseur de Guy de la Brosse. Jacques Gohory et le Lycium Philosophal de Saint-Marceau-lès-Paris (1571-1576)", *Nouvelles Archives du Muséum d'Histoire Naturelle*, 4e Série, T. I, Paris, 1899, p. 6; cf. Du Bellay, *Regrets*, lxxii, and Magny, *Soupirs*, li, lxxxii, cxxxiii. The most complete account of Gohory's life and works is in an unpublished thesis on Gohory, presented at Harvard by Willis Herbert Bowen. Professor Bowen has kindly allowed me to see parts of his thesis; but I have not used it for the present chapter.

[2] *Les Discours* . . ., Paris, 1571; *Le Prince* . . . Paris, 1571.

[3] *Histoire de la Terre Neuve du Perù*, Paris, 1545; cf. an article on this by W. F. Bowen in *Isis*, 1938; it contains a map drawn by Nicolas Denisot.

[4] *Les occultes merveilles et secretz de nature* . . ., Paris, 1574.

[5] *Livres* X (1552), XI (1554), XIII (1571); *Livre* XIV (1575) has a preface by Gohory.

Denisot, Fauchet, Pasquier[1]; and, in defending his translation of the *Amadis*, he proudly mentions their approval[2]. Gohory gives several reasons to justify his translating and publishing such an apparently frivolous work as the *Amadis*; among these, the most important for him was that he believed it to be an alchemical allegory[3]. The same reason accounts for several other of his fictional or mythical publications: a series of engravings of the story of Jason, for which he wrote the introduction and explanatory verses[4]; an edition of and commentary on a mediaeval French poem, *La Fontaine Perilleuse*, which he believed to be the source of the *Roman de la Rose*[5]; he wrote a preface for, and was instrumental in publishing, a French translation by Jean Martin of the *Hypnerotomachia*[6]. All these Gohory interpreted as heavily veiled alchemical treatises.

His original works show the same tendency. His commentary on Paracelsus, which will be discussed later, has a strong alchemical bias, and his little treatise on tobacco is mainly concerned with methods of distillation[7]. His *De Usu & Mysteriis Notarum*, shows a wider range of occult interests; in it he discusses, knowledgeably and approvingly, Trithemius' magic, the Art of Ramon Lull, the Christian Cabala, Camillo's *Theatrum*, the *Ars Memorativa*, Pico's

---

[1] *Amadis, Livre X* (1552) contains liminary verses, in praise of Gohory's translation, by Dorat, Du Bellay and Muret; *Amadis XI* (1554) by Dorat, Belleau, Jodelle, Tahureau; *Amadis XIII* (1571), by Belleau, Pasquier, Baif; Gohory cites Dorat, "amicissimus vir", on the Sybils in his commentary on Paracelsus (*Theophrasti Paracelsi ... Compendium ...*, Basileae, 1568, p. 253); for Denisot v. supra p. 97 note (3); for Fauchet see J. G. Espiner-Scott, *Claude Fauchet*, Paris, 1938, pp. 63 seq.; Gohory also dedicated works to two of the Pléiade's favourite patrons: Marguerite de France (*Amadis*, Livre X, 1552) and Catherine de Clermont, Comtesse de Retz (*Amadis, Livre XIII*).

[2] Foreword to *Amadis, Liv. XIII*.

[3] See Gohory's *Preface au Lecteur contenant exposition generale des chifres des Rommans antiques* to *Amadis XIV* (1575), and the Dedication of *Amadis X* (1552).

[4] *Livre de la Conqueste de la Toison d'or ...*, Paris, 1563; dedicated to the king by Jehan de Mauregard.

[5] *Livre de la Fontaine Perilleuse, avec la Charte d'amours: autrement intitulé, le songe du verger. Oeuvre tres-excellent, de poësie antique contenant la Steganographie des mysteres secrets de la science minerale. Avec commentaire de I.G.P.*, Paris, 1572.

[6] *Hypnerotomachie ou Discours du songe de Poliphile ...*, Paris, 1554; there was another editon of 1561.

[7] *Instruction sur l'herbe Petum ...*, Paris, 1572; cf. article on this by W. H. Bowen in *Isis*, 1938.

Conclusiones, the *Ars Notoria*, and Ficino's *De Triplici Vita* [1]. Gohory was also seriously interested in music. He was a close friend of the great music-publisher and lutenist Adrian Le Roy, for whose treatise on lute-playing he wrote a preface [2]. He also wrote prefatory pieces for several of Orlando di Lasso's works [3]. In one of these, addressed to Charles IX in 1571 [4], he speaks of his own "incredible delight" in music, gives a compressed *laus musicae*, and congratulates the king on his use of music and poetry for recreation—the only poets he mentions are Ronsard and Jodelle. Now this is very odd; Baïf's *Académie de Poésie et de Musique* had been founded only the year before, with the strong support of Charles and his family [5], and one would certainly expect that in such a preface Gohory would at least mention it. We know also that he was on good terms with Baïf at that time ; in 1571 a sonnet by Baïf, addressed to Gohory, appeared in front of the latter's translation of Livre XIII of the *Amadis* [6]. Moreover, in this year, 1571, Gohory started something like a little academy of his own somewhere in the Faubourg Saint Marceau, that is to say not far from Baïf's house in the Faubourg Saint Victor, which was the seat of the latter's Academy. I can only suppose that Gohory's failure to mention Baïf's Academy had something to do with enemies he had at court; in a work of 1572 he complains bitterly of the "abominable ingratitude" of certain literary courtiers who prevent his access to the royal

---

[1] Iac. Gohorius, *De Usu & Mysteriis Notarum Liber* ..., Parisiis, 1550, sig. kij vo (Ficino on spirit in plants and animals), (Civ) (on the *Ars Notoria*, which "solemni obsecrationum ritu à septem Planetis totidem artium (quas liberales vocant) parique dierum numero perfectam & absolutam cognitionem polliceretur. Sed (ut Marsilius Ficinus quae de vita coelitus haurienda per sacrificia, imagines, & annulos scripserat, in epistolis tandem suis interpretatur) non tam sunt haec praecepta credentis vel sperantis, quàm optantis vota"; the last phrase is quoted from Ficino's letter to Poliziano (v. supra p. 54)).

[2] See *Chansons au Luth et Airs de Cour français du XVIe siècle*, ed. La Laurencie, Mairy, & Thibault, Paris, 1934, pp. lvi seq.

[3] Ibid., p. lviii note 4.

[4] Di Lasso, *Secundus Liber Modulorum, quinis vocibus constantium*, Paris, 1571 ("Ego verò qui incredibili musice voluptate afficior").

[5] See Frances Yates, *French Academies*, pp. 19 seq.

[6] Baïf also published it in his *Passetems*, 1573 (Baïf, *Oeuvres*, ed. Marty-Laveaux, IV, 234).

family [1]. Perhaps these also prevented his becoming a member of Baïf's Academy.

Gohory's own institution he called the "Lycium philosophal San Marcellin" [2]. It was in an apothecary's garden, where he prepared Paracelsan medicines, did alchemical experiments, made talismans "suivant l'opinion d'Arnaud de Villeneuve, & de Marsilius Ficinus" [3], and where he received learnèd visitors who admired the rare plants and trees, played skittles, and performed vocal and instrumental music in the "galerie historiée" [4]. Thus there were two Academies going on at the same time and place, and both grew out of the same Neoplatonic tradition, but in divergent directions: Baïf's, encyclopaedic in aim, but predominantly musical and poetic—Gohory's, also encyclopaedic, but mainly alchemical and magical, though including music among its activities. Gohory's "Lycium", which was evidently, unlike Baïf's carefully organized Academy, a quite private, informal affair, presumably ceased at his death in 1576 [5]. It is possibly more than a coïncidence that in that year Nicolas Houel began to work for the foundation of his *Maison de Charité*, which included an apothecary's garden, a medical laboratory, and a music school,

---

[1]   Gohory, *Instruction sur l'herbe Petum*, Paris, 1572, fo 3 vo; cf. similar complaints in Gohory's dedication to the Comtesse de Retz of *Amadis* XIII (1571).

[2]   The only source for this is Gohory's *Instr. sur l'herbe Petum*; cf. E. T. Hamy, op. cit., pp. 15 seq., where the relevant passages are quoted.

[3]   Gohory, *Instruction*, Ded.: "Or ay je entre autres oeuvres des mineraux, vegetaux & animaux composé nagueres des Sig. Astronomiques, suivant l'opinion d'Arnaud de ville-neuve, & de Marsilius Ficinus . . ."

[4]   Ibid., fo 14 ro: "Or j'espere sur le printems qu'il n'y aura simple rare & estrange en ce païs qu'il n'y soit semé ou planté pour donner ce contentement aux gens d'esperit qui souvent se delectent au labyrinthe d'arbres garniz de son donjon au mylieu, & de quatre tourelles d'ormes courbez aux 4 coingz. Les autres, en la fontaine artificielle saillante par conduitz de plomb. Les autres, és fruits des Entes qui y sont de toutes sortes en grand nombre plantees à la ligne de deux costez sur les allées & sentiers. Aucuns à l'orée des deux pavillons, l'un couvert de pruniers l'autre de cerisiers. Autres à l'exercice de la boule ou quilles soubz un long & large berceau de treillage. Et quand quelque assignation les presse de partir, regardant l'heure au quadran horizontal de compartiment. Autres s'addonnent à faire Musique de voix & instrumens en la galerie historiee . . .".

[5]   During this time, 1571-1576, Gohory was also occupied in writing a continuation of Paolo Emilio's history of France, for which he received the 500 livres a year that Ramus had bequeathed for a new Chair of Mathematics (see Hamy, op. cit., pp. 22-4).

and which was situated in the Faubourg Saint Marceau[1].
Gohory's "Lycium" may have been quite an important centre
for the spreading of Paracelsan medicine in Paris. He knew the
most distinguished physicians of his day: Jean Fernel, Ambroise
Paré, Jean Chapelain, Honoré Chastellan, Leonard Botal. He tells
us that he often had long discussions with Fernel on Paracelsism,
and on one occasion had a kind of debate on the subject with
Paré, Chapelain and Chastellan at Botal's house[2]. The discussions
with Fernel must have occurred before the "Lycium" began[3];
But Gohory certainly continued to be friendly with physicians
and to defend Paracelsus.

Gohory was as much aware of the confusion, inconsistency and
general obscurity of Paracelsus' writings as was the latter's chief
adversary, Erastus, and freely admits there is much he does not
understand in them, even that he cannot be sure whether in some
cases they are about alchemy or the soul or astrology or medicine
or something else[4]. He had, I think, two reasons for persisting
nevertheless in trying to understand them, and these reasons
may well have been common to many of his contemporaries who
showed a keen interest in what seemed to Erastus, as it must
to any casual reader, the incoherent *radotage* of a boastful
drunkard[5].

The reasons were: first, that some of Paracelsus' medical

---

[1] See F. A. Yates, "Dramatic Religious Processions in Paris in the late 16th
century", *Annales Musicologiques*, II, 1954, pp. 230 seq.

[2] See Leo Suavius (i.e. Gohory), *Theophrasti Paracelsi Philosophiae et Medicinae
utriusque universae, Compendium, Ex optimis quibusque eius libris: Cum scholijs in libros
IIII. eiusdem De Vita Longa . . .*, Basileae, 1568, pp. 147-9, and Gohory, *Instruction*,
fo 9 vo.

[3] Fernel died in 1558.

[4] Suavius, op. cit., pp. 151 (Paracelsus' style excused because he wrote for the
"rudia ingenia" of the Germans), 169 (Paracelsus' veiling compared to Trithemius'),
309 (Gohory uncertain whether Paracelsus is writing about alchemy or astrological
magic), letter to Louis de Saint-Gelais de Lansac at end of volume (admission:
"nondum ad ipsius sacrarij penetralia deductus").

[5] I can see no reason to doubt the evidence Erastus collects from Oporinus
and others that Paracelsus was hardly ever sober (Erastus, *Disputationum De Medicina
nova . . . Pars Prima*, Basileae, (1571), pp. 236 seq., *Pars Altera*, 1572, p. 12; cf.
Peuckert, *Paracelsus*, Berlin, 1943, pp. 143 seq. for a very different view of Oporinus'
evidence.

works showed first-hand knowledge and contained valuable new
ideas, particularly with regard to the use of chemical remedies [1];
secondly, that Gohory, like many others, was anyway passionately
interested in all occult subjects, and was therefore used to treating
respectfully texts of a baffling obscurity—Paracelsus, after all,
is no more obscure and confused than, say, the *Oracula Chaldaïca*,
the book of *Revelations*, or for that matter, St. Paul. He would
have expected in any work dealing at all profoundly with magic,
religion, alchemy or astrology, to find a heavy "veiling" of the
truth [2]. He prefaces his commentary on Paracelsus with a long
justification of this practice [3], and announces, unfortunately for
us, that he too is going to comment "more platonico", that is,
enigmatically [4].

The work of Paracelsus on which Gohory wrote his commentary
is the *De Vita Longa*, which he took to be in some way derivative
from Ficino's *De Triplici Vita*. This assumption was probably
correct; it is suggested by the title [5], and Paracelsus is known to
have admired Ficino as a physician [6]. Moreover, some of the
contents of the *De Vita Longa* do seem to be a nightmarish
fragmentation of themes in the *De Triplici Vita*. One of its
chapters is headed by Gohory with this *argumentum*: "Aid to
long life is to be sought from the influence of supernatural bodies,
treated by Marsilio Ficino, De Vita coelitùs comparanda" [7].
From the text it appears that man can attract some beneficial
influence from on high, though it is not at all clear what part of
man is influenced, or by what or how. The attraction of this
influence is by means that have wrongly been called incantations
or superstitions, and which are the origin of Greek magic; they

---

[1]   Suavius, op. cit., p. 150; this is conceded by Erastus (*Disp. de Med. Nov.*,
sig. β (*Lectori*)).
[2]   Cf. Walker, "*Prisca Theologia* in France", pp. 221 seq.
[3]   Suavius, op. cit., pp. 159 seq..
[4]   Ibid., p. 170.
[5]   Cf. title of Dorn's edition (supra p. 96 note 4).
[6]   See Peuckert, op. cit., p. 132.
[7]   Suavius, op. cit., p. 89 (*De Vita Longa*, I, vi): "Ex influentia corporum super-
naturalium praesidium petendum longae vitae, tractatum à Marsilio Ficino de vita
coelitùs comparanda".

have something to do with cabalistic magic, by which he seems to mean the magic telepathy in Trithemius' *Steganographia*, and with talismans and *gamaheae* (i.e. naturally formed amulets of stone or mineral), which do not get their power from the stars, but from something higher, and which influence something higher in man than his mortal body.

Gohory's commentary on this chapter helps considerably in clearing up the question of what is influencing what [1]. Throughout this treatise Paracelsus gives man three bodies [2]: natural or mortal, celestial, super- or praeternatural. Although Gohory earlier asserts that the latter two are identical, he here distinguishes all three so that they are roughly equivalent, in Ficinian terms, to: earthly body, spirit, soul or mind. It is the last that is to be influenced by the use of talismans and other magical operations; and the influence is to come, not from the heavenly bodies, which affect only man's earthly body, but from the Intelligences which move them, that is, from planetary angels. This would be in accordance with Agrippa's views, and with the long tradition of mediaeval astrological magic which sought intellectual benefits from planetary angels. But Paracelsus goes one step further than Agrippa in positively excluding planetary influence by cosmic spirit on the human spirit, and thereby removes even the possibility of a natural, spiritual magic. Gohory seems not to notice this difference between the *De Vita Longa* and the spiritual magic of the *De V.C.C.*, though elsewhere he interprets Paracelsus' magic as being primarily directed to the spirit, explicitly connecting this with Ficino [3].

---

[1] Suavius, op. cit., pp. 185 seq..

[2] Cf. Erastus, *Disp.*, *Pars Prima*, pp. 260-1, a passage, reminiscent of James Thurber, on the various bodies, souls and spirits, that appear in Paracelsus' writings; if one adds them all together, man has three bodies (elemental, sideral, celestial), two souls (eternal, vital), four spirits (earthly, sideral, animal, divine); cf. *Disp.*, *Pars Altera*, pp. 220 seq.

[3] Suavius, op. cit., pp. 30 ("... alterius corporis, id est spiritus corporei, vel potius animae, de quo quaedam Marsilius Ficinus scitè ex Platonis sui sententia: Theophrastus noster corpus invisibile appellat"), 327 ("Ex his colligere licet lectori, quanta vis magiae, scilicet naturalis atque honestae consistat in spiritu, in quo Theophrastus noster jure hoc libro totus est. De alia magia, nec ipse quidem, nec Ficinus & Arnaldus sensisse mihi videntur ...").

Here, then, we again find Ficino's magic, as with Agrippa, in a dangerous form: overtly and exclusively demonic, and influencing the intellect instead of the human spirit. Gohory, moreover insists on the derivation of Paracelsan from Ficinian magic [1], and even gives a *Comparatio* of the one with the other. This, in fact, turns out to be a rather sharp criticism of Ficino as being a timid and superficial version of Paracelsus. Gohory recalls with annoyance that Ficino "pretends he is only recounting, not approving of, the magic which he is teaching and establishing" [2]. It was from the same timidity that he made the bad mistake of preferring astrologically prepared medicines to talismans. He is, however, to be praised as a forerunner of Paracelsus in that he "placed beyond doubt" the superiority of astrological medicines over ordinary ones [3]. Gohory sums up [4]:

Say then that Marsilio Ficino believed in images and seals, but from religious fears pretended not to (as one can easily gather from his various utterances); and thereby wrongly hindered many people's belief in, and approval of, these most difficult matters, or caused them to withhold judgment. He and Giovanni Pico had read many books of the Pytha-

---

[1] Suavius, op. cit., p. 186: "Viam autem adipiscendae longę vitae sternit ab imaginibus ac Gamaheis: de quibus Marsilius Ficinus diserte multa & cumulatè ex Platonica disciplina in lib. de vita coelitus haurienda . . . ut illum in eodem quo Paracelsum appareat argumento lusisse".

[2] Suavius, op. cit., p. 187: against removing "vitam animamque mundo, coelo, syderibus per quam influxus coelestes in haec inferiora infunduntur. De quibus scitè Ficinus in Apologia . . . nisi quam nunc docet confirmatque magiam, mox se narrare non probare simularet. Nam ne forte in superstitionem labi videatur, labitur in errorem manifestum, dum praefert concoctiones medicinarum sculpturis lapidum ac metallorum . . ." (cf. supra p. 42).

[3] Ibid.: "At extrà dubitationem meritò ponit unguenta & pharmaca sidereo favore afflata, viribus summis insigniri: In quo Paracelsus Hippocraticam Musam reprehendit, quae inferioribus tantùm rebus insudaverit, nec eas ad normam virtutemque superiorum temperaverit." He then quotes from Ficino on this subject (v. infra p. 168).

[4] Ibid., p. 188: "Dic itaque Marsilium fidem adhibuisse imaginibus & sigillis, sed religionis metu dissimulasse (ut ex illius variis sermonibus colligere facillimum est) multorum interim fidem in ijs rebus difficillimis & assertionem perperàm cohibuisse suspensamve tenuisse. Libros ille & Ioann. Picus Mirandulanus Pythagoreorum Platonicorumque magna mysteria continentes, Zoroastris, Trismegisti, Indorum, Chaldeorum, Egyptiorum, Arabumque legerunt: sed superficiem tantae sapientae delibasse illorum scripta demonstrant, ad intimam eorum mentem penetrasse nulla illorum mirifica opera gestave testantur. Magnam tamen aliis qui prisca illa monumenta non degustarunt, admirationem sui reliquere."

goreans and Platonists containing great mysteries, books of Zoroaster, Trismegistus, of the Indians, Chaldeans, Egyptians and Arabs: but their writings show that they had touched only the surface of this great wisdom, and no marvellous works or deeds of theirs bear witness to their having pierced through to the inward mind of these sages. They were however much admired by those who had no acquiantance with these ancient monuments of wisdom.

For Gohory, then, Ficino was on the right track, namely the *prisca magia*, but, from timidity and religious scruples, he did not go far enough or deep enough; and this is shown, not only in the cautiousness of his writings, but also in his failure to perform any marvellous operations, to become a powerful wonder-working *magus*, like Apollonius or Paracelsus. Here Gohory makes an important point. He is quite right that Ficino did not perform any stupendous works, and he certainly did not want to. His magic is eminently private, individual and subjective, and hence is nearer to being a religion than a bogus science.

As one would expect, Gohory is a firm believer in the magical power of words, characters, figures and incantations. It is also clear that he thinks that Trithemius in the *Steganographia* wrote on a kind of telepathy achieved by the use of invocations to planetary angels and talismans, and mentioned by Agrippa[1]. In defending the efficacy and innocence of such practices against Wier's attacks on Trithemius [2], he asks with astonishment how Wier can dare to contradict so many great ancient philosophers, of whom he gives a list, including Julian the Apostate, Artephius, Roger Bacon, Peter of Abano, Albertus Magnus, Picatrix and Arnaldus of Villanova [3]. It is in fact such authorities that Gohory cites far

---

[1] Ibid., pp. 196-7, 262; cf. also on Trithemius pp. 160-4, 192, 217.

[2] Suavius, ibid., pp. 150-2; Wier, *De Praest. Daem.*, II, vi, cols. 166 seq..

[3] Suavius, op. cit., pp. 250-1: "Negas haec characteristica Wiere, Tu nè es (ô miser) cum tantis Priscis viris ulla ex parte comparandus? ut tantùm hìc novissimos philosophos nominem Appionem Grammaticum, Julianum Caesarem, Artephium, Rogerium Bachonem, Petrum Aponensem conciliatorem, Albertum Magnum, Arnaldum Villanovum, Anselmum Parmensem, Picatricem Hispanum, Cicchum Asculum Florentinum: quorum nullus est qui non te fama doctrinaque longè antecellat." Wier (*De Praest.*, V, viii, col. 535) had written against Gohory's "characteristica".

more frequently than Neoplatonic ones; his own *prisca magia* is predominantly mediaeval, and extremely unorthodox. He then goes on, in a more kindly way [1]:

> I suspect that you (Wier), a man who in my opinion is erudite and neither unskilled not silly, undertook this extremely rash attack on the whole of antiquity out of fear of calumny. Thus did Marsilio Ficino, priest and physician, produce fruitlessly many mystical writings; from which later, with regard both to religion and to medicine, he withheld his positive approval. I indeed, good men, forgive you, and rather deplore the miserable state of this ignorant world . . .

[1] Ibid.: "Suspicor te calumniae metu, virum meo judicio eruditum nec inertem, nec insulsum contra omnem antiquitatem bellum profectò temerarium suscepisse. Sic Marsilius Ficinus sacerdos & medicus, multa scripsit mystica infructuosè; in quibus postea tam in religione quàm medicina suspendit assertionem. Ego verò (viri boni) vos excuso, quin potius seculi miseriam imperiti defleo . . ."

(2) POMPONAZZI

Pomponazzi's *De Incantationibus* [1] is a work in which one might reasonably expect to find discussion, and even approval of Ficino's spiritual magic. For, in spite of their quite different philosophical outlook, they show, when explaining magical effects, the same wish to exclude demons or angels, and the same firm belief in the importance of planetary influences and of the state of the operator's spirit. Moreover, Pomponazzi had read Ficino and quotes a long passage from the *Theologia Platonica* on the magical power of the imagination [2]. Nevertheless, he does not discuss the magic of the *De V.C.C.*, though he does use Ficino as an authority in defending talismans against Thomas Aquinas [3]. Since, however, Pomponazzi's theories are in some respects close to Ficino's, an examination of them here will not be irrelevant.

One of Pomponazzi's favourite explanations of the power of words in incantations, or of characters in talismans, is the *vis imaginativa*, transmitted by spirit, with great emphasis on the importance of credulity both in the operator and the patient. The imaginations of the operator and of the patient are so violently affected by the words or images that their spirits are suddenly and greatly altered. This alteration can produce directly a subjective effect in the patient's body, and it can indirectly produce transitive effects by means of the flow of altered spirits evaporating

---

[1] Pomponazzi, *De naturalium effectuum causis, sive de Incantationibus, Opus abstrusioris plenum, . . . ante annos XXXV compositum, nunc primùm in lucem fideliter editum. Adiectis brevibus scholiis à Gulielmo Gratarolo Physico Bergomate . . .*, Basileae, 1556. Pomponazzi's introductory letter is dated: Bologna, July 24, 1520.

[2] Pomponazzi, *De Incant.*, p. 25 (reference to Ficino, *Theol. Plat.*, IV, i (*Op. Omn.*, pp. 122 seq.), on occult virtues), p. 34 (long quotation from *Theol. Plat.*, XIII, i (*Op. Omn.*, p. 284), on the power of the imagination).

[3] Pomponazzi, ibid., pp. 252-3, an emphatic justification of talismans, ending: "Quod si Ficino nostro fides prestanda est, hoc etiam illustres Platonici voluerunt."

from the operator, which influence the patient's spirit or form
visions in the air. To achieve these results the imagination must
be of a suitable nature or disposition, namely, in a state of receptivity due to credulity; the operator must believe whole-heartedly
in the efficacy of the words he is saying, and the patient must have
complete faith in him and his spells—only thus will their imaginations, and thence their spirits and bodies, be transformed [1]. This
explanation when applied to the subject of prayer comes very
near to the theory of planetary magic in the *De V.C.C.*, namely,
that the rites, invocations, etc., are aimed less at altering the planet,
than at making the operator more receptive to its influence.
Pomponazzi, in discussing the case of a miraculous apparition of
a saint to those who had successfully prayed to him to expell
storms, suggests that the spirits of the congregation, stamped with
the saint's image, may have produced a simulachrum of him by
impressing this image on the air, already made thick and retentive
by the storms. He remarks that prayers, if they are to be effective,

must come from the depths of the heart and be fervent; for thus are
the spirits more strongly affected and more powerful in their effect on
matter—not in order that they may prevail upon the intelligences (for
these are entirely immutable), but in order that they [sc. the spirits]
may be more moved; just as the spittle of an angry man or snake is
more powerful than that of a man or snake who is not angry [2].

I think that "intelligences" must mean the minds that move
the celestial spheres, as in ordinary Aristotelian terminology, and
that Pomponazzi is perhaps thinking of Ficino's planetary rites.
In any case, we have here the core of Ficino's theory of spiritual
magic: the operators, by their invocations, change *themselves*,
rather than the object to which the prayers are directed. Pomponaz-

[1] One of the main sources of this emphasis on credulity is probably Peter of
Abano (*Conciliator*, Difs. 113, 135, 156), to whom Pomponazzi frequently refers
(e.g. *De Incant.*, p. 85).
[2] Pomponazzi, *De Incant.*, p. 255: "Ut preces valeant, ab imo corde debent
provenire, & esse ferventes: quoniam sic spiritus melius afficiuntur, & supra materiam
sunt validiores, non ut flectant intelligentias (quoniam omnino sunt immutabiles)
sed ut magis afficiantur: veluti sputum hominis irati, & sibilus serpentis est potentius
quam hominis & serpentis non irati."

zi later rejects this explanation for this particular phenomenon, but elaborates the same subjectivist theory of prayer in a way that shows clearly the dangers inherent in Ficino's theory if applied to religion in general. There are, according to Pomponazzi, two possible aims in prayer: first, to obtain some external benefit; second, to make oneself more pious. The first of these aims is often frustrated, the second never. Therefore, although God's will has been immutably fixed from eternity and is being carried out through the inflexible revolutions of the heavens, a philosopher should continue to pray because the second aim of his prayers will always be achieved [1].

It is possible that the reason why Pomponazzi did not discuss Ficino's magic was because he positively disapproved of it, not, as was usual, because it might be demonic, but because it was unscientific and could only work with silly and credulous people. He makes a sharp distinction between the ordinary "effects" of music or oratory and those of a magical incantation that is, between the A and B uses of words and music. Incantations lack the beauty and meaning that produce the effects of normal music; they must therefore operate

through the stong faith in the words, held as much by the patient as by the operator; from which faith comes a greater evaporation [sc. of spirits] from the operator, and a better disposition in the patient [2].

This is the same as Pomponazzi's explanation of ordinary Christian prayer, or of any kind of hymn or invocation; he would, therefore, have classed Ficino's astrological singing as a kind of incantation [3], and have condemned it as being based on credulity. Pomponazzi distinguishes three main classes of possible "natural magic":

(1) by use of the natural powers in things,

---

[1]   Ibid., pp. 267-9.

[2]   Pomponazzi, *De Incant.*, pp. 93-4: "... puto in causa esse vehementem fidem habitam verbis illis, non minus ex parte praecantati quam praecantantis: ex qua fide maior & potentior fit evaporatio ratione praecantantis, et melior dispositio ex parte praecantati."

[3]   Ficino himself, of course, denied this (cf. supra p. 43).

(2) by use of the occult powers in things,

(3) by use of the power of imagination (*vis imaginativa*), acting on the spirit and blood of both operator and patient.

(In all three, astrological affinities and timing are of supreme importance). When discussing which, if any, of these kinds of magic should be allowed in a well-run state, he permits, with some reservations, the practice of the first two, but condemns the third on the grounds that it necessarily involves superstition, that is, excessively credulous belief in the power of words and figures. This third kind is also unscientific, because there is no way of knowing *a priori* which individuals will have a suitably (credulously) disposed imagination; no universal rules, therefore, can be established for its use [1].

Pomponazzi, then, though he would perhaps have thought that Ficino's spiritual magic was efficacious and free from demons, would have thought it contemptible because it rested on credulity, and uninteresting because it could not be properly scientific. If he himself believed in his own version of the astrological genesis of religions and religious symbols, he might also have condemned it as being out of date. According to this theory the cross and the name of Jesus, for example, had power only because, for a certain period, the stars were favourable to the growth of this new religion and gave power to these symbols to produce miracles, so that the religion might spread [2]. On this view, Orphic hymns would be ineffective in a Christian era; or, since it is the planets which control all this, would planetary hymns be permanently effective, in any era?

If, as is quite likely, Pomponazzi saw that Ficino's magic was really demonic, he would just have thought he was deluded. Pomponazzi's whole treatise is an attempt to justify Aristotle's disbelief in demons or angels. In the course of doing this he explains every kind of magic effect and marvellous event by "natural" causes, i.e. causes not involving direct divine, demonic

---

[1] Pomponazzi, *De Incant.*, pp. 79-86.
[2] Ibid., pp. 302-310.

or angelic angency. He thus represents in an extreme form the threat of the theory of natural magic to religion, and he is fully aware of this threat. He gives, for example, as one of the objections to his explanations that they would destroy the "laws of Moses and Christ", which rest on belief in the miracles of the Old and and New Testaments [1]. In his answer to this objection he puts forward the ingenious argument, for which he claims the authority of Thomas Aquinas and Augustine [2], that of two identical events one might be naturally, the other miraculously, caused; what is a miracle, and what is not, rests then solely on the authority of the Bible and the Church, to which Pomponazzi humbly submits his judgment [3]. Since the primary function of miracles is to prove the validity of this authority, the argument is circular and entirely destructive in its implications. As an example of such events, he gives the story of Aaron's and the Egyptian magicians' serpents, always a troublesome one for Christian writers on magic [4]. According to Pomponazzi, both lots of serpents were real, but one was produced by divine action and the other by natural magic; they were otherwise identical.

[1] Pomponazzi, *De Incant.*, p. 71.
[2] Augustine and Thomas do mention a small class of abnormal events, externally resembling miracles, but produced with demonic aid by bad magicians; see A. Van Hove, *La Doctrine du Miracle chez Saint Thomas*, Paris, 1927, pp. 16-7, 143-4.
[3] Pomponazzi, ibid., pp. 88-9.
[4] Cf. infra p. 162.

(3) PLATONISTS
GIORGI. TYARD & LA BODERIE. FABIO PAOLINI

I am going now to discuss a few 16th century Platonists who can be said to be within the same philosophic tradition as Ficino and who might therefore provide a favourable climate of thought for the diffusion or developement of his magical theories. Two of these, Diacceto and Agrippa, I have already dealt with, and another, Champier, will appear in the next chapter.

Francesco Giorgi

In the *De Harmonia Mundi Totius* (1525) [1] of Francesco Giorgi, a Venetian Franciscan, one finds something very like the theoretical framework on which Ficino's spiritual magic rests, but not the magic itself. There is not, as far as I know, any direct evidence of Giorgi's having derived his philosophy from the Florentines; but his constant use of Plotinus and the *prisca theologia* makes it likely, as do his frequent cabalistic analyses of Hebrew words in the manner of Pico [2]. The reasons why this framework, in spite of its close resemblance to Ficino's, did not lead Giorgi to any kind of practical magic are, briefly, that his astrology is too Christian, his musical theory too metaphorical, his conception of spirit too comprehensive and hence fluid.

Giorgi's acceptance of astrological influences is quite as whole-hearted as Ficino's, with, of course, the same careful preservation of human free-will; the stars are the medium, the "governors", through which God rules the world [3]. Basing himself mainly on

---

[1] *Francisci Georgii Veneti Minoritae Familiae De Harmonia Mundi Totius Cantica Tria*, Venetiis, 1525.

[2] E.g. Giorgi, op. cit., III, v, i, fo li vo (on *Ruah*); cf. Pico, *Heptaplus*, ed. Garin, p. 374.

[3] Giorgi, op. cit., I, iii, vi seq., fos xliii vo seq.; III, i, viii seq., fos viii ro seq..

Plotinus and Ptolemy, he explains how we may attract favourable influences from the heavens by means of the Soul of the World, "which contains as many seminal reasons as there are ideas in the divine mind" [1]. The sun, like the heart in the human body, is the chief centre of celestial life; "and although man receives benefits from all the heavens, he chiefly draws them from the heart of the heavens which is the sun, since man himself is solarian" [2]. This celestial life is distributed by the sun

> through a certain vital spirit, by which (as the Pythagorean Timaeus says) the whole world lives, continually drawing it in, together with the spirit and power of the other stars. Man, especially, does this through his own spirit, which is by its nature similar to them, and can be made more akin to them by art and forsight, by many rules and aids, of which true sages treat rather by word of mouth than in writing [3].

So far, this seems to lead straight to Ficino's spiritual magic; but Giorgi's conception both of spirit and of stars was very different from Ficino's.

In a long and most interesting discussion on the possible meanings of the term spirit, Giorgi, starting from cabalistic operations on the Hebrew word for it, Ruah (רוח), argues that the central, permanent notion in all its uses is that of a mediation between two extremes; this fits equally well the Holy Spirit, angels as God's, or demons as Satan's, messengers and servants, medical spirits in man, or the medium in which celestial influences are conveyed [4]. Giorgi does in fact use the term in all these senses. The main ambiguities, and the main divergences from Ficino,

---

[1] Ibid., III, i, viii, fo viii ro: "Qui haustus [sc. favoris caelestis] fit (docente Plotino) mediante anima mundi, quę tot rationes seminales continens / quot sunt ideae in mente divina / pręstat unicuique suam particularem vim . . ."

[2] Ibid., fo viii vo: "Et quamvis homo a toto cęlo favorem suscipiat, potissime tamen haurit a corde cęli / quod est sol, cum solaris sit homo".

[3] Giorgi, op. cit., III, i, viii, fo ix: "In sole itaque, mundi praecipua lampade, tanquam in corde est potissime mundani animalis vita: cuius & ipse inter caelica membra est pręcipuus dator / per spiritum quemdam vitalem: quo (ut Timęus Pythagoricus inquit) vivit totus mundus / ipsum continue hauriens / simul cum spiritu, & virtute aliarum stellarum: pręsertim homo per ipsius spiritum illis suapte natura conformem: & arte / atque proudentia [sic], cognatiorem effectum, multis regulis & adminiculis / de quibus veri sapientes potius ore / quam voluminibus pertractant." cf. Ficino, Op. Omn., pp. 531 seq. (De Tr. Vita, III, i).

[4] Ibid., III, v, i-viii, fos li vo seq..

occur with man's spirit. For, although he also accepts this as meaning medical spirits or the Neoplatonic vehicle [1], he prefers that it should mean the rational soul, taken as the mean between the lower, irrational soul and the mind or intellect [2]. This moves it up a place in the ascending series: body, soul or souls, mind . . ., and either makes it incorporeal or the soul corporeal, a difficulty Giorgi cannot quite solve. It also makes spirit a superfluous term, differing only from soul in being more ambiguous.

The stars, for Giorgi, are unusually closely connected with angels. He accepts of course as angels the intelligences which move the celestial spheres, and also associates the latter with the angelic choirs [3]. What is less usual is that, for practical astrological purposes, his angels take over the functions of planets. He recognizes the importance of discovering which planet dominates one's life; but considers that the usual method of doing this, by casting horoscopes, is too lengthy, complicated and uncertain. He suggests, as did Ficino [4], a short-cut by means of observing one's own innate tendencies, which will indicate whether we are Jovial, Saturnian or whatnot. Giorgi thinks that these tendencies are caused by one's guardian angel as much as by one's dominant planet; the influences of the two are always in the same direction. We must,

> having removed all hindrances, submit ourselves to our guiding spirit, which, if we do not resist, will show us the way to which the heavens, our *genius* and the Supreme Ruler lead us [5].

Here "spirit" means man's spirit, and "genius" means guardian angel. The angels lead their *protégés* "in that direction to which their star inclines them" [6], that is, always towards goodness and

---

[1] Ibid., III, v, ii, fo lii vo; III, v, iv, fo liii vo.
[2] Ibid., III, v, iii, fo liii.
[3] Ibid., I, iii, vi, fo xliv; III, viii, ii, fo cvi; I iv, iv seq., fos lix vo seq.
[4] Ficino, *Op. Omn.*, pp. 566-7 (*De Tr. V.*, III, xxiii).
[5] Giorgi, op. cit., III, i, ix, fo x: "breve arripiendum est iter / percontando a nobis ipsis / quod a cęlis facere nequimus. Quod quidem faciemus / si ammotis impedimentis, submittamus nos spiritui / nostro duci / qui nobis non resistentibus demonstrabit iter, quo cęlum, quo genius / immo quo summus Moderator conducit."
[6] Ibid.: "Sentit nam natura: & spiritus noster cęli instinctum, atque favorem: sentit & genii proprii suadelas: quod unicuique datum est, a principio suę nativitatis:

happiness; evil and unhappiness come only from resisting this innate astral and angelic inclination, or from diabolic interference [1]. The ways Giorgi suggests in which man is to make himself more celestial and angelic are innocent and non-magical: cleanliness both of body and soul, and the choice of a suitable place to live in, which is to be found by experiment.

By his identification of planetary and angelic influence Giorgi has made his religion entirely absorb his astrology, so that the latter has no specific characteristics left. His wide use of the term spirit also helps this fusion. Normally planets would act on the spirit and angels on the soul or mind. But Giorgi has merged spirit and soul, so that angels and planets influence the same thing. Instead of astrology and magic contaminating Christianity, as with Agrippa, Christianity has transformed and absorbed Giorgi's astrology. Ficino too had identified guardian angels with dominant planets, but with opposite results; his angels or *daemones proprii* remain clearly astrological [2]. For him angels have become planets; for Giorgi planets have become angels.

Music plays an important part in Giorgi's book; here again, his theories have many resemblances to Ficino's, but do not lead to a similar practical end. The reality of the music of the spheres, the "effects" of music and their importance in preparing the soul for religious contemplation, every analogy between *Musica Mundana*, *Humana* and *Instrumentalis*—all these appear fully and frequently [3]. Indeed Giorgi's whole book, composed of three *Cantica*, each divided into eight *Toni*, is constructed on a vast musical metaphor; and this is why, I think, he never gets to

ut non modo Platonici simul cum doctoribus nostris asserunt, sed infallibilis Veritas sermone profitetur aperto, dum ait. Angeli eorum semper vident faciem Patris. Hi nam suis clientulis favent, illò ducentes / quo & eius sidus inclinat / semper utique ad bonum: nisi homo ab his illecebris, aut mali dęmonis suadelis deceptus, suum obliquet iter."

[1] Ibid.: "Cęli igitur, & genii, vel Angeli proprii (ut catholice loquamur) suasionibus assentiens, aget prospere / & vivet felix. Alioqui, cęlum sentiet, & superos inimicos ... Nam si ingenio tuo, contra genium, & celestium vocem continue invitantem, aliquid professus fueris: frustra laborabis ..."

[2] Ficino, *Op, Omn.*, pp. 566-8 (*De Tr. V.*, III, xxiii); cf. p. 1387 (Socrates' *daimon*),

[3] E.g. ibid., I, viii, xvi seq., fos clxxix vo seq.; *Prooemium*, p. (5); I, v, i-xviii, fos lxxxiv seq.

any practical use of celestial music. The main importance of music for him is as the source of a vast, all-embracing scheme of mathematical analogies. Moreover, many of these analogies are not truly mathematical, but numerological, that is to say, he is not showing that every part of the universe is constructed on the same complex system of proportions (those of musical intervals), but is collecting analogies between sets of things whose only manifest common characteristic is their number. The signs of the zodiac, for example, and the apostles must in some way be connected because there are twelve of each; Giorgi then finds some characteristic in the Hebrew name of each apostle which resembles some characteristic of each sign of the zodiac [1]. The starting-point of this analogy-making is the identity of number, and the further making of secondary analogies is quite uncontrolled and unregulated; the apostles and signs do not correspond in every respect or in any regularly determined respect. These analogies then lead nowhere, either in theory or practice. The knowledge that Matthew corresponds to the Watercarrier in any old way tells us nothing new about either, and suggests no practical operation. If, on the other hand, we know that the distances between the planets and their differences of motion correspond to the intervals of the scale and the proportions of musical consonances, we may, in theory, deduce the former from the latter, and, in practice, we may, by using similarly proportioned music attract the influence of certain planets, since such identities of proportion are physically active, as is proved by the sympathetic vibration of strings. Giorgi uses this *wirksame*, operative kind of analogy as well; but his frequent use of the idle, inoperative kind shows that in general he was not interested in analogies as instruments for some further theoretical or practical operations, but was collecting them because he liked them for their own sake and because they were evidence of an order in the universe—the order of a dictionary, not that of a building or an organic body. This idle, numerological kind

---

[1] Giorgi, op. cit., II, vii, xii, fos cccxii seq.; the analogies are more complex than I have indicated, but no less arbitrary.

of analogy was, of course, extremely common in the middle-ages [1], and continued well into the 17th century. Kepler, whose *Harmonices Mundi* [2] is an example of the use of theoretically operative musical and mathematical analogies, pointed out clearly the fundamental difference between his and Fludd's cosmologies by showing that his own analogies were exact ones of proportion between two systems each having a constant unit of measurement, whereas Fludd's were mostly based merely on an identity of number between systems having no other mathematical characteristic in common [3]. Ficino's analogies between cosmic, musical and human spirits led to magic, Kepler's mathematical ones to science; Giorgi's and Fludd's were not meant to lead anywhere at all.

This distinction is of course too clear-cut. Ficino's analogies and metaphors are often as inoperative as Giorgi's; it is his spirit theory that leads him to practical music, rather then the *musica mundana* built up on the *Timaeus* [4], which he and Giorgi have in common. Conversely, Giorgi's interest in mathematical and in numerological analogies did lead him to practical results, which were, however, architectural, not musical: his design for the church of S. Francesco della Vigna at Venice, which is based on one of the series that constitute the *anima mundi* in the *Timaeus* $(3, 9, 27)$ and on the three perfect consonaces (octave, fifth, fourth) [5].

It must also be remembered that for a Renaissance Platonist, and especially a Cabalistic one, even a bare identity of number

[1] See Huizinga, *The Waning of the Middle Ages*, London, 1924, pp. 188-9.

[2] Kepler, *Harmonices Mundi Libri V.*, 1619, *Ges. Werke*, ed. Von Dyck & Caspar, Bd. VI, München, 1940.

[3] Kepler, *Ges. Werke*, VI, 430-2 (*Apologia* against Fludd, 1622); VI, 375 (*Harm. Mund.*, V, App.: "Ille [sc. Fludd] fisus veteribus, qui vim Harmoniarum ex numeris abstractis esse credebant, sat habet, si quas inter partes concordantiam esse demonstrabit, eas numeris quomodocunque comprehendat, nullâ curâ, cujusmodi unitates illo numero accumulentur: ego nuspiam doceo quaerere Harmonias, ubi res, inter quas sunt Harmoniae, non possunt mensurari eâdem quantitatis mensurâ"). On the controversy between Kepler and Fludd, cf. C. G. Jung & W. Pauli, *The Interpretation of Nature and the Psyche*, London, 1955, pp. 190 seq..

[4] Cf. supra pp. 14-15.

[5] See R. Wittkower, *Architectural Principles in the Age of Humanism*, London, 1949, pp. 90 seq., 136 seq.

between two classes did indicate other resemblances between them, because the numbers themselves had a rich content accumulated by Pythagorean, Platonic and Christian speculation [1]. Giorgi chose the number 3 as the basis for the design of his church not so much because it was a convenient integer for musical proportions [2], as because, it was the "numero primo e divino", that is, the first true number after the Monad beyond being and the infinite Dyad, and because it symbolized the Trinity [3]. Thus 3 is obviously more suitable for a church than, say, 4, which would symbolize the elements and the corporeal world [4]. But the metaphysical content of these numbers is too rich and unsystematized to prevent the analogies drawn from them being to some degree arbitrary; 3 also symbolizes the dimensions of space or man's threefold soul, and 4 also means the Tetragrammaton or the Evangelists.

In Giorgi, then, as in many of the Platonists who preceded and succeeded him, we have a mixture of both exact, possibly operative analogies, and of arbitrary, idle ones. There is a parallel situation in the Neoplatonic and cabalistic exegesis of texts and analyses of language, such as one finds in Pico or Fabio Paolini [5]. You have a significant whole, a text (or a musical scale) which can be analysed into still significant parts, words (or proportions); then you go a stage further and try to find elements of the significance of the whole in single letters (or single notes, or the integers composing the proportions), where in fact they do not exist [6]. What is confusing for us is that the two kinds of analysis and analogy appear tangled up together. At one moment we are watch-

---

[1] Cf. E. R. Curtius, *Europäische Literatur end Lateinisches Mittelalter*, Bern, 1948, pp. 494 seq..

[2] Giorgi uses to express his proportions the numbers, 3, 6, 9, 12, 27; he could obviously just as well have used 1, 2, 3, 4, 9.

[3] See Wittkower, ibid.

[4] Giorgi, *Harmonia*, I, iii, xii, fo 50.

[5] Pico, *Heptaplus*, ed. Garin, p. 374; for Fabio Paolini v. infra p. 126.

[6] Ironically Plato's *Cratylus*, which so carefully established the point I am trying to make, was used to support this cabalistic analysis of language (cf. Walker, "*Prisca Theologia* in France", p. 231).

ing an aimless game with shifting rules [1]; at the next it has turned into an orderly and purposeful train of thought.

The other route that leads from the harmony of the spheres to practical music or magic is Ficino's music-spirit theory. Here too Giorgi's way was blocked; for by making man's spirit the same as his soul, he removed any grounds for supposing a peculiarly close relationship between musically formed air, the human spirit, and cosmic spirit, and he does not in fact suggest that there is.

I have spent so much time on Giorgi because he exemplifies the main reasons why Ficino's magic had so little success with the later Platonists, and because their musical theory was considerably influenced by him. Most of them have the same fondness for inoperative musical or mathematical analogies, and the same breadth and vagueness in their use of the term spirit, if they use it at all. Giorgi's Christianization of astrology by means of angels does not reappear; but later Platonists tend to preserve astrology only as a highly general theory, of the same kind as Pico's, and to distrust or neglect any precise, detailed scheme of celestial influences which might lead to practical use. We must also remember that by the later part of the century Ficino's magic had got mixed up with that of Agrippa and Paracelsus, thereby losing in respectability what it gained in notoriety.

Tyard and La Boderie

From the mid 16th century onwards there were several attempts in France to achieve a poetic revolution—to create a new kind of song which should unite powerfully effect-producing music [2] with poetry of profound religious or philosophical meaning [3]. This aim was common to the early Ronsard, to Baïf's Academy, and to Lefèvre de la Boderie; a symbol of it was Orpheus, *priscus*

---

[1] Cf. Gombrich, "Botticelli's Mythologies", *Warburg Journal*, 1945, p. 38.

[2] Cf. infra p. 137.

[3] On all these movements see F. A. Yates, *The French Academies of the 16th Century*, London, 1947; for Ronsard and Ficino see my article, "Le Chant Orphique de Marsile Ficin", *Musique et Poésie au XVIe siècle*, C.N.R.S., Paris, 1954, pp. 25 seq..

theologus and *magus*, powerful poet and musician. The theory behind these attempts hinged on two themes: the doctrine of the four *furores*, and a wish to revive the emotional or ethical effects of ancient music. Though these themes have many possible sources, there is no doubt that Ficino was for these French poets an especially important one. These poetic revolutions are then in some measure derived from Ficino's general views on music and poetry, but have only a slight connexion with his magic. The astrological aspect of his Orphic singing has disappeared, or survived only as a metaphor, and in consequence we no longer find anything like a magic rite, or any attempt to put "celestial" music into practice by way of planetary modes. The music-spirit theory also survives only vestigially [1]; so that all the specific characteristics of Ficinian magic are gone, except the association of powerful religious song with ancient hymns and the *prisci theologi* who wrote them. The two chief theoreticians of these movements, Tyard and La Boderie, also owe much to Giorgi [2]. It is more from him than from Ficino that they take their huge collections of musico-mathematical analogies. As with Giorgi, these analogies remain inoperative, in spite of the fact that Tyard and La Boderie are, unlike him, interested in practical music. Such analogies could have had an operative connexion with their practical aims only by way of astrology and Ficino's linking of cosmic spirit, musically moved air and man's spirit. With only a highly generalized astrology and no linking spirits, *musica mundana*, *humana* and *instrumentalis* fall apart in practice and remain theoretically connected only by bare numbers and proportions.

Pontus de Tyard's two dialogues on poetry and music, the *Solitaire Premier* (1552) and the *Solitaire Second* (1555), give us the fullest account [3] of the aims of the early Pléiade and foreshadow those of Baïf's Academy. Tyard writes much on music as a

---

[1] Cf. supra p. 27.

[2] See France Yates, op. cit., pp. 43, 88, 91 seq.. La Boderie published a French translation of Giorgi's book (*L'Harmonie du Monde* . . ., Paris, 1579).

[3] There is a similar account by a lesser known Platonist, Louis Le Caron, in his *Dialogues*, Paris, 1556, fos 127 seq., Dial. 4. "Ronsard Ou, de la Poësie"; cf. ibid., fo 126 vo, on the effects of music.

preparation to religious contemplation. The function of the *furor poeticus* is to reduce the soul to a harmonious state by means of song, whence it can pass on to the other, religious, *furores*[1]. This leads up to a demand for the reformation of French poetry and music on the model of antiquity. Poet and musician are to be identical or close collaborators. The music is to be monodic, and the poetry either *vers mesurés à l'antique*, as in Baïf's Academy, or rhymed verse written specially for music[2]. Such song will produce "un veritable ravissement d'ame"[3]. But, although Tyard has long sections on *musica mundana & humana*[4], and although he believed in the reality of astral influences[5], he makes no connexion between this reformed music, its effects on man, and the music of the spheres. Celestial music is for Tyard a collection of decorative analogies; he does not even believe in its reality[6]. Nor has his reformed music anything to do with magic. This is clear from the opening section of the *Solitaire Second*, which is on one of the main subjects of the *De Triplici Vita*: the use of music in achieving a long and healthy life, but which contains only one casual reference to Neoplatonic magic—in discussing various methods of harmonising mental and bodily faculties, he remarks[7]:

Les uns ont appellé à leur aide les carmes de la Magie, par lesquels les Platoniques entendent la loüange chantée à Dieu, duquel la cognoissance esleve l'entendement humain en une merveilleuse tranquillité.

One would certainly have expected that magic would enter into Tyard's conception of the best kind of poetry. He believed in the magical power of words, and cites Zoroaster and Iamblichus on the importance of not changing ancient names in prayers[8].

---

[1] Tyard, *Les Discours Philosophiques*, Paris, 1587, fos 6 vo seq..

[2] Ibid., fos 127 vo seq.; cf. fos 113 vo seq.

[3] Tyard, *Disc. Phil.*, 1587, fo 113 vo.

[4] Ibid., fos 118 seq..

[5] Ibid., fos 146 vo, 196 vo (rejection of judiciary astrology, but assertion of more general celestial influence).

[6] Ibid., fos 122 vo-123; cf. fos 230-1.

[7] Ibid., fo 38 vo.

[8] See Walker, "*Prisca Theologia* in France", *Warburg Journal*, 1954, p. 230.

He mentions in his *Mantice*, a dialogue on divinatory astrology, that he had, when young, tried unsuccessfuly many kinds of magic, apparently demonic kinds[1]; perhaps these had frightened him.

Tyard's proposals for a reformation of song do not mention Orphic or other ancient hymns. But one may suppose he approved of Ronsard's intention of being an "Orphic" poet[2], and later of La Boderie's[3]. In his *Mantice* he quotes some lines from Ronsard's *Hymne des Astres*[4] and compares him to Orpheus, whose Hymns he interprets as veiled astrology[5]. In his *Second Curieux*, where great use is made of the *prisca theologia*, he quotes extracts from three prayers in the *Hermetica*[6], and exclaims: "Que peut on, je vous prie, choisir en David mesmes, de plus pieux, reverend & religieux"?[7]

Still more than in Tyard one would expect to find Ficinian magic in the works of Guy Lefèvre de la Boderie. This learnèd French poet was a great admirer of the writings of both Orpheus and Ficino[8]; he frequently introduced paraphrases of *Orphica* into his own poems, and he published translations of the *De Triplici Vita* and other works of Ficino[9]. He does in fact describe something like Ficino's astrological music in his *Galliade* (1578).

The general theme of the *Galliade* is that the Bards of ancient Gaul were the original source of all good music, poetry and philosophy. It was Bardus, the Gaulish king who instituted the order of the Bards, who first explained the harmonic composition of the Soul of the World, as later expounded in the *Timaeus*, and who

> enseignoit la pratique
> D'attirer icy bas la celeste Musique[10].

---

[1] Tyard, ibid., fo 191 vo.

[2] Ronsard, *Hymne de l'Eternité* (*Oeuvres complètes*, ed. crit. Laumonnier, Paris, 1914, VIII, 246).

[3] V. infra p. 125.

[4] Ronsard, *Oeuvres compl.*, ed. cit., VIII, 150 seq,.

[5] Tyard, ibid., fo 169 vo.

[6] *Hermetica*, ed. Nock & Festugière, I, 17-19; II, 208, 353-4.

[7] Tyard, ibid., fos 315 vo-316 ro.

[8] See D. P. Walker, "*Prisca Theologia* in France", *Journal of Warburg and Courtauld Inst.*, 1954, pp. 226-8.

[9] V. ibid., p. 207 note (7).

[10] La Boderie, *La Galliade*, Paris, 1578, fo 78 vo.

Later followers of Bardus, among whom Orpheus is, of course, conspicuous [1], further elaborated this celestial music:

> Mais les autres plus murs, qui d'un bon contrepois
> Ensemble ont balancé la nature des vois
> Sourdes & enroués, hautes, claires & nettes,
> Avec les qualitez propres aux sept Planetes,
> Ont trouvé une voye & un sentier moyen
> Pour lier leurs accords d'un plus parfait lien [2].

Then we have what is like an expanded version of Ficino's planetary modes, with the addition of two chords or intervals for each planet. Saturn, for example, has a "voix basse, obscure, enrouee", and as intervals the dissonances 2nd and 9th; whereas Jupiter has a "voix grave, aggreable, constante", and the consonances 8th and 15th. The Sun, who "Les Planetes benins beninement regarde,

> Par ses rayons dorez preside aux sons tous purs,
> Venerables, & doux, sonoreux, non-obscurs,
> Et entre les accords comme sienne il affecte
> La Sixiesme et Treiziesme en tous poincts non parfaite;

while Venus has "sons plus mouls, lascifs & amoureux, Espars & dilatez", and the perfect consonances 5th and 12th.

Here there is no suggestion of practical use; but later, after a long narration of classical effects of music [3], there is an impassioned exhortation to "vous Musiciens des Princes & des Rois" [4] to use only salutary, virtuous music. Above all, they are to sing the praises of God [5] and

> Faites-moy tournoyer par nombreuses parolles
> Et les Esprits mouvans, & du Ciel les carolles.
> Entonnez és tuyaux des Orgues longs & ronds
> Des Cieux organisez la Musique & les tons:
> Faites sur le clavier d'une douce Espinette
> Marcher d'ordre & de rang Planete apres Planete

---

[1] Ibid., fo 83 (on planetary character of Orpheus' music and hymns).
[2] Ibid., fo 81.
[3] Ibid., fo 94 seq.
[4] Ibid., fo 96.
[5] La Boderie, *Galliade*, fos 100 vo-101.

> Sous le bal du grand Ciel, qui voit avec tant d'yeux
> Et d'Astres tournoyans au son melodieux
> De la Lyre à Phébus, qui meine en rond leur dance
> Et les fait arriver par nombre à la cadence.

After this planetary music La Boderie recommends the songs of
David, and reaches the climax of his poetic *furor* with [1]:

> Sus sus, Psalterion, sus, sus, ô Harpe encore,
> Tost tost resveillez-vous, j'esveilleray l'Aurore:
> Il me plaist, il me plaist or' le pas avancer,
> Et d'un sault redoublé devant l'Arche dancer,
> Et par un Avant-jeu vous monstrer par exemple
> Comme on doit louer Dieu dedans son sacré Temple [2].

Then, after a lot more reminiscences of the Psalms, we have song
from a singer more ancient than David—a prayer of Hermes
Trismegistus [3].

Is this an attempt to revive Ficino's astrological music, his
Orphic singing, to institute the general use of his magic in order
to save France from her internecine conflicts? The answer is not
a simple one. The connexion here between astrology and music
is, I think, a metaphysical metaphor or analogy, as it normally
was in musical theory before and after Ficino; that is to say,
La Boderie is talking about underlying principles of harmony
and proportion which, on a high level of generality, are the
causes both of the order of the heavens and of musical consonance, but he is not talking about combining practical astrology
with practical music. This is clearer from the full context of the
passages I have quoted, where he heaps up every possible correspondence between microcosm, macrocosm and music; La
Boderie, like Giorgi, is using inoperative, mainly numerological
analogies. On the other hand, I am sure that he is seriously
proposing [4] the public use of a new salutary kind of music and

---

[1] Ibid., fo 103.

[2] Psalms, lvii, 8; cviii, 2; cl.

[3] *Hermetica*, ed. cit., II, 207-8 (*Hymn of Regeneration*); La Boderie, *Galliade*, fos
104 vo-105 vo.

[4] The *Galliade* is an entirely serious poem in spite of the preposterous history
of culture which is its main theme, and in spite of La Boderie's frequent outbursts
of Ronsardian *fureur* (see Walker, "*Pr. Theol.* in France", p. 216 note 9).

poetry, which is at least partly derived from Ficino's Orphic singing.

There were, for La Boderie, two dangerous forces in the music and poetry of his time which his new music was designed to combat: the paganism of the poetry of Ronsard and his followers, and the powerful "effects" of the Protestant Psalms. The remedy against these disintegrating kinds of music, which produced respectively impiety and heresy and hence dissension in the state, was to substitute French versions of Catholic liturgical hymns for the Psalms of Marot and Bèze (and good Catholic translations of the Psalms), and imitations or paraphrases of *Orphica* and *Hermetica* for the themes of classical mythology in the poetry of the *Pléiade*. This programme is indicated in the *Galliade* where, after the exhortation to use only music producing virtuous effects, imitations of the Psalms are immediately succeeded by an Hermetic prayer. It appears still more clearly in La Boderie's *Cantique* "aux Poëtes de ce temps" [1]; in this he begs his contemporaries to abandon "les contes monstrueux d'Hesiode & d'Homere" in favour of the most ancient of Greek singers, Orpheus, and demonstrates his advice by giving verse translations of five Orphic fragments and two Psalms [2]. His *Hymnes Ecclesiastiques* [3] were designed to counteract the effects of the Protestant Psalms, and they contain, besides numerous translations of Christian hymns and appeals to French poets to abandon the pagan Muse, French versions of three Orphic Hymns, one of which is the Hymn of the Sun [4].

This attempt by La Boderie to combine the good musical effects of Catholic hymns and Psalms with those of the hymns and prayers of the *prisci theologi* plainly owes much to Ficino. But there are important differences between Ficino's and La Boderie's Orphic singing. First, La Boderie has, I think, no

---

[1] La Boderie, *L'Encyclie*, Anvers, n.d. (privilege, 1570), p. 189; cf. Walker "*Pr. Th.* in France", pp. 226-7.

[2] See Walker, ibid., p. 226 note 4.

[3] La Boderie, *Hymnes Ecclesiastiques*, 2nd ed., Paris, 1582 (privilege, 1578); cf. Walker, "Le Chant Orphique de Marsile Ficin", pp. 24-5.

[4] La Boderie, *Hymnes Eccl.*, fos 261-2.

practical astrological aims. Secondly, whereas Ficino's magic was a private affair, confined to the circle of Lorenzo, and not fully or openly described in his published works, La Boderie was proposing a kind of public magic—the effects of his Orphic and Davidic music are going to pacify and unite the French people.

The idea of using musical effects for the public good is of course already in one of the main sources of musical humanism— Plato. In La Boderie's case it was probably also suggested or reinforced by the aims and activities of Baif's Academy; Baif's and Le Jeune's *Pseaumes en Vers Mesurez* were composed with the same intentions as La Boderie's *Hymnes Ecclesiastiques*[1]. It seems moreover almost certain that, as Miss Yates has so convincingly argued[2], we have in the Baif-Le Jeune music for the mariage of the Duc de Joyeuse (1581) an example of public magic using not only the effects of music but also practical astrology.

Fabio Paolini and the Accademia degli Uranici

In 1589 Fabio Paolini, a professor of Greek at Venice, published a large volume, entitled *Hebdomades*[3], which is a commentary, divided into seven Books, each containing seven chapters, on one line of Vergil[4]:

Obloquitur [sc. Orpheus] numeris septem discrimina vocum. The commentary, though discursive, is built round two themes: Orpheus in all his possible aspects and the number seven in all its possible meanings. In the course of developing and interconnecting these themes, Paolini presents, with remarkable completeness, not only the theory of Ficino's magic, but also the whole complex of theories of which it is a part: the Neoplatonic

---

[1] See Frances Yates, *The French Academies of the 16th century*, London, 1947, pp. 70-72, 209-210.

[2] Frances Yates, "Poésie et musique dans les "Magnificences" au mariage du duc de Joyeuse, Paris, 1581", in *Musique et Poésie au XVIe siècle* (Colloques Internat. du C.N.R.S.), Paris, 1954, pp. 241 seq..

[3] *Fabii Paulini Utinensis Philosophi, Et Graecas literas Venetijs profitentis, HEBDO-MADES, sive Septem de Septenario libri, Habiti in Uranicorum Academia In unius Vergilij versus explicatione. Ad sereniss. Venetae Reip. Collegium*, Venetijs, 1589.

[4] Vergil, *Aeneid*, VI, 646.

cosmology and astrology on which the magic is based, the *prisca theologia & magia*, the power of music, the four *furores*, and the harmony of the spheres, together with every type of mathematical and numerological analogy. Moreover, although the influence of Ficino is strong and evident [1], Paolini does not merely reproduce Florentine Platonism; he combines it with other later, and often divergent lines of speculation. Indeed, he comes near to resuming the whole tradition as it had grown during a hundred years. Nor does his book represent only the thought of an isolated individual; it consists of a series of orations given in an academy in which he played a dominating part. Paolini's ideas and interest may therefore be supposed to have had quite a wide sphere of influence; for this *Accademia degli Uranici*, though small and short-lived, had some distinguished members, and was by no means merely a private affair. Paolini was also one of the public lecturers on Poetry and Eloquence in the library of St. Mark's [2], and he spread his favourite theories by this means as well as by the Academy [3]; on one occasion he combined his two functions by giving an academic oration as his beginning-of-term lecture to a mixed audience of students and members of the academy [4]. He was such an enthusiastic teacher that during his holidays from public lecturing he held seminars in his house; for the two years we know about they were on Greek and Arabic medicine [5].

As well as this competence in medicine [6] and his professional

---

[1] Cf. infra p. 133; Paolini constantly cites and quotes Ficino, e.g., *Hebd.*, pp. 19, 115, 117, 145, 179, 193-6-8-9, 202, 235, 302, 316, 351.

[2] See Paolini, *Hebd.*, Dedication, & p. 247 (He succeeded "Murettus" (? Marc-Antoine Muret), and in 1589 succeeded his teacher Parthenio (On whom see Tiraboschi, *Storia della Letteratura Italiana*, 2da ed., Modena, 1787, VII, 1498); on Paolini's life and writings, see G. G. Liruti, *Notizie delle Vite ed Opere Scritte da' Letterati del Friuli* . . ., Venezia, 1760, III, 352 seq..

[3] V. infra p. 140.

[4] See Paolini, *Hebd.*, pp. 225-6: "Lib. V. De Arythmetica, numerorumque mysteriis, Habitus in D. M. Bibliotheca in studiorum exordijs" (he was lecturing on the *seven* tragedies of Sophocles and the year was 1587).

[5] See Avicenna, *Canon Medicinae ex Gerardi Cremonensis versione* . . . *Per Fabium Paulinum Utinensem*, Venetiis, 1595, Dedication by Fabritius Raspanus.

[6] Paolini also revised the Latin translation for Galen, *Opera ex Octava Iuntorum Editione* . . ., Venetiis, 1609 (Dedication by "Fabius Paulinus Medicus", dated 1596); his *Tabellae* of ancient anatomy were printed at the end of Vesalius, *Anatomia*, Venetiis, 1604.

interests in Greek and Latin literature [1], especially rhetoric and philosophy, he was a serious student of musical theory [2]; he was a friend of Zarlino, from whom he borrowed unpublished Greek manuscripts on music [3].

The *Accademia degli Uranici* began in 1587 [4]; it seems likely that it had ceased to exist sometime before 1593, when Paolini became one of the nine founders of the *Seconda Accademia Veneziana* [5]. The *impresa* of the *Uranici* was a representation of the eighth sphere, with the motto "Mens agitat molem" [6]. It was officially recognized by the *Signoria* of Venice, and among its members were philosophers, theologians, jurists, historians, orators, ambassadors [7], and many of the Venetian nobility [8]. The inaugural oration, on happiness or the supreme good of man, was given by a well-known Franciscan preacher, Faustino Tasso, on the 10th of June 1587, and was published in the same year [9]. In this oration there is no mention of Paolini or of where

[1]   He was keen that Greek and Latin should be learnt together, and published, for paedagogic purposes, a collection of fables, each with a woodcut and his own Greek and Latin verses (*Centum Fabulae ex Antiquis Scriptoribus acceptae, Et Graecis, Latinisque Tetrastichis Senarijs explicatae à Fabio Paulino Utinensi. Gabriae Graeci fabula, Musaei Leander & Hero, Galeomyomachia Incerti, Sybillae Vaticinium de Judicio Christi, Batrachomyomachia Homeri, Ab eodem latinis versibus è graecis conversa*, Venetiis, 1587); He also published one of his public Lectures, *De Graecis Literis cum Latinis Conjungendis. Fabii Paulini Oratio*, Venetiis, 1586.

[2]   In Lib. II of the *Hebd.*, which is on music, he cites: Zarlino, Vicentino, Guido Aretino, Ptolemy, Martianus Capella, Boethius, Plutarch, and of course Plato and Aristotle.

[3]   Zarlino lent him Greek mss. of: Aristoxenus, Alipius, Briennius (see *Hebd.*, pp. 62, 175). He mentions (ibid., p. 274) going in a gondola, with Parthenio, Fabritio Cechono and Laurentio Massa, to dine with Zarlino.

[4]   Faustino Tasso in his inaugural oration (v. infra note (9)) implies (pp. 8-9) that there have already been sessions of the academy. Paolini, writing in 1587 (*Hebd.*, pp. 4-5), speaks of the "incunabula hujus nostrae nascentis Academiolae".

[5]   See Tiraboschi, op. cit., VII, 178. I have found no publications of the academy later than 1589.

[6]   See Paolini, *Hebd.*, p. 124; F. Tasso, *Oratione della Felicità*, p. 50.

[7]   Rotta, *Oratione* (v. infra p. 129 note (2)), fo 1, gives this list.

[8]   Paolini, *Hebd.*, Ded., "multique ex Venetae nobilitate in ea [sc. Academia] sunt ascripti".

[9]   *Oratione della Felicità e del sommo bene, Del R. P. Faustino Tasso de Minori Osservanti, Da lui composta, e publicamente recitata in Vinetia nell' Academia d'Uranici il giorno decimo di Giugno l'anno 1587. Al Sereniss. Principe Pasqual Cigogna, et Illustriss. Signoria di Vinetia, Vinetia, 1587*. On Tasso, cf. F. Giovanni degli Agostini, *Notizie Istoricocritiche intorno la vita, e le opere degli Scrittori Viniziani*, Vinetia, 1754, II, 509 seq., and Maylender, *Storia delle Accademie d'Italia*, Bologna, 1930, V, 412-3.

the academy held its sessions; but Paolini certainly implies that he himself was responsible for starting it, and states that it regularly met in his own house and that he presided over it [1]. Tasso's oration, Paolini's *Hebdomades*, and an oration on the greatness of man, given in July 1587 by another Franciscan, Isidoro Rotta [2], are the only discourses of the academy I have seen; but we know from Paolini's book that Eustacio Rudi spoke on the seat of the soul, and Camillo Camilli on the meanings contained in the word *Uranici* [3].

Tasso's oration is pious and carefully orthodox, and, although it contains a little innocuous Platonism and an approving reference to Pico [4], it does not point in the direction of Paolini's wholehearted magical Neoplatonism. After an apparent acceptance of Platonic ideas he hastens to say that he must now talk in a more Christian way, for he is in the *Accademia Uranica* at Venice, not in the *Accademia Platonica* at Athens [5]. He even gives an innocent, and rather strained interpretation of the academy's motto, "Mens agitat molem" [6], as meaning the minds of the Academicians which master the whole universe; whereas Paolini firmly puts it in its original context: "Spiritus intus alit . . .", a *locus classicus* for the Platonic *anima mundi*, in which he evidently believes [7].

[1] Paolini, *Hebd.*, Ded. ("operam dedi cum doctis quibusdam viris, ut Academiae hic [sc. Venetiis] quaedam quasi forma excitaretur"), p. 4 ("Academiola, cui me non interesse solum, & ex vestro unum esse numero, sed etiam prǣesse voluisti, domumque meam, quasi musarum Sacellum, atque delubrum constituisti, dum in ea Academiae fundamenta jacienda decrevistis"), p. 120 (that Vicenzo Longo housed the academy until Paolini's house had been got ready for them).

[2] *Oratione della Grandezza dell'Huomo. Del P. F. Isidoro Rotta Venetiano de Minori Osservanti, Da lui composta, e publicamente recitata in Vinetia nell'Academia de gli Uranici, l'ottavo giorno di Luglio l'Anno 1587. All'Illustriss. et Reverendiss. Cardinal Cornaro, Vescovo di Padova*, Venetia, 1587.

[3] Paolini, *Hebd.*, pp. 117, 142. Other members of the academy were: Valerio Marcellino, Ottavio Amalteo, Erasmo da Valvasone (*Hebd.*, pp. 184, 212), Gio. Domenico Alessandri, Chiamei Oligenij; these, and Camillo Camilli, are called *accademici uranici* in Valvasone's Italian translation of Sophocles' *Electra* (Venice, 1588, with a dedication by the *Accademici Uranici* to Giovanni Grimano, Patriarch of Aquilegia), for which they wrote liminary sonnets.

[4] F. Tasso, *Oratione*, p. 39.

[5] Ibid., p. 43, cf. p. 46 ("hora vi parlo come Academico sì, ma come Academico Christiano, e non etnico").

[6] Vergil, *Aeneid*, VI, 727; F. Tasso, *Oratione*, p. 50.

[7] Paolini, *Hebd.*, p. 124 (after the creation of the *anima mundi* and the human soul in the *Timaeus*), cf. ibid., pp. 193, 202.

There was perhaps some clash between these divergent views
on the line the academy was to follow; Rotta's oration ends with
a long plea for concord and unity among the members, and with
hints that the little new-born academy may die in infancy, if these
pleas are disregarded [1]. Rotta himself is much closer to Paolini's
outlook. The main theme of his oration is man as the image of
God, especially the Augustinian reflection of the Trinity in man's
soul, shown in the threefold unity of memory, intellect and will [2];
but he also develops the theme of the microcosm with quite
Pico-like enthusiasm. In the course of doing so he shows an
untroubled acceptance of the equation between the Platonic
intelligible world and the Christian Word, and of its connexion
through the heavens with the sensible world; man, as the link
between God and the lower creation, also contains this mediating
celestial world, as is shown by the planetary correspondences
within him, and by the meanings of the letters *aleph* (divinity),
daleth (celestial nature) and *mem* (corporeal corruptibility) in the
name of the first man [3]. This discourse would have prepared
the Academicians for the full blast of Paolini's seven times seven
orations on Orpheus and the number seven, which he gave in
the same year. It also shows that the liking for Neoplatonic
occultism was not confined to Paolini; indeed, that it was predominant in the whole academy, is of course indicated by the
choice of the motto "mens agitat molem", with its strong asso-
ciations with Neoplatonic cosmology.

Paolini's *Hebdomades* as a whole deals with themes closely
connected with Neoplatonic magic, but the focal point of his
ideas on magic is a long discussion of the "effects" of Orpheus'
music: how could Orpheus' music produce manifest effects not
only on men and animals, but also on rocks and stones and trees?
This problem came up during one of the sessions of the academy
when Paolini was about halfway through his course of lectures.

---

[1]   Rotta, *Oratione*, fos 21-23.

[2]   Ibid., fos 11 vo-17 vo; cf. Augustine, *De Trinitate*, Lib. X, Migne, *Pat. Lat.*,
T. 42, cols. 971 seq..

[3]   Rotta, *Oratione*, fos 5 vo, 7 vo-9, 11 vo (citation of Pico's *Heptaplus*).

He happened to mention casually that Orpheus' attraction of rocks and trees might be explained by supposing them to be animated by the Soul of the World. This remark produced a violent discussion between two members, Valerio Marcellino, a Platonist, who defended Paolini and Orpheus, and Ottavio Amalteo, an ardent Peripatetic (although he too had been "initiated into the mysteries of Platonism"); Paolini therefore promised to treat the subject exhaustively in his next lecture [1].

It seems odd that a group of highly educated adults should spend hours seriously discussing, as if it were historical fact, a story which they knew and admitted to be legendary. It seems odder still that Del Rio, in his massive treatise on magic and witchcraft, should give a lengthy refutation of Paolini's views on the subject [2], and that Campanella should also discuss it at length in the same earnest and factual way. The explanation is, I think, that Orpheus was a uniquely rich and adequate symbol for this kind of Renaissance Neoplatonism in all its aspects [3]— he was a theologian who linked the ancient gods to Christianity, a magician, astrologer, poet, orator, musician, lover both plebeian and heavenly, and child of the sun. By discussing the effects of Orpheus' music one could range, with easy suppleness, over every possible practical application of Neoplatonism, from the whitest to the blackest magic, from the most intellectual religion to the most crude superstition, from the beauty of music to the power of a whispered incantation.

One sign of how seriously Paolini takes the problem of Orpheus' music is that he prefaces his discussion of it with a warning that

[1] Paolini, *Hebd.*, IV, v, p. 184: "Superiori igitur proxima sessione cum in eum sermonem ex aequo loco familiariter loquens incidissem, ut dicerem posse demonstrari Orpheum reapse, & verè potuisse saxa, & silvas ducere sono lyrae, ut de illo praedicatur, saxaque etiam vivere vita communi, & per animam Mundi, negantibusque id Peripateticis, quorum magna nos corona cingebat, acris coorta esset desceptatio inter duo praeclarissima literarum lumina Valerium Marcellinum Platonicum, qui meae sententiae propugnationem susceperat, & Octavium Amaltheum Peripateticę familiae acerrimum defensorem, licet Platonicis quoque sit literis, & quasi sacris initiatus, pollicitus sum hodierno die de hac ipsa re me verba facturum." On Amalteo, see Liruti, op. cit., II, 67 seq..

[2] V. infra p. 183.

[3] See Walker, "Orpheus the Theologian", *Warburg Journal*, 1953, pp. 100-2.

he is going to talk on Platonic principles and that, though these
are close to Christian ones, there are however some discrepancies,
by which his audience must take care not to be misled [1]; and at
intervals throughout the discussion he notes in parentheses that
this or that kind of magic is condemned by Christian theologians
as demonic. These warnings and cautionary statements are
significant of the importance for him of the topic because they
appear nowhere else in the book, although in many places his
presentation of unorthodox Neoplatonic or magical theories
would lead one to expect them [2]. The condemnations of magical
practices are inserted in such a way as to make it evident that
Paolini records them reluctantly; he never gives the arguments
in favour of the condemnation [3] (i.e. why a certain kind of magic
cannot be natural and must be demonic), but he does sometimes
himself argue against it. When discussing talismans, for example,
which are the fourth of the seven ways in which Orpheus could
have attracted rocks and trees, he begins [4]:

that figures are very suited for calling down the power of the heavenly
bodies the writings of all the ancient Philosophers testify (although we,
who reverence truth, believe, with the Theologians, that these are mere
nonsense and dreams) . . .

He then quotes Albertus' approval of talismans, and goes on
to Peter of Abano's medical amulets, to the Neoplatonists [5], and
finally arrives at the *Asclepius* statues animated by herbs, stones
and celestial music [6], "which however it is impious to believe, for

---

[1] Paolini, *Hebd.*, pp. 184-5: "in Platonica penetralia confugiendum, quae licet
sint parum à nostra plerumque religione dissentanea, interdum tamen parum con-
gruunt . . . praefandum mihi judicavi, & profitendum me semper Platonicè locuturum,
& disputandi, sive proludendi tamen gratia"; Platonic views must be accepted only
in so far as they agree with Christianity, "in reliquis fabulosa omnia existimanda,
& quasi Poetica, vel saltem Philosophorum somnia, & ego solenni ista pręmissa
professione aggrediar . . ."

[2] Paolini's *Ad Lectorem* ends with a conventional submission to theological
censure, if he has said anything not "pietati Christianę consentaneum", but he does
not think he has.

[3] This was what annoyed Del Rio, cf. infra p. 183.

[4] Paolini, *Hebd.*, pp. 207-8: "Quod autem figurae aptissimae essent ad cęlestium
vim devocandam, omnium veterum Philosophorum scripta testantur (licet nos
veritatis cultores meras esse nugas cum Theologis, & somnia credamus) . . ."

[5] Ibid., p. 208.

[6] V. supra p. 40.

the Theologians (such as St. Thomas) deny that this could be done by the simple influx of the stars", and say it must be the work of demons [1]. But Thomas is then immediately contradicted:

but that the influx and power of the heavenly bodies and certain natural benefits could be attracted means by of these images, constructed in a legitimate astrological way, it is less impious to admit, at least in so far as that could be achieved by herbs and other means. And if this may be done by material shapes, so much the more must we believe that mathematical figures will be effective, which are nearer to the divine Ideas [2].

He ends the discussion with the plainly regretful qualification: "although all these things are forbidden us by the decrees of the Councils and Popes" [3].

Paolini's exposition of Ficino's musical magic is much less uneasy; apart from an occasional parenthesis—"I am still speaking as a Platonist", "although the Theologians think otherwise"—when dealing with the *spiritus mundi* [4], there are no cautionary remarks. Ficino's magic contributes the chief way in which Orpheus might have produced his effects [5], namely by astrologically powerful music. Paolini quotes in full Ficino's rules for composing planetary music [6], and expands Ficino's preface to them in a significant manner. Ficino had written, in a phrase that reads merely like becoming modesty, that, though it was difficult to discover what kind of music fitted which planet, he had succeeded in doing so by his own diligence and by some

---

[1] Paolini, *Hebd.*, p. 208: "quod tamen nefas esset credere, id nam fieri potuisse negant Theologi (ut D. Thomas) per simplicem stellarum influxum".

[2] Ibid., p. 209: "sed coelestium influxum, & vim per has imagines legitima Astrologiae ratione constructas, & naturalia quaedam bona attrahi posse minus impium concedere, saltem quantum herbis, aliave ratione praestari posset. & si per materiales figuras id fieri licet, multo magis per mathematicas credendum est".

[3] Ibid.: "licet hęc omnia Concilijs, & Pontificum decretis prohibita nobis sint, & exerceri sanctissima lege non possint."

[4] Ibid., p. 203: "(Platonicè semper loquor) . . . (licet aliter sentiant Theologi, sed nos nunc Platonicè loquimur, ut sumus ab initio professi) . . ."

[5] It constitutes the first three ways, by musical sound, by song, by astrology, which are really all the same and are only separated so as to bring the total up to seven.

[6] Ibid., p. 199 (introduced thus: "Tres autem dicunt Astrologi esse regulas cognoscendi convenientiam tonorum cum sideribus teste Ficino"); for the rules, v. supra p. 17.

divine good chance, as Andromachus had discovered the *theriaca* (an antidote against snake-bites) [1]. Paolini expands "divine good chance" into "with divine help and command", and adds:

For when in any great matter, necessary or extremely useful to the human race, man has worked as hard as he can to achieve his aim, what still remains to perfect it, God Himself accomplishes and, as it were, donates [2].

This gives a divine origin and approval to the planetary music, and an importance for humanity, which Ficino had never claimed for it.

The whole theoretical basis for the magic is also fully expounded: the harmony of the spheres, the cosmic spirit, sympathetic vibration. But Paolini is less careful and consistent than the Ficino of the *De V.C.C.* in confining direct celestial influence to man's spirit; indeed, except where he is quoting verbatim from Ficino, it is for him the rational soul which draws in the cosmic spirit and receives its celestial benefits [3]. He puts more emphasis than Ficino on the provocation by music of greater planetary influxes, and considerably less on the subjective preparation of the spirit and making it receptive to influxes [4]. Moreover, Paolini's magic aims even higher than the stars; he hopes for miraculous help from the *anima mundi*. As it is the operator's soul or mind, not just his spirit, that is to benefit, so the operation is to attract not merely cosmic or astral spirit, but the cosmic soul or the ideas in it; by this inspiration man will be able to accomplish marvellous works that would be impossible with

---

[1] V. supra p. 15 note 4.

[2] Paolini, *Hebd.*, p. 199; Ficino's "divina quadam sorte" becomes "divina etiam ope, & nutu"; Paolini goes on: "cum nam in aliqua re praeclara, & humano generi necessaria, sive perutili, quantam in ipso est, dederit operam homo, ut conficiat rem, quod restat ad perfectionem Deus Opt. Max. absolvit, & quasi elargitur . . ."

[3] Paolini, *Hebd.*, pp. 202-3: "hic autem spiritus [sc. mundi] ab anima rationali facillimè suscipitur, & hauritur, ut ex Plotini doctrina Marsilius affirmat . . ."; (attracting cosmic spirit by the use of material objects) "multo magis anima rationalis, quae magis est illi [sc. animae mundi] consentanea, & majorem mundani spiritus copiam haurire diversis rationibus potest."

[4] Ibid., p. 200, Paolini summarizes two passages where Ficino suggests that the music will provoke a greater influx from the planet by making it vibrate in sympathy (*Op. Omn.*, pp. 563-4) and which in their original context are quite inconspicuous.

his own natural powers, such as producing nearly perpetual motion in hard, recalcitrant materials—clocks could never have been invented without the help of the *anima mundi* [1].

Paolini's version of Ficino's spiritual magic is, then, no longer mainly subjective and carefully confined to the spirit; the effects of his magic are directed to the rational soul and they reach up to the stars and beyond. He has combined the practices of the *De V.C.C.* with the demonic magic of Ficino's other writings. Moreover, between Ficino's time and Paolini's lies the revival of mediaeval astrological magic, the magic of Trithemius, Agrippa, Paracelsus and others—the invocations which compel planetary angels or spirits to do something extraordinary, the transmissions of thoughts by sending them up to the stars and down again, the magic which aims at intellectual benefits, at universal knowledge and power, not just at a healthy condition of the spirits. Paolini was an admirer of Trithemius; he quotes from his letters [2], and his treatise on planetary angels [3], and believes that he understands the secrets of the *Steganographia* [4]. It is, I think, Trithemian magic which has contaminated his conception of Ficino's magic and which he describes on two occasions as another possible explanation of Orpheus' effects. Paolini does not name Trithemius in this connection, nor does he ever cite Agrippa; but the follow-

---

[1] Ibid., p. 203 (after passage quoted above p, 134 note (3)): "quare nihil videmus hominibus denegatum, nihilque tandem aggressos, quin summo adhibito studio, & industria, animae mundanae opera adjuvante, & quasi inchoatum opus sua perficiente divinitate, atque potestate fuerint assecuti, quodque etiam inaminis rebus motum tribuere potuerint, & possint, facile declarat domesticum, & vulgatissimum Horologij exemplum, ac testimonium, in quo durissimo omnium rerum metallo, nempe ferro, videmus perpetuum quasi motum certa ratione assignatum . . . quod nisi divino nutu humanis faventi operibus, & industriae factum [non] esse arbitramur." Cf. passage quoted in note (2) of previous page.

[2] Paolini, *Hebd.*, pp. 120-1, quotes from Trithemius' letter to Germain de Ganay of 24 Aug. 1505 (Trithemius, *Epistolarum familiarum libri duo* . . ., Hagonoae, 1536, fo 92 vo) a passage on an ascent by nine stages, of which the last two are *potentia* and *miracula*, to a "supercoelestis harmonia" of body and soul.

[3] Paolini, *Hebd.*, pp. 313-4, gives the names of the planetary angels, citing Trithemius' *De septem Secundadeis*, and states that their subservient demons transmit planetary gifts to men.

[4] Paolini, *Hebd.*, p. 452, states that the *Stegan.* is an "unveiled" version of the *Polygraphia*.

ing operation is clearly the same magic that Agrippa ascribed to Trithemius [1]:

Some people assert that the feelings and conceptions of our souls can by the force of the imagination be rendered volatile and corporeal, so that, in accordance with their quality, they can be carried up to certain stars and planets (e.g. Jovial thoughts to Jupiter), and, affected and strengthened by the power of the planet, they will come down again to us and will obey us in whatever we want [2].

After the second description of this operation Paolini asks whether it implies that the stars must have sense, memory and choice, "in order to carry out for men such prayers (*vota*)" [3]. He finds the answer in Plotinus or Ficino's Commentary on him [4]: no, this operation can be accounted for by the "vital energy flowing from the living limbs of the world into everything, but more copiously into those things which have been made more receptive by the prayer (*votum*) and other suitable acts"; or perhaps the "intellectual souls" of the planets may hear the prayers and grant them [5]. From this it appears that the operation involves a prayer to the planet or its angel, by which the operator's imagination becomes receptive to that planet's influence and is enabled to solidify and project thoughts up to the stars. The operation also requires a talisman, or some image of the planet; for Paolini goes on:

[1] V. supra p. 88.

[2] I have conflated the two descriptions: Paolini, *Hebd.*, pp. 206-7, "traduntque nonnulli, & asserunt animi nostri sensus, conceptionesque reddi posse volatiles, corporeosque vi imaginationis, eosque pro sui qualitate ad sidera, & planetas ferri, qui rursus planetarum virtute affecti, & corroborati descendant nobis obsecuturi in his, quę volumus"; ibid., pp. 216-7, "volunt vehementes animae nostrae motus, & desiderium, per communem mundi vitam, atque animam ubique vigentem ... diffusa, ad ipsa mundi numina perduci, vicissimque horum numinum motus per eandem animam, atque vitam ad nos trahi, vel ex ea ratione qua diximus in Astrologia, quod scilicet animi sensus quidam putant reddi imaginatione corporeos, & aligeros, & ad planetas evolantes, pro suo quosdam ordine, nempe Joviales ad Jovem, eorum affici potestate, & ad nos reverti obsecuturos ad omnia."

[3] Ibid., p. 217: "ut vota hujusmodi hominibus perficiant".

[4] Plotinus, *Enn.*, IV, iv, 42; Ficino, *Op. Omn.*, p. 1748; cf. infra p. 165.

[5] Paolini, *Hebd.*, p. 217, "Vitalis vigor ... ex vivis mundi membris ... derivatur in omnia, uberius in ea, quae ad accipiendum aptiora fuerint facta per votum, & alia convenientia"; the "intellectuales animae", carrying out the eternal decrees of God, may "consulere rebus humanis, & supplicum preces audire ...".

Some impious and criminal people, in declaring this prayer (*votum*) and emotion, even add worship, venerating as spirits (*numina*) the bodies of the stars, and, offering to images of the stars that adoration (*latria*) which they owe only to God the Supreme Creator, have given opportunities to bad demons to pretend to be attracted or repelled by their sacrifices and, as it were, magic machines, and thus lead them to eternal perdition [1].

The use in this context of the technical term *latria* points to the *Opusculum* of Thomas Aquinas where it is stated that prayers or acts of reverence may be directed to planetary angels with *dulia*, but not with *latria*, that is, with the veneration proper to saints (their departed souls or their relics), but not with the worship that is proper to God alone [2]. I think that Paolini approves of this magic provided that, first, one does not direct one's imagination only towards the body of the star, instead of its angel or the *anima mundi*, and secondly, that one only reverences it as a powerful creature and does not worship it as a God.

What kinds of practical activity may have resulted from Paolini's versions of Ficinian and Trithemian magic? Let us consider first the Ficinian, primarily musical magic. Paolini does occasionally suggest reforms of modern music that will make its effects more powerful. He notes with regret that the music of his own time in its use of softening, decadent modes and a multiplicity of instruments is the exact opposite of the ethically good music advocated by Plato in the *Laws* and Aristotle in the *Politics* [3]. This criticism is perhaps more serious in intention than the conventional denigration of modern at the expense of ancient music [4];

[1] Paolini, *Hebd.*, p. 217: "Quidam verò impij, & scelesti ad declarandum hunc [sic] votum, & affectum, adorationem etiam adhibuerunt, ipsa corpora stellarum venerantes, ut numina, & quam Deo summo ipsi Opifici debent latriam, imaginibus stellarum praestantes, occasiones malis demonibus attulerunt, ut fingentes se eorum sacrificijs & magicis quasi machinis trahi, vel pelli, eos verè in perniciem secum ducant sempiternam . . ." The last clause is taken from Ficino, *Op. Omn.*, p. 1748 (*Comm. in Plot.*).

[2] Thomas Aquinas, *Opusculum* IX, (*Op. Omn.*, ed. S. E. Fretté, Paris, 1875, Vol. xxvii, p. 260). This passage was also referred to by Agrippa (*De Occ. Phil.*, III, xv, p. ccxxxix) and Campanella (v. infra pp. 226).

[3] Paolini, *Hebd.*, p. 92; cf. Walker, "Musical Humanism", *Music Review*, 1941-2.

[4] See James Hutton, "Some English Poems in Praise of Music", *English Miscellany*, ed. M. Praz, 2, Rome, 1951.

for we must remember that Paolini was a contemporary and compatriot of the Gabrielis and must have heard their huge instrumental compositions, with their brilliant, predominantly major harmony. He also regrets that modern songs do not preserve the metrical rhythm of poetry, and believes that this defect could and should be put right[1]; he had not presumably heard any of Baïf's *musique mesurée à l'antique*[2] or Andrea Gabrieli's choruses for the *Edippo Tiranno*, performed at Vicenza in 1585[3]. The only suggestion of a musical reform leading to specifically magical effects occurs after one of his several descriptions of the celestial power of Orpheus' music, which results from the proper, astrologically determined mixture of sounds :

if the musicians of our time also knew how to do this, they would produce not inferior effects, since we see that some of them, perfect within their own limits, have accomplished wonders, but none has produced effects superior to Orpheus'[4].

But we hear no more of this revival of Orphic music. Not does he connect the Orphic Hymns or other Orphic writings with Ficinian magic. He believed, however, that the Hymns contained "divine mysteries", and quotes several of Pico's *Conclusiones* about them, which are unmistakeably magical[5]. His faith in Orpheus as a *priscus theologus* was firm and untroubled—indeed his "liberal" acceptance of the whole *prisca theologica* equals that of the boldest of Catholic syncretists, Steuco, whom he frequently cites with approval[6]. It is therefore surprising that he does not

---

[1]   Paolini, *Hebd.*, pp. 158-9.

[2]   See F. A. Yates, *French Academies*, pp. 36 seq..

[3]   Leo Schrade will shortly publish a work on this performance, including an edition of the music, in the series *Le Choeur des Muses*, directed by J. Jacquot for the Centre National de la Recherche Scientifique.

[4]   Paolini, *Hebd.*, p. 221: ". . . perfectissimum omnium fuisse Orpheum judicamus, & hinc factum, ut propter admixtionis suę excellentiam tantam sibi vim cęlitus vindicavit, quod si nostrates quoque Musici scirent efficere, non minora praestarent, cum videamus quosdam pro suae perfectionis gradibus miranda effecisse, neminem verò Orpheo praestitisse majora."

[5]   Paolini, *Hebd.*, p. 445, 368 (quoting Pico, *Concl. Orph.*, Nos. 3, 4, 5, 13, 17, 20).

[6]   Lib. VII of the *Hebd.* is devoted to showing "quoòd Orpheus fuerit Theologus etiam Christianus. Christianos autem intelligo eos quoque qui adventurum Christum crederent, antequam venisset" (p. 364); of Steuco (,,Theologus praestantissimus") he says, quite truly, "manibus atque pedibus in hanc venit sententiam, ut omnium

in fact suggest that Orpheus produced his effects by singing his own Hymns.

Although he was widely read in musical theory and a friend of Zarlino [1], Paolini was evidently much more interested in oratory than in music, and, as far as the practical production of magical or other effects is concerned, one may say that for him oratory has taken the place of music. Orpheus too was an orator, and Paolini writes of the effects of his oratory in terms which are exactly those traditionally used to describe the effects of music; he also gives a long list of the effects of ancient orators [2]. Moreover, he believed that, just as a proper mixture of tones could give music a planetary power, so a proper mixture of "forms" could produce "celestial power" in an oration. In one of his public beginning-of-term lectures Paolini described how this celestial power was obtained in oratory by attracting the *anima mundi*, and his description is exactly parallel to his exposition of the Ficinian attraction of *spiritus mundi* by means of music [3]. The *anima mundi* contains seminal reasons, corresponding to the Ideas in the Divine Mind, and by means of these gives forms to things in the sensible world; by collecting together a suitable set of things one can attract into them the corresponding seminal reasons (or even the Ideas), by which they were originally shaped [4]. But what is a

fcrè veterum Theologiam cum nostra congruere ostendat, sed potissimum Orphei." (p. 373); on Stcuco cf. Walker, "Orpheus", pp. 116-7.

[1] V. supra p. 128.

[2] Paolini, *Hebd.*, pp. 7 seq., 46, 221-2 (,,Hac vi divina orationis mentes allicit, voluntates impellit Orator, quo vult, & unde vult deducit . . . quid majus divinitatis argumentum, quam flectere animos pugnaces, & obstinatos, & quocunque velis detorquere?". On the effects of oratory cf. F. A. Yates, *French Academies*, pp. 166, 170, 194.

[3] Paolini, *Hebd.*, pp. 202-3, summarizing Ficino, *De Tr. V.*, III, i (*Op. Omn.*, p. 531).

[4] Ibid., p. 47: "Quod vcrò cx ista formarum dicendi admixtione eloquentiae divina facultas comparetur, à me fuit demonstratum in ea, quam tertio abhinc anno habui, de literarum divinitate, orationem in exordijs studiorum, in qua ita disputavi, ut dicerem divinam quandam adhiberi vim posse orationi à coelesti illa, & divina eloquentiae forma per hanc admixtionem deductam, quia anima mundi, cujus munere hoc assequimur . . . totidem habet rationes rerum, & semina divinitus sibi data, quot exempla, & species sunt in mente divina, per quae has inferiores in rebus species gignit, & hinc fluxa haec divinis illis è regione singulis singula respondent, & possunt illarum ctiam vires, si se illis aptè conformarint, allicere tanquam igitur

suitable set of what things? The set has something to do with the number seven, and some of the things are the sounds of words, figures of speech, and Hermogenes' seven 'Ιδέαι, i.e. general qualities of good oratory, such as clarity, gravity, truth[1].

Now Paolini was, of course, obsessed with the number seven to an almost psychotic degree, and it is dangerous to draw any inferences from any particular application of it. But it is true that he connects oratory with 7 with unusual earnestness and persistence; the connexion appears conspicuously in his otherwise normally rhetorical or philological *Scholia* on Cicero's *De Oratore*[2]. It is also, I think, true that the prime non-mathematical content of 7 is the planets, and the whole theory of planetary influences and correspondences. If we are right in supposing that Paolini considered oratory to be closely parallel to music, that he was applying Ficinian magical theories to oratory instead of music, then it is obvious why 7 is so important in oratory, and what the sets of things are that will attract the *anima mundi* and give a celestial force to an oration: on the model of Ficino's planetary modes of music, Paolini is aiming at planetary modes of oratory. The general subject, the various topics, the figures of speech, the sounds and rhythms of words, will all correspond to a certain planet or combination of planets. It is of course normal that the seminal reasons of the *anima mundi* should be passed downwards through the planets. In Hermogenes' Περι 'Ιδεων, for which he had a great admiration and on which he had written a commentary[3], he found every aspect of rhetorical composition and style grouped under seven general types or forms (ἰδέαι) of oration; with very little juggling these forms could be made to fit the characters of the planets.[4]

sulphurea fax ad ignem exposita flammam repentè concipit, ita optimi Oratoris mens, si divinum commodè subsequatur exemplum vim trahit affectione, & in optimè affectam, aptamque mentem tota ipsa ideae virtus affatim redundat, & influit."

[1] Hermogenes, Περι 'Ιδεων, passim; Paolini, *Hebd.*, pp. 34 seq.

[2] *In eundem M. Tullii Ciceronis, Dialogi de Oratore Librum Primum. Fabii Paulini Utinensis Scholia*, Venetiis, 1587 (together with A. Maioragius' *Comm.* on the same; Paolini had lectured on this the previous year), fos. 5vo, 7vo, 9ro-vo, 18vo.

[3] Paolini, *De Gr. Lit. cum Lat. Conj.*, fo 22 vo.

[4] The seven forms are: σαφήνεια, μέγεθος, κάλλος, γοργότης, ἦθος, ἀλήθεια, δεινότης.

This planetary oratory is only my conjecture; but it receives considerable support from the fact that Paolini was a great admirer of Giulio Camillo; he cites him, in connexion with oratory and 7 and Hermogenes' forms, in his *Scholia* on Cicero [1]; in the *Hebdomades* he praises him enthusiastically and quotes from his works [2]. One of these works is Camillo's *Idea del Teatro* [3]. This was a scheme for ordering everything in the universe in an amphitheatre with seven gateways, which were the seven planets; thus all objects, activities and ideas were arranged according to their planetary characters. The theatre was an astrologically centred mnemonic system, and its prime purpose was to enable one to give an oration on any subject. It was the sevenfold, planetary construction of Camillo's theatre as applied to oratory that interested Paolini; for the sentence he quotes [4] describes this general structure, and he quotes it in the section of his book that deals with Orpheus' oratory. Paolini's interest in Camillo and Hermogenes may have come from his teacher, Parthenio, who admired Camillo and associated him with Hermogenes [5].

This planetary oratory will also give us the answer to the question of what was the practical aim of Paolini's version of Trithemian magic. By means of this magic you gave a planetary character to a given thought or mental image, which would

[1] Paolini, *Scholia in Cic.*, fo 7 vo: "nam septem dicendae formae constituuntur ab Hermogene, quod hoc uno numero contineatur universa eloquentia, quod non solum Veteres illi animadverterunt, ut multis nos demonstrabimus alio loco, sed ex recentioribus quoque multi, ut Julius Camillus in Topicis, & in suo Theatro eloquentiae, quod hoc uno numero construxit, ut ex illius idea, quae extat, apparet".

[2] Paolini, *Hebd.*, p. 27, 422, 429.

[3] Camillo, *L'Idea de Theatro*, Fiorenza, 1550.

[4] Paolini, *Hebd.*, p. 27, quotes from Camillo, *Theatro*, p. 14: "Ma per dar (per così dire) ordine à l'ordine con tal facilità, che facciamo li studiosi come spettatori, mettiamo lor davanti le dette sette misure sostenute dalle sette misure de sette Pianeti in spettacolo, ò dir vogliamo in Theatro distinto per sette salite" (the first 7 measures are the first seven *sefirot*); cf. above note (1). Camillo also was interested in Hermogenes, whose Περι 'Ιδεων he translated into Italian (*Le Idee, overo Forme della Oratione Da Hermogene considerate, & ridotte in questa lingua Per M. Giulio Camillo Delminio Friulano*, Udine, 1594). For Camillo, and probably for Paolini, the number 7 as an Idea in God, of which the highest emanations are the 7 *Sefirot*, is prior to the planets; but, from the point of view of the terrestrial world and practical magic, the planets are the highest manifestation of 7 about which anything precise and useful is known (cf. Camillo, *Theatro*, p. 10).

[5] Bernardino Parthenio, *Della Imitatione Poetica*, Vinegia, 1560, pp. 70-1, 89, 174-6.

then obey you, do whatever you wanted. What would you want a thought to do for you if you were an orator? First, to be available whenever you needed it; secondly, to produce a powerful effect on your audience. By Trithemian magic, then, you affect a thought, say of a lion, with its appropriate planetary character, that of the Sun, and fit it into your planetarily constructed mnemonic scheme (Camillo's Theatre); having been made active by the planetary affect, it will spontaneously appear whenever you think or say anything solarian. You will use it in an oration which has been constructed on Solarian principles (on the analogy of Ficino's planetary music), and the activated lion-thought will powerfully affect your audience, making them leonine, which effect is part of the total effect of making them solarian.

As I have put it here, baldly but I hope clearly, the whole business seems crude and childish; but if one translates this magic into more modern and familiar terms (and I think it can legitimately be so translated), one can see that it was a serious, if mistaken, attempt to use psychological forces which are not directly under conscious control. The Trithemian magic begins by using the imagination and ends in a thought being "affected" (emotionalized) by a planet; in Ficino's magic the operator must vehemently concentrate his emotions (*affectus*) on the planet. Now one of the primary meanings of the planets was as symbols of psychological types, or categories of emotional states and tendencies. If you try magically to stamp a thought with a planetary character, one of the things you are trying to do is to give that thought a specific and permanent emotional charge or affective tone. The content of the thought (an object, activity, idea) will be inherently more fitted to one type of emotion than another; you must therefore arrange everything you can think about in certain broad categories of emotional character—in other words, construct a planetary scheme of the universe. It would be generally admitted nowadays that every mental process, however abstract, has an accompanying emotional tone, and that this tone bears some relation to the content of the process, but that this relation is unstable, since the emotional tone is also conditioned by the general and constantly changing state of the whole psyche. There would be obvious practical advantages if this relation between the content of mental events and their emotional charge could be made permanent, appropriate and ordered. On the one hand, it would provide an extra kind of linkage for memory, that is, would reinforce logical and associative connexions; on the other, it would provide a method of controlling and ordering one's own emotions, —by deliberately following a train of thoughts or images belonging to a certain planet, one could colour one's whole emotional state with the type of affect belonging to that planet. With regard to Ficinian magic, it is evidently reasonable and possible, if one considers the planets primarily as types of emotional tone, to produce a song or an oration that is, as a whole and in all its parts, expressive of a certain type; it can be combined with Trithemian magic by composing the song or oration of ideas or mental images that have already been charged with the appropriate planetary affect.

The crudity and error have not been explained away; but we can see now that they lie in the following two defects. First, this way of controlling affective states is rigid and over-simplified; there is no good reason for cramming our whole emotional life into seven immutable categories. Secondly, the system of ordering all mental contents under these seven headings is obviously in some measure arbitrary; there is always *some* reason why any given thing is, say, solarian, but the kinds of reason differ wildly and meaninglessly—lion, because of kingship and yellowness; honey, just because of yellowness; heart, because it is the source of life and spirits; cock, because it sings to the rising sun, etc.. This does not in itself matter, provided the system is widely and firmly established—any more than it matters that our words have no real likeness to what they designate. The system of planetary correspondences was in fact like a language, in that it was understood and worked only as long as people went on learning it and speaking it. The error lay in supposing that it was not largely founded on convention and tradition, but that it had an objective reality; it was therefore at the mercy of anyone who exposed its arbitrariness and conventionality. It did in fact eventually become obsolete as a language, though very gradually and certainly long after its objective reality was universally disbelieved. It still exists, in petrified fragments, in our own ordinary language (saturnine, jovial), and it is a language we must learn if we wish to understand the past.

CHAPTER V. FICINO'S MAGIC IN THE 16th CENTURY. II. CONDEMNATIONS. G. F. PICO. J. WIER. ERASTUS. CHAMPIER & LEFÈVRE D'ETAPLES. BODIN. DEL RIO.

Among those who condemned Ficino's magic on religious grounds, we may distinguish one homogeneous group. The members of this can be described as evangelical hard-heads; those who believe all magic to be demonic or diabolic and illusory; who tend to be sceptical about the reality of supernatural phenomena; who distrust all pagan philosophy, particularly Neoplatonism; who take the Bible as their supreme authority whenever possible; who in general have a sensible, no-nonsense outlook on things, usually based on a moderate, Christianized Aristotelianism. The chief members of this class, for our purposes, are Gian-Francesco Pico, Johann Wier, and Erastus. These do constitute a real tradition of thought about magic; they mention each other with approval and are conscious of having the same outlook [1].

The other anti-magical writers I shall deal with belong to various, more liberal traditions: Symphorien Champier, a keen Platonist, but a carefully orthodox Catholic; Lefèvre d'Etaples, a rather timid evangelical, interested in the *Hermetica* and *Dionysiaca*; Jean Bodin, overtly a Catholic, but really believing in a curious sort of demon-ridden Judaïsm; Del Rio, an immensely erudite Jesuit.

[1] Both Erastus and Wier frequently quote from G. F. Pico; e.g. Wier, *Histoires, Disputes et Discours, des Illusions et Impostures des diables . . .*, n.p., 1579, pp. 128 (II, iv), 496 (V, viii, on Alkindi), 499 (V, ix, on Ficino); Erastus, *Disputationum De Medicina nova Philippi Paracelsi Pars Prima . . .*, Basileae, 1571, pp. 130, 133; and Erastus praises Wier's book (Erastus, ibid., p. 187).

(1) G. F. Pico. Johann Wier. Thomas Erastus

G. F. Pico

In the Epilogue to the first Book of his *Examen Vanitatis Doctrinae Gentium* G. F. Pico wrote [1]:

If in one tray of the balance were placed one dogma from Mosaïc, Evangelic or Apostolic writings, and in the other everything that could be collected from pagan thought, the former would far outweigh the latter.

This sums up the conclusions of a vast work demonstrating the variety, confusion and folly of all pagan thought about religion and philosophy. The method used, and a great deal of the matter, are taken from Sextus Empiricus. Since the object of this revival of ancient scepticism is to establish the absolute pre-eminence of the Judaeo-Christian revelation, G. F. Pico's attack is directed with particular vehemence against the *prisci theologi*, most of whom, it will be remembered, were also *prisci magi* [2].

For G. F. Pico the *prisca theologia*, far from being a precious corroboration and illumination of Christian truth, as it was from Ficino and Giovanni Pico, is a persistent tradition of superstitious error, with idolatry, magic and astrology going hand in hand. He takes it as conclusive proof of Giovanni Pico's later rejection of all magic that, in the *Adversus Astrologiam* [3], he denies the divine origin of astrology and makes disparaging remarks about Zoroaster [4]. The theory of the *prisca theologia* is back again at its patristic origins [5]: all pagan religion is diabolic; what grains

---

[1] G. F. Pico, *Op. Omn.*, Basileae, 1573, p. 814 (*Examen*, I, xx): "quando unum dogma ex Mosaicis, Propheticis, Evangelicis, Apostolicis literis in examine positum, omnibus quae in altera lance collocari queant Gentium doctrinis, longe praeponderet."

[2] Cf. supra p. 93.

[3] Giov. Pico, *Adv. Astr.*, ed. Garin, p. 484 (XII, i).

[4] G. F. Pico, *Op. Omn.*, p. 633 (*De Rerum Praen.*, VII, ii).

[5] Cf. Walker, "Orpheus", pp. 104, 110, 114.

of truth it contains are stolen from Moses; it is the same as, or indissolubly mixed with, black magic.

These are the main grounds for G. F. Pico's very detailed attacks on astrology and magic in his *De Rerum Praenotione*. These attacks, with a few exceptions, are not overtly directed against modern magicians; but that he had the Florentine Platonists in mind is indicated by his choice of ancient and mediaeval authors as subjects for detailed refutation. Among the *prisci theologi* or *magi* Orpheus comes in for a particularly heavy battering. He gave the Greek gods their names and instituted their cult, i.e. the worship of demons, and invented paederasty, which, like St. Paul, Pico believes is closely connected with bad religion [1]. Even the legend of Euridice is defiled—it is just an example of necromancy; Euridice in the underworld was an illusory shade evoked by black magic [2]. This special dislike of Orpheus may well be due to Pico's knowledge of the important part he played in Ficino's and Giovanni Pico's magic. Among the Neoplatonists he chooses out Proclus, whose *De Magia* [3] he summarizes fully, and among the Arabs Alkindi, whose *De Radiis* [4] he refutes in great detail. Roger Bacon and Peter of Abano are taken as continuing the tradition of Proclus and Alkindi [5]. Peter's planetary invocations [6] he derives from the *Picatrix*, "a most vain book, full of superstitions" [7].

The direct attack on Ficino (though Pico does not actually name him) occurs in a chapter against Apollonius of Thyana. Apollonius was a particularly vulnerable *magus* because it was known from Eusebius that he had been compared to Christ [8].

---

[1] G. F. Pico, *Op. Omn.*, pp. 471-2 (*De Rerum Praen.*, IV, iv); Paul, *Romans* I, v. 26-8; cf. Walker, "Orpheus", p. 114.

[2] G. F. Pico, ibid., p. 490 (*De Rerum Praen.*, IV, ix).

[3] V. supra p. 37. [4] See Thorndike, op. cit., I, 643.

[5] G. F. Pico, ibid., p. 658 (*De Rerum Praen.*, VII, vii).

[6] On these see Thorndike, op. cit., II, 900 seq.; cf. supra p. 90.

[7] G. F. Pico, ibid., p. 662.

[8] Eusebius, *Adv. Hieroclem* (Migne, *Pat. Gr.*, T. 22, cols. 795 seq.); the main aim of Artus Thomas' voluminous commentaries on Philostrates' *Life* of Apollonius is to demonstrate that he was a wicked sorcerer and nothing like Christ (Philostrate, *De la Vie D'Apollonius Thyaneen en VIII. Livres. De la Traduction de B. de Vigenere . . . enrichie d'amples Commentaires par Artus Thomas Sieur d'Embry Parisien*, Paris, 1611).

After mentioning Apollonius' talismanic rings [1], in order to show that he was a magician rather than a philosopher, Pico goes on to say:

It is regrettable that even in our own times there are many who have reached such a degree of folly that they have golden ornaments made under certain constellations and have images engraved on them. It is regrettable that, also in our time, far too much has been written about astrological images by a certain man, otherwise learnèd and of the highest authority among Platonists, when he was inanely trying to draw long life from the heavens. I would have confuted this man with all my power in this chapter, and still more in the 5th Book [against astrology] (nor would I have been withheld from performing this duty by the friendship that was between us during his life-time, nor by his praises, both written and spoken, of myself and my uncle Giovanni), if he had persisted in his opinion; for I would have put truth and love of our religion above friendship. But he prefaced his work by saying that he intended to assert nothing against religion, nor to write anything other than what the church would approve of; though it would have been better if he had in fact written what was right and in conformity with tested theologians [2].

Pico then quotes from Ficino's *Ad Lectorem* to the *De V.C.C.* the feeble excuse that he was merely recounting, not approving of, his magic remedies [3], and recalls that he had written against astrologers in his commentary on Plotinus [4]. He concludes:

We must then reject this superstition of talismans, which cannot adequately be defended by his prefatory excuses. For in things that

---

[1] Cf. Philstrate, *Vie D'Apollonius*, ed. cit., I, 679, where Thomas, commenting on these, cites Del Rio (v. infra p. 185) against Ficino's use of talismans.

[2] G. F. Pico, *Op. Omn.*, pp. 668-9 (*De Rerum Praen.*, VII, x): "Displicet autem quod nostra etiam tempestate in id insaniae devenerint plerique ut fabrefieri aurea gestamina sub syderum configurationibus curent, & imagines illis insculpi. Displicet quòd aetate quoque nostra à quopiam docto alioqui viro, & inter Platonicos eximiae auctoritatis de imaginibus Astrologicis nimis multa conscripta sunt, cum inaniter sibi vitam de coelo prorogaret, quem hoc loco, & quinto maximè libro pro viribus confutassem (nec me ab hoc munere, aut ea quae inter nos dum vixit amicitia intercessit, aut in mei nominis & dictae ab eo & scriptae laudes, sed & Joan. Patrui apud eum praeconia revocassent) si perstitisset in dogmate, amicitiae quippe & veritatem & amorem religionis nostrae praetulissem. Sed contra illam nihil à se assertum velle ille ante praefatus est, nec praeter id aliud quàm comprobaret ecclesia, quanquam satius erat & recte, & Theologis probatis consentaneae scribere ..."

[3] V. supra p. 42, and infra p. 168.

[4] V. supra p. 54.

are or might seem new or doubtful such excuses are evidently necessary; in things that are manifestly good and true there is no need of them; in things that are manifestly bad and false they are a mockery [1].

Ficino, then, is finally convicted of dangerous superstition, but, in consideration of his submissive attitude, is let off a public exposure. However, much that Pico has to say about Alkindi applies to Ficino's spiritual magic, if one substitutes the term "spirit" (as Pico sometimes does) for Alkindi's "rays". From the weakness of his arguments one can see that his rejection of natural magic is based, not on disbelief in its possibility, but on the feeling that it is somehow threatening to Christianity.

It will be remembered that the basis of most theories of natural magic is the power of the imagination, aided by planetary influences and the *vis verborum, musices*, etc., and that this can work in two ways, subjectively or transitively. The first leads to Ficinian magic, where the effects remain within the operator; the second leads to fascination, telepathy, medical incantations, and most of the operations of witchcraft. It is Alkindi's theory of transitive natural magic that Pico attacks.

Alkindi, says Pico [2], supposes that the stars operate by rays and that the human imagination has similar rays which can operate in the same way, that is, impress on an external object an image conceived in the imagination, where such images have an "actual" existence. Pico's answer is: there are no rays in the

---

[1] G. F. Pico, ibid.: "Reijcienda igitur haec Astrologicarum imaginum super-stitio, quae nec illa praefatione honoris defendi satis commode potest. Namque in ijs quae aut sunt, aut quoquomodo videri possunt, vel nova & ambigua, apertè requiritur, in manifestè bonis & veris non oportet, in manifestè malis & falsis irrisio est ..." Pico then goes on to Thomas Aquinas' condemnations of talismans (v. supra p. 43).

[2] G. F. Pico, *Op. Omn.*, p. 651 (*De Rerum Praen.*, VII, vi): "Imaginationem deinde ponit radios habere, mundi radijs apprimè conformes, quod fieri ut facultas ei sit in rem extrariam imprimere, quodque in ea concipitur actualem, ut inquit, existentiam habere in spiritu imaginario, quapropter extra produci posse quod conceptum est ... Multa hic falsa, multa impossibilia, neque enim insunt imaginationi quos fingit radij: Sed quicquid ex ab homine, ex corporeis spiritibus provenit, quibus tanquam instrumentis utitur anima: eò autem impensius feruntur, & quodammodo proijcitur [sic], si vehemens desiderium fuerit ..."; Alkindi, *De Radiis Stellicis* (or *Theoria Artis Magicae*), MS Harleian 13 (Brit. Mus.; 13th century), fos 168 vo col. 2 -169 ro col. 1.

imagination; the only things that can be projected outside a man are the corporeal spirits, which the soul uses as instruments. If some strong desire leads to these spirits being emitted, they may produce an external effect; concupiscence may produce a seminal emission and hence a child, or anger may result in fascination (evil eye) and hence a disease. But these effects can be produced only at a very short distance and in suitably receptive material (in these cases: the womb, the eyes). Since, then, Pico concedes that at least some transitive effects can be produced by the power of the imagination through an alteration of the spirits, he would *a fortiori* have to admit the possibility of the subjective effects of Ficinian magic.

Alkindi admits that effects from imaginative power can usually only be produced if the imaginative effort is accompanied by words or manual gestures. Words and voices have their own particular rays, which also derive their operative power "from the celestial harmony"; in consequence "some voices strengthen the operations of Saturn, some those of Jupiter, some those of Mars . . ." [1]. In reply to this Pico attempts a general refutation of the magical power of words and sounds (*vis verborum & musices* B), beginning contemptuously:

This exceeds all folly, to say that certain voices correspond with certain images in the heavens, and that certain words uttered with solemnity, can change the senses of animals and men . . . [2].

If the power lies in the meaning of the words, then they must be addressed to an intelligence and the operation is demonic. If it lies merely in the sound, then why should the human voice be more effective than other sounds? If it lies in the articulation of speech, then in which syllable, and why in one more than another? These arguments fail to refute the basis of Alkindi's theory, which is the familiar one we have already met in Ficino,

---

[1] Pico Ibid., p. 652: "easdem voces effectum suum enancisci ex harmonia coelesti . . . voces alias Saturni operationes confortare, Jovis alias, alias Martis . . ."

[2] G. F. Pico, ibid., p. 652: "Illud autem superat omnem stultitiam, quasdam voces cum quibusdam coeli imaginibus convenire, & verba quaepiam cum solemnitate prolata mutare sensus brutorum & hominum . . ."

namely, that the metre of verse and the intervals of music have proportions which correspond with the movements of the heavenly bodies, and that the active power of such proportional correspondence is proved by the fact of the sympathetic vibration of strings.

Pico's line of argument also has another weakness: "if one of those who think themselves clever should apply this argument to the most sacred words used in performing baptism and conse-crating the eucharist" [1]. Pico is evidently embarrassed by this; he answers that theologians are not agreed on this point—the words may have no efficacy, or they may be the sign of a pact made by God (i.e. to effect transubstantiation if, and only if, certain words are said) [2]. He does not cite Thomas Aquinas, as he freely does in the rest of the treatise, no doubt because Thomas does ascribe power, as an "instrumental cause", to the words of consecration (the prime cause being direct divine action) [3]. It is indeed difficult to see how he could avoid doing so, since he maintains that the consecration is valid if only the words "Hoc est corpus meum" and "Hic est calix sanguinis mei" are spoken and no others, even if they are spoken by a priest who is a heretic or in a state of mortal sin or with evil intentions, and is not valid (i.e. transubstantiation does not occur), if they are not spoken [4]. Pico returns again to this question, when discussing the tetra-grammaton [5], and later when trying to deal with Peter of Abano's connexion of the eucharist with the *ars notoria* [6]. It was in fact a difficult and dangerous question, whether one asserted or denied the magical power of words.

---

[1] G. F. Pico, ibid., p. 653: "Si quis verò ex ijs qui sibi sapientes videntur hoc ipsum argumentum & ad baptismi conficiendi & ad euchristiae consecrandae verba sacratissima transferret ..."

[2] Cf. infra p. 181.

[3] Thomas Aquinas, *Summa Theologica*, P. III, q. 78, a. iv.

[4] Thomas Aquinas, *Sum. Th.*, P. III, q. 78, a. i. ad 4.; q. 74, a. 2; q. 64, a. 5 & 9; q. 85, a. 5 & 7.

[5] G. F. Pico, ibid., pp. 654-5, beginning: "Sed iterum videre mihi videor, sciolos illos qui verba sacra, quae formas dicimus sacramentorum nobis ingesserunt."

[6] G. F. Pico, ibid., pp. 660-1; cf. supra p. 36, and infra p. 182.

Johann Wier

Like G. F. Pico, Johann Wier takes the *prisca theologia* as a tradition of evil superstition from which mediaeval and modern magic derive. Being a somewhat aggressively anti-Catholic Protestant, he goes further in this direction than Pico. Even the Sibyls, who for Bellarmin are still of almost canonic status [1], were inspired by the Devil, who passed on to them prophecies from the Old Testament about the coming of Christ, in order that they might later mislead Christians into believing they were divinely inspired [2]; here, as elsewhere, the double-crosses of Wier's Devil are so subtle as to make it almost impossible to distinguish him from God. The visits of the Greek sages to Egypt resulted in their learning, not the Mosaïc tradition of true theology, but bad Egyptian magic. In the preface to his *De Praestigiis Daemonum* Wier congratulates himself that his education was not like Plato's "chez ces superstitieux Egyptiens & prognosti-queurs Memphitiques: ou bien Procle aupres de Marc, esclave du diable" [3].

Wier is still famous in our time, and was exceptional in his own, for his disapproval of witch-burning; but this was not because he believed magic and sorcery to be anything but diabolic. Nearly all the operations of witchcraft were, he thought, subjective delusions induced by evil demons. Since the witches, being female and usually senile, were too silly to be anything more than passive victims of the Devil, they should not be so severely punished; the same leniency should not be extended to male magicians, who often voluntarily entered into commerce with demons. Though he grudgingly concedes the possibility of good,

---

[1]   See Walker, "*Prisca Theologia* in France", p. 256.

[2]   Wier, *De Praestigiis Daemonum, & incantationibus, ac veneficiis Libri sex, postrema editione sexta aucti & recogniti. Accessit Liber Apologeticus, et Pseudomonarchia Daemonum*, ..., Basileae, 1583, I, viii, cols. 40-2; the first edition is of 1566; I shall also quote sometimes from the French translation: *Histoires, Disputes et Discours, des Illusions et Impostures des diables ... par Jean Wier medecin du Duc de Cleves ...*, n.p., Pour Jaques Chouet, 1579.

[3]   Wier, *Hist., Disp.*, Pref., and II, iii, pp. 123-6 (*De Praest.*, cols. 146-150).

natural magic [1], he does in fact condemn all kinds of magical practices as involving demons and producing only illusory effects; by magic the Devil buys men's souls, but his currency is worthless.

Wier reproduces G. F. Pico's arguments against Alkindi's theory of the magical power of words, sounds and figures [2], and Thomas's arguments against talismans [3], namely, "Il est bien vray que les choses naturelles prennent leurs formes & vertus des choses celestes, mais les images artificielles ne peuvent attirer aucune puissance de l'art", and are therefore addressed to demons [4]. The other great Dominican theologian of the middle-ages, Albertus Magnus, had long been a stumbling-block for anti-magical writers; but, whereas the two Picos try to excuse him by doubting the attribution of the *Speculum Astronomiae* or claiming he changed his mind in old age [5], Wier is able flatly to reject him as a superstitious maker of talismans. It is as a follower of Albert that Wier casually condemns Ficino, "otherwise a most learnèd philosopher"; he then refers the reader to G. F. Pico's condemnation [6].

It was obviously out of the question that Wier should have the slightest sympathy for Ficino's magic. One hidden source of this was the magical elements in Christianity, and Wier wanted a religion cleared of all such elements. We have already seen Pico trying to take the magic out of the words of consecration of the host; in Wier this tendency has developed enormously. Quite a large proportion of his treatise is directed not against secular magic, but against Catholic practices and ceremonies

---

[1] Wier, *De Praest.*, II, iii, col. 151.

[2] Wier, *De Praest.*, V, viii, cols. 534-5.

[3] V. supra p. 43.

[4] Wier, *Hist.*, *Disp.*, V, xiii, pp. 112-3 (*De Praest.*, cols. 550-2).

[5] G. F. Pico, *Op. Omn.*, 1573, p. 633 (*De Rerum Praen.*, VII, ii); Giov. Pico, *Adv. Astr.*, ed. Garin, Lib. I, p. 94. Earlier, in the *Apologia* for his *Concl.*, Pico used Albert as one of the "summi theologi" who approved of natural magic (Pico, *Op. Omn.*, 1572, p. 166).

[6] Wier, *De Praest.*, V, ix, col. 538: the supporters of talismans "objicient & Albertum sui semper similem, & horum annulorum sigillorumque à veritate saepe-numerò divaricantem fabrum. Accedet quoque Marsilius Ficinus, doctissimus alioqui philosophus, & plerique alij . . ."

which he regards as superstitious, and hence, at least potentially, demonic [1]. These include most forms of exorcism, the use of the scriptures or the names of God or relics in curing diseases, the wearing of scriptural amulets, the baptism or consecration of bells and images.

Now, if one believes that the effects of magic are illusory, that is, exist only subjectively in the imagination, and if one also wishes to have a non-magical religion, where the effects of words and ceremonies are also purely subjective, consisting solely in a change of heart or illumination of mind, then the main distinction between diabolic magic and true religion lies in the private nature of religious effects, which, unlike many magical ones, cannot be shown to be hallucinatory. It is nonsense to say that someone has a delusion of being comforted by reading the Gospel, but one could demonstrate that someone's belief that he had magically induced measles was a delusion. Thus Wier, and other radical Protestants, are on safer ground when trying to distinguish magic from religion than are the Catholics; they have a valid criterion for magic producing manifest effects, even if they do not always apply it.

But there were still dangers. For, by making subjective the effects of both magic and religion, Wier comes very near to admitting that they are produced in the same way, namely, by credulity or faith suitably disposing the imagination. Just after, with Pico's help, he has refuted Alkindi's theory of the power of words, he writes [2]:

The words are uttered from the priest's mouth, but they are consecrated by the power and grace of God; if magical whispers have any efficacy, they have some occult power from a firm belief in the devil. There is indeed no efficacy in these words; but God most justly, on account of

---

[1]   Nearly the whole of Book V of the *De Praest.* is about current Christian superstitions; cf. infra pp. 180-2.

[2]   Wier, *De Praest.*, V, viii, col. 535; the first sentence is quoted from Chrysostom, *De Prod. Iudae Homil. I & II*, Migne, *Pat. Gr.*, T. 49, cols. 380, 389; "Verba sacerdotis ore proferuntur, Dei autem virtute consecrantur & gratia: & magici susurri si quid habent efficaciae, id occultae virtutis habent à certa fiducia in diabolum. Nulla verò inest ijs verbis efficacia: sed qui ijs fidunt, hos ob impiam confidentiam saepe illudi à Satana sinit justissimus Deus."

their impious belief, often allows those who trust in them to be deluded by Satan.

And later we find an exact parallel drawn between this credulity in superstition and faith in religion. After condemning as idolatrous the use of relics for curing disease, Wier quotes, as if it were his own, the following passage from Agrippa's *De Occ. Phil.*[1]:

Superstition requires credulity, just as true religion requires faith. Deep-rooted credulity is so powerful that it may even, in false beliefs, be thought to perform miracles. For, if anyone believes most firmly that his religion is true, even if it is in fact false, he raises his spirit by reason of that very credulity, until it becomes like the spirits who are the leaders and princes of that religion, and seems to perform things which are not perceived by those in a normal and rational state.

Since Wier holds the normal patristic view that the gods of all pagan religions were demons, this is an exact parallel between the modes of operation of religion and magic; the distinction between faith and credulity is a purely verbal one. The examples of "how superstition imitates religion", given immediately after and taken overtly from Agrippa [2], show how the above criterion for distinguishing magic from religion applies. They are: the excommunication of locusts and the baptism of bells. These must be magical or superstitious because they cannot produce any private, unverifiable effect either on the locusts and bells or on the congregation; for, whatever the subjective delusions of the latter, any person not in a state of credulity could see whether excommunicated locusts go away or not, and whether baptized bells repel storms better than unbaptized ones.

But this criterion is only my deduction from Wier's attitude to magic and religion. Moreover, it cannot be successfully applied

---

[1] Wier, *De Praest.*, V, xvii, col. 569; Agrippa, *De Occ. Phil.*, III, iv, pp. ccxvi-ccxvii: "Credulitatem requirit superstitio, quemadmodum fidem vera religio. Tantum potest obfirmata credulitas, ut etiam miracula operari credatur in opinionibus falsis. Quilibet enim in sua religione, etiam falsa, modò firmissimè credat veram, spiritum suum ea ipsa credulitatis ratione elevat, donec assimiletur spiritibus illis qui ejusdem religionis duces sunt & principes: eaque videatur operari, quae natura & ratio non discernunt."
[2] Cf. supra p. 94.

to the miracles performed by Christ, and when Wier discusses these he gives his own criterion: these miraculous effects of religion are beneficial to man (curing of diseases etc.), whereas those of magic are either useless (e.g. Simon Magus flying) or harmful (diseases produced by witchcraft, etc.). There seems no valid reason why, on these grounds, he should admit the reality and goodness of Christ's miracles, and condemn contemporary religious cures of diseases. The task of taking all the magic out of Christianity was an impossible one; it was there right from the beginning.

Thomas Erastus

Erastus' critique of magic continues the tradition of G. F. Pico and Wier. But his attack on the theoretical bases of magic is more thorough and radical, his condemnations of magical practices are more violent, and the influence on his reasoning of his particular kind of religion is still more pervasive and evident. The efficacy of his attack is strengthened by his tendency to argue from experience. Empirical arguments had very rarely been applied before to this subject, and they were capable of destroying many of the "facts" on which magical theories were based. But his other arguments against magic lead him into very difficult positions. His hard-headed Protestantism shows itself not only in the effort, also made by G. F. Pico and Wier, to explain away the magic in Christian ceremonies, but also in his frequent use of the Bible, interpreted as literally as possible, as the supreme authority in philosophic and scientific matters [1].

These characteristics can be seen in the refutation of the astrological basis of natural magic which Erastus gave in his treatise on occult virtues [2]. The existence of these he takes as proved by experience, remarking that "it is idle to enquire the

---

[1] Erastus also goes further than Wier in rejecting the authority of Albertus Magnus, whom he considers an impious magician, as superstitious as the Platonists (see Erastus, *Disputationum De Medicina nova Philippi Paracelsi Pars Prima* . . ., Basileae, n.d. (circa 1572), pp. 49, 111, 128, 162).

[2] *De Occultis Pharmacorum Potestatibus* . . ., Basileae, 1574.

opinion of the best and shrewdest philosophers, when our own
senses can enlighten us"[1], and he gives the usual Aristotelian
derivation of them from the substantial forms of the things which
possess them; but he will not take the further step of deriving
these forms from the celestial world. He is aware of the solid
body of tradition, both Aristotelian and Platonic, he is opposing[2]:

Thomas Aquinas, together with nearly all the moderns, decreed that
the separate substances or intelligences, by means of the heavenly
bodies, imprint on things the forms contained in their intellect.

And of much the same opinion are[3]

those who invent some celestial spirit or other, which pervades all
things and from which everything in the universe takes its nature and
power.

But from the first chapter of *Genesis* we know that God created
plants before the heavenly bodies[4]; vegetable forms at least, then,
cannot have a celestial origin. Moreover, whereas God did tell
animals to multiply after their own kind, he gave no directions
to the stars about transmitting forms or seminal reasons. It is
God, not the heavens, who is the giver of forms[5]. The heavens,
by their light, may help to conserve life, as a general (equivocal)
cause of generation; but, says Erastus, boldly contradicting the
famous dictum of Aristotle[6], "not the sun, but man gives form
to the nascent man"[7], or rather passes on the form God has
given him. To allow the celestial intelligences or planetary

---

[1] Erastus, *De Occ. Ph. Pot.*, pp. 4-5: "Sed frustra quid senserint summi & acutis-
simi philosophi quaeratur, ubi nos sensus nostri erudire possunt".

[2] Ibid., p. 32: "Thomas Aquinas cum recentioribus ferè omnibus statuit, separatas
substantias sive intelligentias apud se intellectas formas, corporum coelestium
virtute, rebus imprimere". For a full astrologically based account of occult virtues,
see Jean Fernel, *De Abditis rerum Causis*, Paris, 1548; Erastus criticizes Fernel sharply
(ibid. pp. 22, 42-3).

[3] Erastus, *De Occ. Ph. Pot.*, p. 32: "Cum eadem [sc. sententia] ferè faciunt,
qui nescio quem spiritum coelestem rebus omnibus permisceri fingunt: à quo
naturam vimque suam omnem universa mutuentur".

[4] Erastus, ibid., p. 35; *Genesis*, I, 11-17.

[5] Erastus, Ibid., pp. 33, 36, 8 ("jussit ergo Deus quamque speciem se individuo-
rum eisdem viribus praeditorum multiplicatione propagare: non imperavit sideribus,
ut vel formas vel earum vires proprias creatis rebus imprimerent").

[6] Aristotle, *Physics*, II, 194 b 13: "ἄνθρωπος ἄνθρωπον γεννᾷ καὶ ἥλιος."

[7] Erastus, ibid., p. 35: "Non Sol, sed homo, nascenti praebet homini formam".

angels (whose existence he denies [1]) to be the transmitters and preservers of specific forms opens the way to polytheism [2]:

What is this but the invention of Platonic godlets, to whom God has delegated the management of the work He began?

This admission of occult qualities, coupled with the refusal to derive them astrologically, points directly towards Baconian empiricism, the patient investigation of natural phenomena, guided by no hypotheses. For if these qualities, or the substantial forms to which they correspond, depend solely on the will of God, it is impious as well as impossible to make any *a priori* assumptions about the way they are grouped and ordered; the only guides are experience and the Bible [3].

After this denial of astrological influence, far more radical than Giovanni Pico's or Bacon's, we are not surprised to find Erastus denying in an equally sweeping manner the reality of all the effects of all magic as being demonic delusions; this explanation he takes from Wier, though, unlike him, he is in favour of burning witches [4]. The only kind of magic which might produce real effects and be free of demons consists in practical natural philosophy concentrated on unusual experiments which seem, only to the ignorant, to be marvellous; he gives Porta's *Magia Naturalis* as an example of this [5]. This concession is only apparent: for if effects are truly marvellous, they are hallucinations produced by demons; if they are not marvellous, they are not magical.

Erastus' main attacks on magic occur in his *Disputationes de Medicina nova Philippi Paracelsi* [6]. Paracelsus is taken as the culmination of a magical tradition which includes the most diverse members: Avicenna, Alkindi, Ficino, Pomponazzi, who have

---

[1]   Erastus, *Disp. de Med.*, pp. 121-2.

[2]   Erastus, *De Occ. Ph. Pot.*, p. 36: "Quid hoc aliud est, quàm Deunculos fingere Platonicos, quibus incepti operis partem demandarit Deus?"

[3]   On Erastus and 17th century science, cf. R. Lenoble, *Mersenne ou la Naissance du Mécanisme*, Paris, 1943, pp. 212 seq..

[4]   Erastus, *Disp.*, pp. 107, 197 seq..

[5]   Ibid., p. 133; even in Porta a great deal is to be rejected as superstition.

[6]   These were published in four Parts at Bâle, 1572-3; I shall quote only from the First Part, in which most of the discussions on magic occur.

however the common characteristic of basing their magic on the power of the imagination and planetary influence. Erastus differentiates them according to the medium of transmission by which they suppose the imagination and the stars produce effects: Avicenna, directly by the mind; Alkindi by rays; Pomponazzi and Ficino, by spirits; Paracelsus, also by spirits [1]. Paracelsus is said to differ from the others in that he believes, not only that the heavens influence our imagination, but that the power of our imagination can alter, infect the stars and compel them to produce effects [2]. Ficino is attacked here, as elsewhere in Erastus' book, not by himself, but in conjunction with another magician, in this case, Pomponazzi, whom Erastus links with him by reproducing the passage on the *vis imaginativa* from the *Theologia Platonica* that Pomponazzi had quoted in the *De Incantationibus* [3]; at the same time Ficino is usually given a special rebuke of his own as a representative of the credulous and superstitious Platonists [4]—as G. F. Pico had said, Aristotelians believe too little, and Platonists too much [5].

Erastus gives a detailed refutation of the possibility of producing transitive effects by the power of the imagination conveyed in emissions of spirit. He accepts the reality of subjective effects, both psychological ones and the more ordinary psychosomatic ones. But, he says [6],

certainly no one in their right mind will think that an image fashioned in the spirit of my fantasy can go out of my brain and get into the head of another man.

[1] *Erastus, Disp.*, pp. 53-5.

[2] Erastus, ibid., pp. 54-7 ("Imaginationes nostras sursum attolli putat, astraque non aliter inficere, quam illa nos radijs suis afficiunt"; it is peculiar to Paracelsus "quod Imaginationi potestatem attribuit coelum & astra cogendi, ijsque pro libidine ad res nequissimas abutendi"); he is referring to Paracelsus, *De Imaginatione*, in *Philosophiae Magnae . . . Collectanea Quaedam . . . Per Gerardum Dorn . . . Latinè reddita*, Basileae, n.d., pp. 208, 210.

[3] Erastus, ibid., p. 78; for Pomponazzi v. supra p. 107.

[4] Erastus, ibid., p. 80: "Fuit enim vir ille, ut Platonicorum, ita etiam omnis Platonicae superstitionis plus satis studiosus, nimisque credulus".

[5] G. F. Pico, *Op. Omn.*, 1573, pp. 642-3 ("ex ferventiori Platonis amore in superstitiones, ex nimio Aristotelis affectu in impietatem non difficilis est lapsus").

[6] Erastus, ibid., p. 65: "Certè ex meo cerebro imaginem in spiritu phantasiae effictam exire, inque alius hominis caput subire, nullus sanae mentis putabit".

His position is based partly on empirical grounds. He refuses to admit, for example, the classic example of menstruating women tarnishing mirrors, and even suggests that experiments could easily be made to prove that they do not [1]. He denies the reality of fascination produced by an ejection of spirit; but concedes that evil spirits, whenever, with God's permission, they cause disease by troubling the spirits and humours, are wont to persuade wretchèd old women that they themselves have done such works [2].

He believes that some diseases may be transmitted by infected spirits; and asserts that the mother's spirits affect her unborn child [3]—but this can of course be regarded as a subjective effect. His arguments against the possibility of fascination, telepathy, etc., produced by emissions of spirit are as follows. First, the transmission is impossible: spirits are never voluntarily ejected; they are inanimate, and therefore powerless, once they have left the body (like blood); they could not be directed, but would be dissipated in the air almost at once [4]. It is difficult to see how, from this position, Erastus could have explained the successful transmission of ordinary speech and music. Secondly, he denied that the images or "species" produced by the imagination permanently change the nature of the spirit; he compares the spirit to a mirror which cannot be said to be red only because it is reflecting a red object. Moreover, the species in the spirit are mere effigies or shadows of things, and can therefore only "figure, signify, represent", but not produce any physical effects [5]; in slightly more modern terms, the species of the imagination have secondary, but not primary qualities. These two negative propositions have the disadvantages of making memory and all psychosomatic phenomena, including all voluntary motor-activity, inconceivable, and of being hopelessly inconsistent with Erastus' own acceptance

---

[1] Ibid., p. 91.

[2] Erastus, *Disp.*, p. 107: "Solent nequam spiritus, quoties permissu Dei per agitationem spirituum & humorum morbum accenderunt, infoelicissimis aniculis persuadere, ipsas talium operum fuisse effectrices."

[3] Ibid., p. 86, 98.

[4] Ibid., pp. 83-103.

[5] Ibid., pp. 60-4.

of subjective effects produced by the *vis imaginativa*. He should have stuck to his purely empirical denials; for in fact the ordinary current medical conception of spirits and their modes of action was compatible with a belief in telepathy, fascination, etc., and such magical effects could have been disproved only by experiment.

The application of these arguments to religion produces curious results, which indicate that Erastus' basic motive for attacking magic was the same as G. F. Pico's and Wier's, namely, the wish to achieve a non-magical Christianity. When discussing the use of Christian prayers or ceremonies in magical operations [1], he insists that this is not only blasphemous but ineffective;

for there is no power in ceremonies but that of representing. For ceremonies have been instituted for the sake of representation, or indeed of order and splendour, so that, striking the eyes of the less educated, they might help both the understanding and the memory [2].

The omission here of any effect on the imagination is plainly deliberate; it is of course implied in the second sentence, but this also implies that intelligent Christians with good memories do not need any ceremonies. Erastus also denied that "sacred words" have any power; they merely tell us what the will of God is [3]. This approaches near to the "religion purement mentale", which Montaigne both criticized as neglecting most men's need for anthropomorphic imagery in religion, and praised as being true and leading to a purely subjective Deism [4]. Protestants like Erastus escaped deism and the danger that they might see that their religion "fût eschappee et fondue entre leurs doigts" [5], by their absolute faith in the divine inspiration of the Bible. This obliged them, with whatever inconsistency, to accept the

[1] E.g. in Trithemian magic (v. supra p. 87).

[2] Erastus, *Disp.*, p. 134: "Etenim ceremoniarum vis alia nulla est, quam repraesentandi. Quippe repraesentationis, aut certé ordinis & ornatus causa institutae sunt ceremonię, ut in oculos incurrentes imperitiorum intelligentiae pariter & memoriae serviant. Equidem majore intentione observant, quae dicuntur & aguntur, fideliusque memoria retinent".

[3] Ibid.

[4] Montaigne, *Essais*, ed. Villey, Paris, 1922, II, 248, III, 195; cf. Walker, "Ways of dealing with Atheists", *Bibl. d'Hum. & Ren.*, 1955, p. 271 note (1).

[5] Montaigne, ed. cit., III, 195 (speaking of Protestantism as an "exercice de religion si contemplatif et immateriel").

reality of at least some marvellous events. The miracles in the New Testament differ from magical effects in being real, not illusory; how do we know this? because they were performed by the power of God; how do we know this? because we are told so in the Bible—there is no other criterion. Unfortunately the Bible also contains accounts of some marvellous events which are plainly not divine miracles. When dealing with the competition between Aaron's and Pharaoh's magicians, Erastus has to decide, with some reluctance, that Aaron's serpents were real, being miraculously created by God, and those of the magicians illusory [1]; this is proved, rather oddly, by the real serpents' eating up the illusory ones.

Erastus' most violent attack on Ficino is as a follower of Avicenna. Avicenna had attributed the powers of prophecy and miracle-working, possessed by certain noble souls, to the influence of the Intelligences which move the heavenly bodies [2]; Erastus takes the following passage from Ficino's *Commentary* on Plato's *Laws*, which he quotes, as an explanation of how this influence is transmitted [3]:

> The superior spirits, therefore, act on our spirits, as on their companions, by the influxes of their images, as faces are reflected in a mirror; and by acting on them they form them and make them like to themselves, to such a degree that [our] souls often act in almost as marvellous a way as the celestial souls are wont to do.

---

[1]   Erastus, *Disp.*, pp. 39-40; *Exodus*, VII, 10-12; cf. Pomponazzi on this, supra p. 111. Erastus (ibid., pp. 81-2) also takes Jacob's method of producing ring-straked and speckled cattle (*Genesis*, XXX, 37-42) as miraculous; which is odd, since he admitted the effects of pregnant females' imaginations on the foetus. The serpent question has a long and complicated history, on which see the references given in Godelmann, *Tractatus de Magis*, Francoforti, 1591, pp. 25 seq..

[2]   Erastus, *Disp.*, p. 116; Avicenna, *Opera*, Venetijs, 1508, fos 20 ro-vo (*De Anima* (same as *Sextus Naturalium*), IV, iv), fos 107 vo-108 (*Metaph.*, X, i); cf. Andreas Cattanius, *Opus de Intellectu et de Causis Mirabilium Effectuum*, n.p., n.d., sig. (e vi)-(e viii) (the whole of this work is based on Avicenna).

[3]   Erastus, *Disp.*, p. 116: "Modum, per quem animae Idearum Intelligentiarum participes fiunt, exponit Marsilius Ficinus his verbis, Spiritus ergo superiores in nostros, utpote consortes, imaginum duntaxat suarum influxibus operantur, quemadmodum vultus in speculum: atque agendo in eos formant, similesque efficiunt: usque adeò, ut animae saepè tam fermè mirabiliter, quam coelestes soleant, operentur" Ficino, *Op. Omn.*, p. 1501.

These "superior spirits" are the planetary Intelligences or their subsidiary demons [1]. Ficino then describes how one must prepare oneself for receiving such influences. The body must be made like to the heavenly bodies; the mind must be directed towards the celestial intelligences with faith, ardent love and hope—"then miracles, dreams, prophecies and oracles will come "[2]. Both Plato and Avicenna, says Ficino, believe that our souls can thus do even more marvellous works than the heavens themselves; and these confirm the words in the Gospel about the faith that can move mountains [3].

In Erastus' eyes this use of Christ's words puts Ficino in the same class as Paracelsus, who had also used them to support the importance of credulity in magical operations [4]; anyway the whole theory is typical of the Platonists' impious presumption and superstition:

Would you think this man a Priest of God, as he wished to appear, and not rather the patron and high-priest of Egyptian mysteries, thus raving unrestrainèdly against true piety? Certainly there have never lived under the sun (I am speaking of Philosophers) more diligent worshippers of demons than the Platonists. And are we to say that the words of truth are confirmed by their execrable lies? Ficino was so addicted to these loathsome and clearly diabolical fables, that he preferred to lick up the stinking spittle of the Platonists, rather than taste the most sweet honey of truth [5].

[1] Ficino, ibid.: "spiritus, qui vel vivificant, vel movent coelum, vel vivificantium & moventium sunt consortes".

[2] Ficino, ibid.: "Tunc prodigia, somnia, vaticinia, oracula veniunt".

[3] Ficino, ibid.: "Verùm si quando integra virtute sua ad certum opus utantur, sicut & ignis tota intentione naturae comburit, & coelum toto agit influxu, tunc Plato non dubitat, mirabiliora nostris mentibus, quàm ab igne, vel coelo, facillimè proventura. Non dubitant & Avicenna, Alazelesque, nescio qua sorte saepe Platonici. Sed de his in Theologia latius disputamus. Quibus evangelicum illud de fide montes permutatura, maximè confirmatur". The reference is to the *Theol. Plat.*, XIII, iv (*Op. Omn.*, pp. 298 seq.).

[4] Erastus, *Disp.*, p. 118: "Quid quod hac Philosophia Christi verba de fide montes transferente confirmari opinatur? (Pulchrè cum eo convenit Paracelsus alicubi, in horum verborum expositione)"; Paracelsus, *De Summis Naturae Mysteriis Libri Tres, ... Per Gerardum Dorn è Germanico Latinè redditi*, Basileae, 1570, p. 34.

[5] Erastus, *Disp.*, p. 118: "An tu Sacerdotem Dei, qualis videri voluit, ac non potius Aegyptiorum sacrorum approbatorem & Antistitem esse putabis ita licenter in pietatem insanientem? Certum est, nullos sub hoc Sole (de Philosophis loquor) vixisse majores & officiosiores Daemonum cultores Platonicis. Et horum execrandis

This diatribe is quite as violent in tone as any that Erastus launches against Pomponazzi and Paracelsus—he considers the former a militant atheist, and the latter a drunken, drivelling blasphemer[1]. It is certainly in part because he was associated in Erastus' mind with these two very diverse, but both religiously suspect, magical traditions, that Ficino is here attacked with such vehemence. Though his language is often intemperate, Erastus' disapproval of Pomponazzi and Paracelsus was not without good grounds; it is difficult for us now, after reading the *De Incantationibus*, to believe that Pomponazzi was a Christian, and there is no doubt that Paracelsus was muddle-headed and expressed religious views offensive to an orthodox member of any church[2]. But it was not only because Pomponazzi had quoted from the *Theologia Platonica*, and because Gohory had connected the *De Triplici Vita* with Paracelsus' *De Vita Longa*[3], that Erastus considered Ficino's magic a danger to religion. We must remember that the magic in the *De Triplici Vita* is only very precariously non-demonic, and that in his other works, as we have seen, he is much less cautious about demons and ways of attracting them[4]. Thus Erastus, even if he had not connected Ficino with Pomponazzi and Paracelsus, would have been bound to see in Ficino's work as a whole a most suspicious interest in "platonic godlets"; and it would seem, from the reference to "Egyptian mysteries", that he saw in the *De Vita coelitùs comparanda* an attempt to revive the idolatry of the *Asclepius*[5].

Even when Erastus judges Ficino in the more respectable company of Plotinus, his condemnation is harsh and contemptuous. It occurs after a refutation of the magical power of words. Erastus begins with a typically empirical argument against the natural or

mendacijs veritatis verba confirmari dicemus? Ita his tetris & planè Diabolicis fabulis addictus fuit Ficinus, ut foetidam Platonicorum salivam lingere, quam dulcissimum veritatis mel gustare maluerit."

[1] On Pomponazzi, cf. Erastus, *Disp.*, pp. 75, 111, 178; for his opinion of Paracelsus, cf. supra p. 101.

[2] Cf. Lenoble, op. cit., pp. 142-3.

[3] V. supra p. 102.

[4] Cf. supra pp. 45-53.

[5] Cf. supra pp. 40-42.

real connexion between words and things: if human speech were not conventional but natural, then deaf-mutes would be able to talk. All apparent effects produced by incantations are due to demons; this is shown by the barbaric, meaningless words they contain, which are meaningless only to us, for the demons understand them, and by their being in the form of supplications or threats. That so many learnèd men believe in the power of words is the fault of the superstitious Platonists [1]. Plotinus, though he really knew that incantations were demonic, ascribed their power to the universal sympathy of things, to the Soul of the World, or the forces of the human soul;

> Ficino, drunk with his [sc. Plotinus'] madness, believed that powers could be obtained from the conjunction of words, just as from a mixture of material things [2].

The passage Erastus refers to is in Ficino's *Commentary* on Plotinus [3]. The theory put forward is the same as that with which Ficino introduces his planetary music in the *De Vita Coelitùs Comparanda*, namely, that by putting together words and sounds of the same planetary affinity, one can make a song that will attract the influence of a certain planet. But, says Erastus triumphantly:

> He adds at length: 'I indeed suspect that perhaps crafty Demons pretend to be attracted or repelled by certain magic devices' [4]. I would refute his theory [of the power of words], were it not that he himself plainly betrays his doubt and hesitation, and that I have already exploded it.

This is a skilful and deliberate misrepresentation of what Ficino was saying. Before Ficino's remark about crafty demons

---

[1] Erastus, *Disp.*, pp. 169-177.

[2] Erastus, *Disp.*, p. 177: "Ficinus ejus insania ebrius ex verborum conjunctione, quemadmodum res materiatae ex mixtione, vires adipisci credidit."; Ficino, *Op. Omn.*, p. 1749.

[3] Ficino, *Op.*, *Omn.*, pp. 1748-9.

[4] Erastus, *Disp.*, pp. 177: "Tandem adijcit. Ego verò suspicor, ne fortè Daemones subdoli simulent Magicis quibusdam machinis vel allici vel expelli. Refellerem ista, nisi & palàm ipse dubitationem hęsitationemque suam prodidisset, & jam antè solidè diluta fuissent"; Ficino, ibid.

there is a substantial passage, not quoted by Erastus, where he discusses magic that is overtly demonic, both beneficent and maleficent; and the sense of his remark is that such magicians probably do not really succeed in compelling demons, but are merely deluded by the demons into believing they do—a perfectly normal and orthodox explanation of black magic. That Ficino was not applying this explanation to his own theory of the *vis verborum*, outlined at the beginning of the passage [1], nor to the magic of the *De Vita coelitùs comparanda* is quite clear from what follows his remark on demons. Having noted that the Neoplatonists gave warnings against the craftiness of bad demons, he adds [2]:

But in what way from the universally living body of the world, from the living stars, and other living parts of the world, we may, in a natural manner, like farmers or doctors, absorb vital vapours, we discuss fully enough in the Third Book of the *De Vita*.

Nevertheless, although in this particular case he interprets Ficino dishonestly, and although in general he treats him with a complete lack of understanding and sympathy, Erastus' criticism was, from a Christian point of view, justified. The demons, though they may have been good solarian ones, are lurking even in the *De Vita coelitùs comparanda*, and Ficino knew they were. Erastus, by finding and quoting the remarkably indiscreet passage in the *Commentary* on the *Laws*, showed that in Ficino's mind the apparently innocent practices of the *De Vita Triplici* were closely connected with plainly demonic, thaumaturgic magic.

---

[1] There are other, much fuller expositions of the *vis verborum* in Ficino, e.g. *Op. Omn.*, pp. 1217-8, 1309 seq. (*Comm. in Cratyl.*).

[2] Ficino, *Op. Omn.*, p. 1749: "Qua [orig.: quia] ratione ex corpore mundi ubique vivo, vivisque tum stellis, tum caeteris mundi partibus naturale quodam, quasi agricolarum, medicorumque more vitales carpere auras [orig.: aures] valeamus, satis in libro de Vita tertio disputamus."

(2) Champier and Lefèvre d'Etaples

The Lyonnais doctor Symphorian Champier was the earliest and most active transmitter of Ficinian Platonism in France. But, like many French Platonists, he was acutely aware of the dangers to religion that might result from too whole-hearted an acceptance of Neoplatonism and the *Prisca Theologia*[1]. His *De Quadruplici Vita* (1507)[2] is presented as an imitation and extension of the *De Triplici Vita*, and in his *Epistola prohemialis* to it he proclaims himself a disciple of Ficino[3]. Nevertheless, although in this work he discusses at length the question of astrological influences and reaches much the same conclusions as Ficino—namely, that the stars can incline but not determine corporeal things, and can only affect the soul indirectly, through the body[4]—there is hardly a mention of the spirit, and all Ficino's elaborate methods, dietetic, musical and magical, of nourishing it and attracting to it beneficent astral influxes, are omitted. He does, however, deal with Ficino's talismans. These "are thought by the learnèd to be more superstitious than true; which can very easily be proved"[5]; and he reproduces Thomas Aquinas' arguments to prove that anything effected by them must be due to demons, and not to astrological influence[6]. Their use is a sign of a tacit pact with the Devil; the use of "suffumigations and invocations" is a sign of a manifest pact[7]. Thomas does not

[1] Cf. Walker, "Prisca Theologia".
[2] *Liber de quadruplici vita | Theologia Asclepij hermetis trismegisti discipuli | cum commentarijs eiusdem domini Simphoriani . . .*, Lugduni, 1507.
[3] Champier, *De Quadr. Vita*, sig. b ro-vo.
[4] Ibid., sig. (c v) ro seq..
[5] Ibid., sig. d iij ro: "magis superstitiosa quam vera a doctis esse creduntur [sc. imagines astronomicae]: quod facillime probari potest."
[6] Thomas Aquinas, *Contra Gentiles*, III, cii-cvi.
[7] Thomas Aquinas, *Summ. Th.*, 2da 2dae, q. 96, art. ii; *De Occultis Operibus Naturae* (*Opusc.* xxxiv). Cf. supra p. 43 and infra p. 221.

mention suffumigations, and perhaps Champier inserted them to show that he also disapproved of Ficino's Orphic singing, with its special incense for each hymn [1]. He then exclaims: "Alas, how much impiety lies hid under the cover of astrology" [2]. But he makes some attempt to defend Ficino, by quoting from the *Ad Lectorem* of the *De Vita coelitùs comparanda* [3]:

If you do not approve of talismans, which were however invented to benefit men's health, but which I myself do not so much approve of as merely describe, then dismiss them, with my permission, even, if you wish, on my advice. But at all events, unless you disregard life itself, do not disregard medicines strengthened by some celestial support. For I have long since discovered by frequent experiment that there is as much difference between medicines of this kind and those made without astrological selection as between wine and water.

On this Champier makes the shrewd comment: "See the way Marsilio himself speaks, as if uncertain of his own mind (*ut ambiguus*)" [4]. He then recalls that the *De Vita coelitùs comparanda* purports to be a commentary on Plotinus [5] and may therefore be taken as merely an exposition of Plotinus' views, and finally he quotes Ficino's conventional declaration of submission to the judgment of the church.

Elsewhere Champier condemns Ficino's magic emphatically and without reserves [6]:

---

[1] Cf. supra p. 23.

[2] Champier, *De Quad. V.*, sig. d iij ro: "Heu quanta impietas sub umbra astrologiae latitat. Misereor secte huius miserrime; que sui nescit misereri. Et dum alijs salutem & bona eventura presagire frustra laborat: ipsa elephantino [sic] morbo tabescens: cancrum quoque usque ad anime sue interiora serpere sinit."

[3] Ficino, *Op. Omn.*, p. 530: "Si non probas imagines astronomicas alioquin pro valitudine mortalium adinventas, quas & ego non tam probo quam narro, has utique me concedente, ac etiam si vis consulente dimittito. Medicinas saltem celesti quodam adminiculo confirmatas, nisi forte vitam neglexeris, ne negligitote. Ego enim frequenti jamdiu experientia compertum habeo tantum interesse inter medicinas huiusmodi atque alias absque delectu astrologico factas, quantum inter merum & aquam."

[4] Champier, ibid., sig. diij vo: "Vide qualiter ipse Marsilius ut ambiguus loquatur."

[5] V. supra p. 3.

[6] Champier, *Libelli duo. Primus de medicine claris scriptoribus . . .*, n.p., n.d., fo viij vo: "Herbas gemmasque sanitatis gratia sine ulla incantatione deferre concessum est. Ymagines vero astrologorum characteresque preter signum crucis penitus damnantur. De quibus etiam apud nostros theologos & philosophos multa reperies: & precipue apud marsilium ficinum platonicum libro tertio de triplici vita: sed hec

(in the first two sentences he is summarizing the *Decretum Gratiani*) [1] It is allowable to administer herbs and gems for reasons of health, but without any incantations. Astrological images and characters, except for the sign of the cross, are absolutely condemned. You will find much about these even in the works of our own theologians and philosophers; and especially in Marsilio Ficino the Platonist, in the third book of the *De Triplici Vita*; but this is what I wanted to say briefly: that in our times we see several who, depraved by these wicked arts, having secretly entered into friendship with the devil, seduce many people and involve their souls in the gravest errors. But we, who are resolved never to depart from Catholic purity, care nothing for such things; we prefer to be perpetually ill rather than be healthy by contempt for our Saviour.

Here Ficino is certainly not classed among the sorcerers who have entered into a pact with the devil; but he is, I think, considered to be one of those who have been seduced by them and led into grave errors.

Champier also makes an ineffectual attempt to excuse the Hermetic source of Ficino's magic. He published the *Asclepius* together with his *De Quadruplici Vita* and added commentaries which are supposed to be his own; in fact, they are reproduced verbatim from those of Lefèvre d'Étaples. He defends the god-making passage in the *Asclepius* by noting beside it that it is probably an interpolation or distortion due to the supposed translator, Apuleius [2], and he omits entirely Lefèvre's strong condemnation of it in his commentary [3].

Lefèvre had written by the side of this passage "PROPHANA HEC ALIUS LAPSUS HERMETIS", and sharply rebuked Hermes for admiring men for their greatest wickedness, that is, for attracting "demonic spirits" into "images"; Hermes is writing

---

breviter dixisse volui: quod hac nostra tempestate plerosque videmus his malis artibus depravatos, clam inita cum diabolo amicitia quam plurimos seducere & gravissimis erroribus animas implicare. Nos autem quibus propositum est nunquam a catholica puritate discedere: talia floccipendimus: eligentes nos magis semper egrotare quam cum salvatoris contumelia sanos esse."

[1] *Decretum Gratiani*, Pars II, Causa xxvi, Qu. V, c. iii, and Qu. VII, c. xviii (Migne, *Pat. Lat.*, T. 187, cols. 1346, 1372).

[2] Champier, *De Triplici Disciplina*, 1508, sig. (II vii) vo, cf. hh ij ro, (II v)vo, (II vii) ro.

[3] Champier, ibid., sig. (II vii) vo (on *Ascl.*, xiii).

about herbs, stones, and aromas, symphonies and hymns, by which they [sc. the Egyptian priests] propitiated those spirits put into statues and images. This some sorcerers are still wont to do (O unhappy times!), who think they have spirits shut up in rings or vessels, a most impure race of men, hostile to God and man . . . [1].

It seems unlikely that Lefèvre is here referring to Ficino, on whose translation of the *Hermetica* he is commenting [2] and whom he "venerated as a father" [3]; but, for anyone who had read the *De Triplici Vita*, this might well be taken as a warning against Ficino's magic. The cap would fit Lazarelli even better; but this also seems unlikely, since Lefèvre published the *Crater Hermetis* in his 1505 edition of the *Hermetica*. But then, Lefèvre himself, in about 1492, had written a long treatise on astrological magic, which he never published [4]; he was perhaps being harsh on his own errors [5].

[1] Lefèvre, edition of the *Pimander*, *Asclepius* and Lazarelli's *Crater Hermetis*, Paris, 1505, fos 57vo-58vo: "de herbis / lapidibus et aromatibus / concentibus et hymnis: quibus propiciarent spiritus illos statuis imaginibusque inditos. Quod adhuc facere solent / nonnulli phitonici (o seculum infelix) qui aut in annulis / aut vasculis se spiritus clausos habere putant / genus hominum impurissimum / deo hominibusque infensum . . ."

[2] Lefèvre's first edition of this was published by the University of Paris in 1494. From 1516 onwards Lefèvre's commentaries frequently appear in editions of Ficino's translation of the *Pimander* as if they were by Ficino (see Kristeller, *Suppl. Ficin.*, pp. cxxx-cxxxi).

[3] Lefèvre, *Pimander*, 1494, sig. e iij ro: "Curavit . . . Faber Stapulensis ex viciato exemplari hoc opus reddere castigatum: tum amore Marsilij (quem tanquam patrem veneratur) tum Mercurij sapientie magnitudine promotus."

[4] See Lynn Thorndike, *A History of Magic and Experimental Science*, IV, Columbia U.P., 1934, p. 513.

[5] This change in Lefèvre's attitude may be due to the condemnation in 1494 of the astrologer Simon de Phares (see Thorndike, op. cit., IV, 153-4, 545 seq.).

(3) JEAN BODIN

Jean Bodin, like the other writers discussed in this chapter, disliked magic because of his religious beliefs. But his religion was very different from theirs, and so in consequence was his attitude to magic.

By the end of his life Bodin had ceased to be a Christian, and believed in a kind of simplified, archaïc Judaïsm [1]. This seems to me quite clear from his unpublished dialogue on religion, *Heptaplomeres* [2], which he finished writing in 1593 [3]. I cannot be sure that he already held these beliefs when he wrote his treatise on magic, the *Démonomanie* [4], published in 1580, but I think it highly probable. His last published work, *Le Theatre de la Nature Universelle* (1597) [5], though it is not overtly unchristian, is certainly written from the same standpoint as the *Heptaplomeres*, and contains many of the same very odd and unorthodox doctrines; it was, he tells us [6], composed during the civil wars—which takes us back to the late 1580's. The *Démonomanie* is not so evidently unorthodox as the other two works; but the opinions in it fit exactly with what we know to have been his later religious convictions, and it seems therefore reasonable to assume that he already held these at the time of writing it [7].

[1] I have not the space here to demonstrate the truth of this statement, but hope to do so in another work. The best discussion of Bodin's religious views remains that of Roger Chauviré in his *Jean Bodin Auteur de la "République"*, Paris, 1914 (see especially pp. 157 seq.).

[2] Bodin, *Colloquium Heptaplomeres de rerum sublimium arcanis abditis*, ed. Lud. Noack, Suerini Megaloburgiensium, 1857; this is a poor edition, but the only complete one; where possible, I shall cite the Chauviré edition of a partial French translation of the *Heptaplomeres*: *Colloque de Jean Bodin ...*, Paris, 1914.

[3] See *Colloque*, ed. Chauviré, Introd., pp. 3-4.

[4] Bodin, *De la Demonomanie des Sorciers ...*, Paris, 1580.

[5] Bodin, *Le Theatre de la Nature Universelle ... Traduict du Latin par M. François de Fougerolles ...*, Lyon, 1597; *Universae Naturae Theatrum ...*, Lugduni, 1596.

[6] Bodin, *Univ. Nat. Th.*, sig. a 5.

[7] Chauviré (op. cit., pp. 160-1) thinks it likely that Bodin's religious views had

The *Heptaplomeres* is a search, conducted by a Catholic, a Lutheran, a Calvinist, a pagan, a Jew, a Mohammedan, and a Naturalist, for the *Urreligion*, the ancient nucleus of religious truth, which is included in all their religions, and which, restored to its original simplicity, will reunite them all. This nucleus is eventually found in the decalogue, which is "ipsissima lex naturae" [1]. The principles by which this search is guided, as well as its conclusion, are Judaïc: the true religion must be absolutely monotheistic, and it must provide a Law, a rigid and precise ethical system based on rewards and punishments. Christianity fails on both counts and is rejected [2]. The absolute transcendance and uniqueness of God is preserved by making Him the only incorporeal being in the universe; all souls or minds, angelic, demonic and human are corporeal, very subtle and "spiritual", but extended and localized [3]. The break in the continuity of the chain of being between God and the created world is made as complete as possible. In consequence, all the functions performed by an immanent God are thrown on to the higher created beings, the angels and demons. God, after the act of creation, is idle, and the work of ordering and preserving the universe is carried out, in accordance with His immutable will, by these higher corporeal souls, most of which are invisible [4]. The visible angels or demons are the heavenly bodies [5]. Demons are evil, but nevertheless fulfil God's will; they are the avengers, who

already reached the final stage of their evolution as early as 1566 (date of Bodins' *Methodus*).

[1] Bodin, *Colloque*, ed. Chauviré, p. 94, cf. ibid., pp. 67, 87, 94-8; from here on (*Hept.*, ed. Noack, p. 146) to the end the dialogue is a defence of Judaïsm as the true natural religion.

[2] E.g. Bodin, *Coll.*, ed. Chauviré, pp. 141 seq. (attack on authenticity of Gospels, based on Marcion), 161 (impossibility of Incarnation), 163 seq. (against ethics of Gospels), 166 seq. (against Trinity), 181 seq. (against Original Sin and Redemption); *Hept.*, ed. Noack, pp. 213 seq., 249 seq., 261 seq., 268 seq., 297 seq.

[3] Bodin, *Theatre de la Nat.*, pp. 737-771 (*Univ. Nat. Th.*, pp. 511-535); *Hept.*, ed. Noack, pp. 37-41.

[4] Bodin, *Hept.*, ed. Noack, pp. 48-50, 55 seq.; *Th. de la Nat.*, p. 773, 913 seq. (*Univ. Nat. Th.*, pp. 536, 631 seq.).

[5] *Hept.*, ed. Noack, pp. 91 seq.; Bodin thinks that after death good human souls become angels or stars, and bad ones demons (ibid., pp. 93-4, 100-1; *Th. de la Nat.*, pp. 771-784, *Univ. Nat. Th.*, pp. 535-544), cf. infra p. 197.

execute divine justice by punishing, tormenting and destroying [1].

Since for Bodin demons and angels take over all the work of *natura naturans*, it is not surprising that he should believe that all magic is demonic and efficacious [2]. He could, for example, have no difficulty in believing that a man cause a storm by demonic magic, since he had no doubt that all storms were caused by demons anyway [3]. His passionate disapproval of all magic comes from his fear that it will lead to the worship or veneration of created beings. It is to be expected therefore that he should attack the Neoplatonists, ancient and modern, with particular vehemence, since their magic or theurgy is based on the theory that one can reach God by ascending a continuous chain of being, which leads up from the sensible world, through the stars and their *daimones*, to the higher emanations of the divinity. They are a far more dangerous threat to the purity of monotheism than ordinary sorcerers, who, by employing bad demons show plainly they have turned away from God. Speaking of [4]

ceux qui veulent lier la partie du monde inferieur à la partie superieure, pour marier le monde (comme dict Picus Mirandula) [5] couvrant soubz un beau voile une extreme impieté, & par le moyen des herbes, des animaux, des metaux, des hymnes, des caracteres & sacrifices, attirer les Anges & petits Dieux, & par ceux cy le grand Dieu Createur de toutes choses:

Bodin remarks that "pour obvier à ceste impieté"

Dieu semble avoir defendu bien expressement, qu'on ne feist point de degrez pour monter à son autel, ains qu'on vint droict à luy: ce que les Platoniques n'ayant pas bien entendu, ont voulu par le moyen des Daemons inferieurs, & demy-dieux attirer les Dieux superieurs, pour attirer en fin le Dieu Souverain [6].

---

[1] *Hept.*, ed. Noack, p. 89; *Th. de la Nat.*, pp. 913 seq. (*Univ. Nat. Th.*, pp. 631 seq.).

[2] *Demon.*, passim; *Hept.*, ed. Noack, pp. 12-20.

[3] *Hept.*, ed. Noack, pp. 63-4.

[4] *Demon.*, fo 20 ro.

[5] G. Pico, *Op. Omn.*, 1572, p. 121 (*Apologia*; cf. *De Hom. Dign.*, ed. Garin, p. 148).

[6] Bodin, *Demon.*, fo 20 ro-vo; *Exodus*, XX, 26 (Neither shalt thou go up by steps unto mine altar, that thy nakedness be not discovered thereon); cf. same use of this verse, ibid., fo 53 ro, *Th. de la Nat.*, pp. 685-7 (*Univ. Nat. Th.*, pp. 547-8).

Bodin does not mention Ficino in this connexion [1], but only Agrippa, Pico and the "nouveaux Academiques", that is, the ancient Neoplatonic writers on magic, whom Ficino had been the first to translate. Agrippa, he says [2],

compose des caracteres, qu'il dit propres aux Daemons de chacune planette, lesquelz characteres il veut estre gravez au metal propre à chacune planette, à l'heure qu'elles sont en leur exaltation ou maison, avec une conjonction aimable, & veut alors qu'on ayt aussi la plante, la pierre, & l'animal propre à chacune planette, & de tout cela qu'on face un sacrifice à la Planette, & quelquefois l'image de la Planette, & les Hymnes d'Orphee le Sorcier, ausquelles le Prince de la Mirande s'est trop arresté sous ombre de Philosophie, quand il dict les hymnes d'Orphee n'avoir pas moins de puissance en la Magie, que les hymnes de David en la Cabale . . . & se vante d'avoir le premier decouvert le secret des Hymnes d'Orphee [3].

This condemnation of planetary magic combined with Orphic Hymns is relevant to Ficino not only because it describes his magic quite accurately, whether Bodin was aware of this or not, but also because the passages in Agrippa referred to by Bodin are largely based on Ficino, and are in many cases copied word for word [4]. Though Bodin would in any case have disapproved of this Neoplatonic magic, the fact that he finds it in Agrippa makes his condemnation harsher. For he habitually calls Agrippa "le Maistre Sorcier" and believes that the spurious 4th Book of the *De Occulta Philosophia* is the key to all the rest [5]. If Agrippa practised this magic, it was plainly diabolic; whereas Bodin thinks that the ancient Neoplatonists were genuinely, if misguidedly, trying to reach God, and should be classed as idolaters rather than as sorcerers [6].

---

[1] He does sometimes cite Ficino, e.g. *Demon.*, fo 72 vo; *Th. de la Nat.*, p. 703 (*Univ. Nat. Th.*, p. 506).

[2] Bodin, *Demon.*, fo 19 vo-20.

[3] G. Pico, *Op. Omn.*, 1572, p. 106: "Conclusiones numero xxxi secundum propriam opinionem de modo intelligendi hymnos Orphei secundum Magiam, id est secretam divinarum rerum naturaliumque sapientiam à me primum in eis repertam"; ibid., *Concl.* No. 4: "Sicut hymni David operi Cabalae mirabiliter deserviunt, ita hymni Orphei operi verè licitae & naturalis Magiae."

[4] V. supra p. 92.

[5] Bodin, *Demon.*, fo 51 vo; cf. fo 20 (Agrippa's black dog).

[6] Ibid., fo 20: "Jaçoit qu'il semble que les Academiques, que j'ay dict, en [sc.

Bodin regarded the Orphic Hymns as peculiarly dangerous, not only because, as he rightly saw, they played an important part in modern Neoplatonic magic, and because he took Orpheus to be one of the chief *prisci magi*[1], but also because he himself believed in the magical power of words. This belief was based partly on the theory of "natural" language; the usual derivation of this language from Adam's giving things their true Hebrew names has, of course, especial force for Bodin—the Jews alone have the real, sacred language[2]. But the power of words in magical operations works, according to Bodin, demonically: the demons who produce the effects respond to one particular formula of words for one particular effect. For example, as every peasant knows, a certain verse of a certain Psalm will, through demonic agency, stop butter being made[3]. The magical power of Hebrew words is shown by the impious use magicians make of them: Agrippa "& ses complices souïllent ce grand & sacré nom de Dieu [tetragrammaton] en le meslant en leurs caracteres"[4]. The only good use of this power is a religious one. The Hebrew Psalms are the only good ancient hymns; all the speakers in the *Heptaplomeres* are able to unite in singing these praises of the One God, whereas all other hymns are addressed to lesser, so-called gods, who are really creatures—and here Bodin gives a list of pagan gods, but ending with Jesus, Mary and the saints[5]. Orpheus, traditionally compared with David[6], represented, I think, for Bodin the supremely evil use of the power of words and music;

de la Magie] usoient par ignorance, & par erreur, & y alloient à la bonne foy pensant bien faire: mais Agrippa en a usé par impieté detestable: car il a esté toute sa vie le plus grand sorcier qui fut de son temps"; ibid., fo 20 vo: "Nous disons donc que les Platoniques, & autres Payens, qui par une simplicité de conscience, & par ignorance adoroient, & prioient Jupiter, Saturnus, Mars, Apollo, Diane, Venus, Mercure & autres demy-dieux vivans saintement, prians, & jeusnans, & faisans tous actes de justice, de charité, & de pitié, ont bien esté idolastres, mais non pas Sorciers, ny ceux qui sont en pareil erreur, encores qu'ilz s'efforçassent de sçavoir les choses futures par moyens Diaboliques, attendu qu'ils pensoient faire chose agreable à Dieu."

[1] Bodin, *Demon.*, sig e iij vo.
[2] Bodin, *Coll.*, ed. Chauviré, pp. 86-7, 135-6.
[3] *Demon.*, fo 55.
[4] Ibid., fo 62, cf. fo 55 vo.
[5] *Coll.*, ed. Chauviré, pp. 153 seq. (*Hept.*, ed. Noack, pp. 238 seq.).
[6] Cf. Walker, "Orpheus the Theologian", *Warburg Journal*, 1953, p. 101.

In contrast with the religiously powerful monotheistic songs of David, Orpheus' hymns were the demonically powerful liturgy of a diabolical, polytheistic *prisca magia* [1].

Bodin's belief in astrology is necessarily moderate, stopping short of exact predictions and horoscopes, because there are so many invisible demons and angels doing things all the time, that observation of just the visible angels, i.e. the stars, could not suffice to know the future. He does nevertheless defend the reality of planetary influences, and approves of astrology being used in medicine and natural science, citing Thomas Aquinas and Calvin as authorities for this "droict usage" of astrology [2]. He defines his own position by giving G. F. Pico and Melanchthon as two extremes to be avoided [3]:

Mais il y a de grans personnages qui pour n'avoir pas separé le droit usage d'Astrologie de l'abus, ont tiré plusieurs en erreur: c'est à sçavoir Jean François Pic, Prince de la Mirande, qui l'a blasmée outre mesure, & Philippe Melancton, qui s'est par trop arresté à l'Astrologie divinatrice.

But the real danger of astrology is that it may be another path leading to Neoplatonic magic and polytheism:

Mais je ne puis passer par souffrance, ce que Jean Picus Prince de la Mirande, aux positions Magiques escript, que la Magie naturelle n'est que la pratique de la Physique, qui est le filet auquel Sathan attire les plus gentils esprits, qui pensent que par la force des choses naturelles on attirera, voire on forcera les puissances celestes [4].

Bodin then gives a sinister interpretation of one of Pico's Orphic

---

[1] Cf. Bodin, *Demon.*, fos 2 vo (on Satan, "Orphee l'appelle aussi le grand Daemon vengeur: Et comme il estoit maistre Sorcier il luy chante un hymne"), 20 (on Pico and Orphic Hymns, "on void que ces hymnes sont faicts à l'honneur de Sathan, à quoy se raporte ce que dict Picus, *Frustra naturam adit, qui Pana non attraxerit*", cf. infra p. 177). Bodin of course accepts the ordinary Moses-Plato part of the *prisca theologia* (*Hept.*, ed. Noack, pp. 49-50, 66, 70, 187), which can be used to prove that Judaïsm is the *Urreligion*.

[2] Bodin, *Demon.*, fos 30 vo-33; cf. *Th. de la Nat.*, pp. 790-901 (*Univ. Nat. Th*, pp. 549-623).

[3] *Demon.*, fo 209 ro-vo.

[4] *Demon.*, fo 37 vo; G. Pico, *Op. Omn.*, p. 104.

Conclusiones: "He who has not attracted Pan will approach Nature in vain" [1]:

Pour neant on use des choses naturelles, qui n'aura attiré Pan, c'est à dire, qui n'aura invoqué Sathan. Car tous les anciens ont entendu par le mot de Pan, ce que les Hebrieux appellent Sathan . . . [2].

[1] G. Pico, *Op. Omn.*, p. 106 (v. supra p. 176 note (1)).
[2] Bodin, *Demon.*, fo 37 vo.

(4) DEL RIO

Del Rio's encyclopaedic book on magic [1] is representative of Catholic anti-magical views of a moderate and well-informed kind. He was intelligent and liberal enough to convert Justus-Lipsius [2]. His sober criticism of Ficino carries therefore greater weight than the stronger condemnations of extreme anti-magical writers, such as Erastus or Bodin, who were, moreover, judging him from a non-catholic standpoint.

Like most of the opponents of magic, Del Rio concedes the theoretical possibility of a good, natural magic, but in fact condemns all secular magical practices as superstitious and demonic. He claims that the prevalence of magic and sorcery in his own time is due to the spread of heresy, which they follow as a shadow does a body [3]—a rather rash statement in view of some of the Catholic practices he has himself to defend against the charge of superstition. Bad magic derives ultimately from Zoroaster, Orpheus, and the other *prisci magi* [4]; but Del Rio also accepts, parallel to these, a good *prisca magia* deriving from Adam, by which he means natural science, including "good" astrology [5]. This "good" astrology has very narrow limits, which are the same as those of Pico's *Adversus Astrologiam*, of which he expresses his approval [6]. He firmly denies that the heavens are animated, and that occult qualities are astrologically caused [7],

---

[1] *Disquisitionum Magiacarum Libri Sex, . . . auctore Martino Del-Rio Societ. Iesu Presbyt. I. L. Licent. et Theol. Doct. olim in Academia Graetcensi, et Salmanticensi, publico S. Script. Professore, . . .* Coloniae Agrippinae, 1679; earlier editions: Lovanii, 1599-1600 (1st ed.); Venetiis, 1616 (considerably expanded), and many subsequent ones.

[2] See *Dict. de Théol. Cath.*, art. Del Rio, T. 4, col. 262.

[3] Del Rio, *Disq. Mag., Proloquium*: "Haeresibus profectò, ut umbram corpori, sic magicam spurcitiem ancillari, adeò manifestum est, ut proterviae sit negare."

[4] Del Rio, *Disq.*, I, iii, pp. 8 seq.; I, iv, qu. ii, p. 53.

[5] Ibid., I, iii, p. 9.

[6] Ibid., I, iii, qu. i, p. 13.

[7] Ibid., I, iv, qu. ii, pp. 47-9.

thus removing the bases for both demonic and natural, or spiritual, planetary magic. Another essential basis of natural magic, the transmission of the *vis imaginativa* by the human spirit, is denied on much the same grounds as Erastus'[1].

It is interesting that he argues against a natural explanation of the magical force of words, music and images, by making a clear distinction between the A and B uses of them. When dealing with the figures on talismans, he refutes the argument that these might operate through their beauty producing joy, or their ugliness sorrow, by denying that they are either beautiful or ugly[2]. That incantations produce effects by the beauty or meaning of words or music is also emphatically denied. Pomponazzi had put forward as one of his several defences of them that they worked like music and oratory, and gave long lists of the effects of ancient musicians and orators to support this argument[3]. Del Rio answers that the effects of oratory are produced by rational persuasion, and as for musical effects:

the sweetness itself of the concert, and the harmonious modulation, distract the soul from thoughts of pain, and, by inciting to joy, soothe and temper the humours; what is there like this in the horrific and hissing whistles and whispers of the magicians[4]?

That is to say, you cannot defend the B uses of words and music by claiming A effects for them. By this argument Ficino's talismans would be condemned, but not his Orphic singing, which was certainly not meant to be a whistle or a whisper.

[1] Ibid., I, iii, qu. iii-iv, pp. 18-22. Del Rio believed, of course, in the effects of the mother's imagination on the foetus, about which he tells the following unusual anecdote (ibid., I, iii, qu. iii, p. 21): "Paderbornae mulier haeretica ante annos sexdecim plus minùs (res ibi tum nota) peperit filium modo Ecclesiasticorum palliatum & pileatum; quae ex vehementi odio in Papistas, ut vocant, obviis semper maledicebat. Sed hoc fortè divinae ultionis fuit."

[2] Del Rio, *Disq.*, I, iv, q. i, p. 41; he goes on to refute Caietano's ingenious arguments in favour of the purely physical action of talismans (cf. infra p. 222-3).

[3] Pomponazzi, *De Incant.*, pp. 91-3; Pomponazzi himself refutes this argument by making the same distinction between A and B uses of words and music (cf. supra p. 109).

[4] Del Rio, *Disq.*, I, iv, q. iii, p. 56: "ipsa concentus suavitas & harmonica modulatio distrahit animum à doloris cogitatione, & ad laetitiam provocans lenit & contemperat humores: cui quid simile in horrificis ac stridulis sibilis atque susurris magorum?"; cf. ibid., I, iv, q. ii, p. 46.

In the course of his refutation of the *vis verborum* Del Rio attacks the "natural" theory of language. Although Hebrew may be a sacred language, it has no especial power; it was Adam, not God, who gave Hebrew names to things. "Whatever the Platonists may say, names have been given by human choice"; God, however, does know the real names—but no one else does [1].

Del Rio, then, although he is unusually credulous about supernatural occurrences [2], destroys the bases of natural magic in much the same way as the other writers we have discussed in this chapter, and, like them, tends to regard all magical practices as demonic and diabolic. But, unlike them, he had the additional task of trying to show that certain Catholic practices were essentially different from magical operations. This he was obliged to do, since these practices had already been attacked as magical by Protestants such as Wier, Erastus and Godelmann, and had been presented as magical by the equivocal Agrippa [3]. With regard to amulets worn round the neck, for example, Del Rio has to assert that, if they are talismans, any effects produced are due to the devil, but that, if they are Christian amulets, the same effects are due to the beneficence of God. After a formal summary of his arguments that talismans can have no natural power from figures, words or planetary influences, and can produce effects only by demonic agency, he writes [4]:

[1] Ibid., I, iv, q. iii, p. 58 ("Quicquid enim Platonici dicant, nomina sunt hominum arbitratu indita"), I, iv, q. i, p. 36.

[2] Among many possible examples I give the following charming story (*Disq.*, II, q. xiv, p. 173): "Verissimam narrationem his adjungo. In hoc ipso Belgio fuit nefarius quidam; qui vaccae se commiscuit. Post visa bos praegnans, & post aliquot menses edere masculum foetum, non vitulum, sed puerum: adfuêre non unus, deque matris vaccae cadentem utero adspexerunt, levatumque de terra nutrici tradiderunt, adolevit puer, baptizatus, & institutus Christianae vitae praeceptis, pietati se addixit: & pro patre, seriò poenitentiae vacat operibus: homo quidem perfectus, sed qui sentiat in animo propensiones vaccinas, pascendi prata, & herbas riminando."

[3] Cf. supra pp. 161 (Erastus), 154 (Wier), 94 (Agrippa); in answering the attacks on baptized bells, Del Rio (*Disq.*, Vi, ii, s. iii, q. iii, p. 1073) asserts their efficacy in dispelling demons and storms, but denies that they are baptized—they are merely blessed and named.

[4] Del Rio, *Disq.*, I, iv, q. iv, p. 60: "Quando ipsis verbis modo scriptionis, crucium numero, figura vel similibus spes non ponitur: pium & sanctum est, reverentiae causa Sanctorum reliquias, cereas agni Dei effigies, Evangelium S. Joannis, Psalmum Davidis, & similia Scripturae testimonia secum gestare collo appensa:

When no hope is placed in merely the words themselves of the writing, in the number and shape of the crosses, or in suchlike, it is pious and holy, as an act of reverence, to carry hung round the neck relics of saints, waxen images of the *Agnus Dei*, the Gospel of St. John, a Psalm, and other testimonies of the Holy Scriptures; but the effect, if any arises thence, will be supernatural and must be attributed to the beneficence of God.

This is an attempt to distinguish between talismans and Christian amulets by denying that the efficacy of the latter depends on the magical power of words or figures (*vis verborum & imaginum* B). But this denial cannot so easily be made about set prayers and forms of words, especially in the sacraments, because here, undeniably, the effect follows on one certain formula of words and no other. When dealing with the ritual curse described in *Numbers* V, Del Rio denies that its effects (the swollen belly and rotting thigh of a guilty wife) are produced by the words of the curse or by the "bitter water" drunk by the woman [1]:

but whatever efficacy it [sc. the curse] had, it had from above; much as today liturgical prayers, the formulae of the Sacraments and Sacramentals and of exorcism, have supernatural power from having been instituted by God, or from the action of His grace coinciding with them.

This is the Scotist, as opposed to the Thomist, explanation of the efficacy of sacramental formulae, namely, that God has made a promise or pact to produce a certain effect if, and only if, certain words are pronounced [2]. With either explanation the distinction between magical and sacramental formulae rests solely on authority. One cannot claim, for example, that the effects of magical incantations are good miracles

because neither has God promised, nor revealed to the Church, any such things as the magicians boast of [3].

sed effectus, qui inde oritur, erit supernaturalis, Dei beneficientiae adscribendus"; cf. ibid., III, P. II, q. iv, s. iii, pp. 471 seq..

[1] Ibid., I, iv, q. iii, p. 54: "quicquid habebat efficacitatis, de sursum habebat: ferè sicut hodie, preces Ecclesiasticae, formulae Sacramentorum & Sacramentalium; & exorcismi, vim habent supernaturalem ex Dei institutione, vel gratioso concurrendi modo".

[2] See *Dict. de Théol. Cath.*, art. *Eucharistie*, T. V, cols. 1317-8; on Thomas cf. supra p. 151.

[3] Del Rio, *Disq.*, I, iv, q. iii, p. 56: "quia Deus nihil tale promisit, nec Ecclesiae revelavit, quale Magi jactant".

This is the same kind of distinction as that made by the Protestants between miracles and magical operations[1]; but their authority was the Bible alone, whereas Del Rio also has to include "what has been revealed to the Church", an authority which, of course, his Protestant adversaries did not accept. Thus when he has to answer this attack by Godelman on transubstantiation[2]:

That by the utterance of these five words, *hoc est enim corpus meum*, spoken aloud, they alter the substance of the bread, that they draw the body of Christ down from Heaven, and that they change the bread into it, this they [sc. the Catholics] persuade themselves and others in a plainly magical way.

Del Rio can only cry out in horror at such blasphemy, jeer at Chemnitz' similitude of the Real Presence being contained in the bread as in a purse or a jar[3], and then give a long list of authorities (Theologians and Councils) to support the doctrine of transubstantiation[4].

On these grounds alone Del Rio was bound to condemn Ficino's magic; for there is no authority, either in the Scriptures, nor in the traditions of the Church, for claiming that God ever promised to do anything in response to the Orphic Hymns, or even the most monotheistic of the Orphic fragments. Moreover, Del Rio, like Bodin[5], connects these with Agrippa, who for him

[1] V. supra pp. 156, 162.

[2] Johann Georg Godelmann, *Tractatus de Magis, Veneficis et Lamiis, deque his rectè cognoscendis et puniendis* . . ., Francoforti, 1591, I, vi, p. 57: "prolatione horum quinque verborum, hoc est enim corpus meum cum halitu facta, se panis substantiam mutare, corpus Christi de coelo detrahere, & in hoc illum convertere, planè magicè sibi & alijs persuadent."

[3] Martin Chemnitz, *Secunda Pars Examinis Decretorum Concilii Tridentini* . . ., Francofurti ad Moenum, 1599, p. 140; the Lutherans, with their vague and ill-defined doctrine of the Real Presence, were not in a good position for throwing this kind of stone.

[4] Del Rio, *Disq.*, VI, iii pp. 1087-8: "O linguam eradicandam stirpitus! os impurum & blasphemias evomens assiduè! ergò Christus Dominus Magus? . . . sanè Christum velut dolio aut marsupio includis: dignus hoc nomine, qui insutus culleo vel dolio in profluentem conjicieris . . . Non est etiam Magicum, putare panem in corpus Christi converti: immo est fidei articulus, ab initio Ecclesiae semper retentus." Cf. ibid., III, P. II, q. iv, s. viii, pp. 487-8 (refutation Felix Maleolus, who had used the power of the words of consecration as an argument in favour of beneficent incantations).

[5] Del Rio did not approve of Bodin; he lists the *Démonomanie* among the bad books on magic, together with the *Picatrix*, Agrippa, Pomponazzi, etc., and writes

too is the chief of the black magicians, the "Archimagus". Del Rio quotes Agrippa on the greater efficacy, in incantations, of sentences rather than of single words [1],

"because the truth (says the *Archimagus*) contained in the sentence is added [sc. to the power of the single words]; the power of this truth is greatest when the formula or song contains a celebration of the virtue and operation of the star or spirit (*numen*) to which we are praying."

Del Rio then exclaims:

O Satan, Satan, how perpetually you remain the same! you still continue with this weapon to obtain divine honours. Is this not quite clearly shown by the examples your initiate seeks, which are from the hymns of Orpheus and the writings of Apuleius, full of idolatry?

It is no use Agrippa pretending that such incantations increase the power of the operatoi's imagination and thereby produce a more copious flow of spirit on to the object addressed [2]. Such natural, spiritual explanations are "not worth a farthing", coming from this diabolic magician.

Del Rio's main attack on Ficino is not, however, connected with the Orphic Hymns, though it has an indirect connexion with Orpheus. It occurs in his detailed refutation of Paolini's long discourse on the ways in which Orpheus' music might have attracted inanimate things [3]; he considers this a necessary task because, as he truly remarks, Paolini, though he mentions that various kinds of magic are condemned by the theologians, does not say why [4]. The chief of these ways, it will be remembered,

of his *Universae Naturae Theatrum*: "plus in eo corpore Rabbinicorum esse deliriorum; quàm solidae philosophiae; multa quoque cum Theologicis placitis adeò pugnantia, ut qui lenius de illis loqui velit, erronea & prorsus temeraria cogatur vocare" (*Disq.*, I, iii, p. 11).

[1] Agrippa, *De Occ. Ph.*, I, lxxi, p. xci; Del Rio, *Disq.*, I, iv, q. iii, p. 59: "*quia veritas* (inquit Archimagus) *in ipsa propositione contenta hic accedit: cujus veritatis vis maxima est, quando formula seu carmen virtutis ac operationis astri seu numinis, quod comprecamur, continet commemorationem.* O Satan, Satan tibi quàm perpetuo similis es? pergis hoc telo Divinos honores consequi. Nonnè satis hoc indicant, quae mystes ille tuus, exempla petit, ex Hymnis Orphei & Apulei scriptis, idololatriae plena?"; cf. *Disq.*, II, q. ii, iii, pp. 108, 111, on Agrippa's recantations in the *De Van. Scient.*, ending: "Haec miser ille, qui videns meliora, in finem usque vitae deterioribus adhaesit".

[2] Del Rio, *Disq.*, p. 59 ("Quae vana sunt, ned empsitanda titivillitio").

[3] V. supra pp. 130 seq.

[4] Del Rio, *Disq.*, I, iv, q. ii, pp. 46-7.

was by Ficinian magic, and Del Rio quotes from Paolini Ficino's rules for composing planetary music. On these he comments: "All these we reject as futile and as the coverings and wrappings of forbidden magic"[1], which, as we have seen, they were. His reasons for believing that Paolini's and Ficino's music and magic were demonic follow from his general rejection, already mentioned, of the principles on which theories of natural or spiritual magic were based, especially his denial of planetary correspondences and affinities, and need not be examined here.

Del Rio evidently has no particular dislike of Ficino, and, on occasions, even does his best to defend him. Speaking of astrological medicine, he says[2]:

> Ficino, who when he was younger defended these things (in the *De Vita coelitùs comparanda*), later confessed that he wrote them, not to recommend them, but that, with Plotinus, he might deride the follies of the astrologers.

and then refers to Ficino's apologetic letter to Poliziano[3]. This goes much further than Ficino himself, who, even in his most disingenuous excuses, never had the effrontery to claim that the *De V.C.C.* was an anti-astrological work. Nor did Del Rio really think it was. When condemning Paracelsus' use of waxen images for curing magically caused diseases, he remarks that this superstition is of a different kind from that "which Marsilio Ficino imbibed from the astrologers "[4]. A little later he returns to

> that planetary manufacture of images, which Marsilio Ficino, in the *De Vita coelitùs comparanda*, rashly passed on from Plotinus and the Arabs; in which book he does not seem to have given an adequate antidote to the poisons there displayed. For he behaves like an unskilful and foolish host, who places before his guests many healthy dishes, but also many tainted with poison, and merely says: eat the healthy ones, leave the

---

[1] Ibid., pp. 50-1: "quae omnia nos, ut futilia & magiae vetitae quaedam tegmina & involucra, reijcimus".

[2] Del Rio, *Disq.*, IV, iii, q. i, p. 612: "Marsilius Ficinus, qui junior ista defenderat [side reference to the *De V.C.C.*], eadem postea fatetur scripsisse, non ut probaret, sed ut cum Plotino astrologorum ineptias rideret."

[3] V. supra p. 54.

[4] Del Rio, *Disq.*, VI, ii, q. i, p. 967: "est [sc. haec superstitio] dissimilis illi, quam ex Astrologis Marsilius Ficinus obtrusit, de quo postea."

harmful ones; and does not indicate which, among so many dishes, and so variously spiced, that they can hardly be told one from another, are those from which he thinks one should abstain. This would be to make a mock of one's guests and to injure them. A wise guest, then, would rather depart fasting, than run such evident risk to his life. I think the same about this book, that it is better to believe nothing in it, as far as these images are concerned, rather than to let anything dangerous enter into one's soul [1].

This condemnation specifies only Ficino's talismans, but we already know, from Del Rio's attack on Paolini, that one of the highly spiced, but poisonous, dishes is the planetary music. This verdict on the *De Vita coelitùs Comparanda* seems to me moderate, and, from a Catholic point of view, just.

[1] Del Rio, *Disq.*, VI, ii, q. i, p. 972: "... & imaginum illam fabricationem planetariam, quam ex Plotino & Arabibus periculosè tradidit Marsilius Ficinus lib. de vita coelitus comparanda. quo libro non videtur venenis exhibitis satis idoneum antidotum addere. facit enim perinde ac inscitus & ineptus convivator, qui convivio apponeret cibos multos salutares, multos etiam veneno imbutos, & duntaxat diceret, vescimini salutaribus, relinquite noxios: nec indicaret, qui in tàm multis, tàm variè conditis ut dignosci vix queant, sint illi noxii à quibus abstinendum censeat. Ludere hoc convivas esset, & laedere. Sapientis convivae tunc foret incoenatum abire potius, quàm tàm apertum vitae discrimen subire. Idem ego censeo, de libro illo praestare nihil ejus quoad imagines illas credere: quàm cum periculo aliquid in animum admittere."

PART III. TELESIANS

CHAPTER VI. TELESIO. DONIO. PERSIO. BACON

(1) TELESIO

Donio, Persio, Bacon and Campanella, (the last-named will be treated separately in the next chapter) are all in some measure followers of Telesio, whose influence on their philosophy is evident and, except for Donio, is openly acknowledged by them. Telesio's philosophy, though it had roots in antiquity [1], was, I think, a novel system with respect to mediaeval or Renaissance traditions of thought. In spite of its claim to be based on sense-experience [2], it is an *a priori* construction of startling simplicity and rigidity; every occurrence, both mental and material, is explained as a conflict between two principles, hot and cold, both of them endowed with sense and a desire for self-preservation. In expounding this philosophy, which is an attempt to overcome the dualism of nearly all earlier systems—to remove the transcendence of mind over matter, Telesio was inevitably faced with almost insuperable difficulties of terminology, since most traditional terms implied the dualism he was trying to avoid. But there was one set of terms, spirit and its derivatives, which had long been used to bridge the gap between body and soul, and these terms play a very important part in his system. In their traditional, stop-gap, uses they are crudely and immediately self-contradictory: spirit is matter so tenuous that it has become soul, is sentient,

---

[1] It has obvious affinities with ancient Stoïcism; Bacon (*De principiis atque originibus secundum fabulas Cupidinis et Coeli, Works*, ed. Spedding, Ellis, etc., London, 1857-1901, III, 94) suggests Plutarch, *De Primo Frigido*, as a probable source; cf. N. C. Van Deusen, *Telesio The Frist of the Moderns*, New York, 1932, pp. 15 seq..

[2] Bernardino Telesio, *De Rerum Natura iuxta propria principia. Libri IX*, Neapoli, 1587, pp. 1-2 (Prooemium): "sensum videlicet nos, & naturam, aliud praeterea nihil sequuti sumus"; modern scholars seem still to be misled by this claim to empiricism.

or soul so gross that it has become matter, is extended [1]. This implies that there is only a difference of degree between mind and matter, in which case the notion of spirit is superfluous, since its function was to connect two categories differing absolutely in quality. For Telesio this difficulty does not arise, since everything is both sentient and extended. He is not using spirit as a bridge-concept, but in order to account for centralized systems of activity, particularly animals and men. Every individual part of man can feel, think, react, like all other matter; but man evidently performs these functions as an organized whole. To explain this Telesio uses medical spirits, which were traditionally hot and rarified, and therefore, according to his own principles, especially sentient and active. By means of these spirits Telesio accounts for the organic unity of nearly all human functions and activites, both bodily and mental.

There is evidently no logical room in Telesio's philosophy for an immaterial and transcendent soul or mind—indeed it seems specially designed to avoid it. He does nevertheless introduce one; not merely, I think, because he wishes to keep within the bounds of Christian orthodoxy, but because he sees that his monistic system does not comprehend all the activities of man. His two principles, hot and cold, and his spirit, the most efficaciously hot kind of matter, tend always and only toward their self-preservation; the wholes built out of them, animals and men, must do this and no more. Thus, in this system, all man's actions, thoughts and desires should be purely utilitarian. In a remarkably eloquent chapter, particularly in view of the porridge-like quality of his style, Telesio points out that in fact man persistently desires and seeks things that do not lead to his preservation or pleasure; that he is always "anxiously", restlessly, looking for what is far beyond these, for useless knowledge, for God, for eternity [2].

---

[1] Cf. Ficino, *Op. Omn,*. p. 535, quoted above p. 13 note 3.

[2] Telesio, *De Rerum Nat.*, V, ii, p. 178: "Non scilicet animalium reliquorum ritu, in earum rerum sensu, cognitioneque, ac fruitione, è quibus nutritur, servaturque, & voluptate afficitur, acquiescere homo videtur; sed aliarum quarumvis, vel earum, quae nullo ipsi usui esse, quin quae nullo prorsus comprehendi possunt sensu, &

The functions, then, of the immaterial, God-given soul in Telesio's philosophy are limited to non-utilitarian contemplation and feeling; the spirit by itself does all ordinary, practically orientated, feeling, perceiving and reasoning. The relation of the soul to the spirit is that of a transcendent, other-wordly force pulling an animal up from its normal, natural behaviour.

The position of the concept of soul in this system is obviously insecure; give a little more to spirit, allow its reasoning or feeling to be more than utilitarian, and it will absorb the soul, make it unnecessary. The rôle of spirit in Telesio's philosophy is important for us, because his disciples, though in other respects their philosophies diverged considerably from his, retained spirit as a cardinal notion in their physiology and psychology, and because Ficino's natural magic is also centred on spirit, as the medium which links together stars, music, talismans, hymns, and man, without the intervention of demons or angels. The Telesians do comprise two undoubtedly Ficinian magicians: Persio and Campanella, and one philosopher, Francis Bacon, whose views on magic are relevant to Ficino. The relation of spirit to soul is particularly crucial in this magical tradition. It is only if the transcendence of soul or mind is maintained that the danger of demonic magic can be avoided. If the spirit absorbs the soul, if the two are identified, then any spiritual magic must either be demonic or absolutely coextensive with ordinary religion. This danger was already present in Ficino; his Orphic singing does have an intellectual content, and his human spirit and cosmic spirit are really stages on the way up to the mind of man and the *anima mundi*. It is only by constant emphasis on these stages, rather than on the ultimate goal, that he prevents even his spiritual magic being quite obviously a religion, and therefore hopelessly unorthodox. Even for the Telesians, such as Bacon and Campanella, who kept an incorporeal soul, it was much more difficult to achieve a non-demonic magic, since their spirit was not merely,

divinorum etiam entium, Deique ipsius substantiam, operationesque summa inquirit cum anxietate."

as for Ficino or any medical theorist, an instrument used by the soul for feeling and thinking; the spirit itself felt and thought, and differed from the soul only by having lower, more practical objects of thought and feeling. For these who, like Donio and perhaps Persio, did identify soul and spirit magic inevitably became religion, or religion magic.

(2) DONIO

Donio, in his *De Natura Hominis* (1581), announces that he is going to treat of man from the point of view of a natural philosopher, that is, not taking revealed truth into account [1]. Thus we are not surprised to find throughout the book no mention of an incorporeal soul infused by God, but a psychology and physiology based solely on a Telesian spirit. Right at the end, however, Donio does try to bring his natural philsosophy into agreement with Christianity. In accordance with Telesian principles, he states that the spirit, like everything else, gains pleasure from any activity that leads to its own preservation, which is best achieved by uniting itself with similar or identical substances. Its ideal situation would therefore be one where it was entirely surrounded by hot, lucent, subtle substances; but in the body it is encompassed by cold, dark, crass flesh and bones, and is therefore engaged in a constant, anxious and only partially successful effort at self-preservation. A sign of its unhappy condition in the body is that its natural state is so altered that it cannot bear the direct light of the sun, which should be eminently congenial to it [2]. But when, in a perfected form, it leaves this body, it will, in a place far from all contrariety, and surrounded by like substances, perpetually enjoy, with inconceivable delight, its own state of union with light and warmth [3]. The place where the spirit

---

[1] *Augustini Donii Consentini Medici & Philosophi, De Natura Hominis Libri Duo: In quibus, discussa tùm medicorum, tùm philosophorum anteà probatissimorum caligine, tandem quid sit homo, naturali ratione ostenditur. Ad Stephanum Sereniss. Regem Poloniae,* Basileae, 1581, pp. 5, 56-9; on Donio's connection with Telesio see Francesco Fiorentino, *Bernardino Telesio,* Firenze, 1872, pp. 321 seq.; Bacon writing on the spirit (*De Augm. Scient.,* IV, iii, *Works,* ed. cit., I, 606) calls Donio the disciple of Telesio. On Donio see Delio Cantimori, *Italienische Haeretiker der Spätrenaissance,* Basel, 1949, p. 479.

[2] Donio, op. cit., II, xxiii, pp. 120-2.

[3] Ibid., p. 122: "Ubi verò magis adhuc perfectus de hoc corpore evolârit, seque

will do this is evidently the sky; for he had earlier stated that the substance most like man's spirit is the aether of the heavens [1]. Then comes Donio's *Peroratio*:

I have set down here all that natural philosophy can tell of man's nature and spirit. If indeed this spirit is the soul itself, to which God has promised (if it keeps His law) the enjoyment of celestial goods, and for whose salvation CHRIST JESUS GOD, KING AND OUR LORD, died, then we Christians must resolve, overcoming nature with God's help, to keep our spirit while in this body entirely uncorrupted by all adverse forces, so that after leaving the body it may have that fate which God Himself shall give it [2].

If spirit and soul are not identical, Donio goes on, then the nature of the latter is absolutely unknowable, though we may, if we like, suppose that the functions of the spirit are in some way due to the soul.

etiam nobilioribus cognatis sociârit, si eo loci erit, quo contraria sint procul; ibi verò immutatus, incorruptus, suoque statu fruens, usque à similibus fotus & vegetatus, & lumine aeternùm exhilaratus; integer, aequus, clarus, hilaris, convenientissimam, jucundissimamque exercens operationem, summis omnibus fruens bonis, nihil extrà quaerens ampliùs, nunc incomprehensibili voluptate, perpetuùm agitabit."

[1]   Ibid., II, iv, p. 66.
[2]   Donio, *De Nat. Hom.*, pp. 122: "Haec habui, REX Serenissime, quae naturali philosophia magistra scriberem tibi de natura hominis, deque humano spiritu. Qui quidem spiritus si est ea ipsa anima, cui à Deo (modo custodiat eius legem) fruitio coelestium bonorum promissa est: & pro cuius salute CHRISTUS IESUS DEUS, REX ET DOMINUS NOSTER, mortuus est: statuendum nobis christianis, eum, DEO sic providente, potentia naturam superante, sub hoc corpore ab omni vi impetentium servari omninò incorruptum: & post discessum à corpore habiturum eam sortem, quam ipse dederit DEUS."

(3) PERSIO

There is no mention of magic in Donio. His importance for us is in proving that this development of Telesio's psychology, the absorption of soul by spirit, was in fact possible and could be asserted in a religious context[1]. I think the same development occurs in an early work of Antonio Persio, his *Trattato dell'ingegno dell'huomo* (1576)[2], which does deal with magic of a kind; but I am not quite sure—Persio is both more cautious and more inclined to use metaphorical language than Donio. The cautionary note at the end of his book indicates that he was aware that he had at least tended to confuse soul and spirit. It reads[3]:

Tutto questo che ho detto, Sign. Piero [Contarini], intorno allo spirito per ispeculation naturale, non intendo che per cosa del mondo debba crear pregiudicio, od esser interpretato per contradicente alla sana opinione che portiamo, come la mente sia a noi infusa da Dio ...

This request must now be disregarded.

Persio finds the fundamental cause of differences of *ingegno* (by which he means mental capabilities, particularly inventiveness) in the spirit, rather than in the complexion or in planetary influences, which he also discusses[4]. This dismissal of astrology is by no means absolute; the astrological and humoral explanations "in molte cose dicono il vero"[5]. Moreover we are told that the nature of the spirit resembles the heavens, and that in very ingenious people it becomes so subtle and celestial that there is

[1] Nor was this peculiar to Telesians; it occurs, e.g., clearly in Melanchthon *De Anima*, Lugduni, 1555, pp. 4-16.

[2] Antonio Persio, *Trattato dell'ingengno dell'huomo, Al Clariss. Sign. Pietro Contarini* ..., Vinetia, 1576; on this work and Persio's close connections with Telesio, Patrizi, and Campanella, see E. Garin, "Nota telesiana: Antonio Persio", *Giorn. Crit. d. l. Fil. Ital.*, 1949, and the literature there cited.

[3] Persio, *Trattato*, fo 129 vo.

[4] Ibid., pp. 19-23.

[5] Ibid., p. 23.

a danger that it may fly up to heaven to its father the Sun, as occurs in cases of ecstasy [1]. There is a cosmic spirit, centred of course in the Sun, but permeating everywhere, and by nourishing our spirit with those things that contain most of it we can give ourselves "il piu bel ingegno di huomo nato".

> Onde ci hanno consigliato certi savi, che chiunque vorra donar virtu all'anima sua, & anche spirito di mondo secondo la qualita che e'vuole apprendere, habbia gli occhi alle membra del gran mondo, & scielgasi quel membro di quella qualita che egli cerca, come in essempio se vorremo far lo spirito nostro solare, o partefice di virtu solare, useremo le cose solari [2].

Then follow lists of solarian things, closely modelled on Ficino's, and we are told to do the same for Jupiter, Venus and Mercury. But, since man is primarily solarian, it would be better to concentrate on the sun, from which we shall acquire the virtues of all the heavens; and our spirit,

> quanto più s'assomigliera a quello del sole, tanto ci fara piu ingegnosi, & inventivi & giudiciosi, sendo tutto lucente, caldo, tenue, bianco, mobile, & vivace [3].

So far we have nearly the whole of Ficino's spiritual magical theory and practice, but lacking the essential elements of the hymn and the planetary music [4]. The hymn we shall perhaps find later. Music is only mentioned casually as delighting the spirit by making it move [5]. Persio is more interested in using visual means of influencing the spirit: beautiful pictures and people, clean and graceful rooms and churches [6]. Odours are especially beneficial, being of a like nature to our spirit and being able

---

[1] Ibid., pp. 32-3: if the pores of the body are not closed, there is "gran pericolo che il detto spirito sottilissimo divenuto non si risolva, & lievissimo essendo, cio è quanto piu puo celeste, se ne voli in ciel al suo padre Sole".

[2] Persio, *Trattato*, p. 35.

[3] Ibid., pp. 38-9.

[4] There is a cautious acceptance of talismans, after a mention of the planetary rings of Apollonius of Thyana, whose spirit was particularly solarian (ibid., pp. 39-40).

[5] Ibid., p. 25.

[6] Ibid., pp. 109-110, 119; cf. p. 98, about Titian's spirits becoming ecstatically concentrated on his subjects.

conveniently to reach its main seat, the brain, through the nostrils [1]. This is why incense is used in churches,

cio è per disporre gli spiriti delle persone all'innalzamento della mente a Dio, accioche l'aria sparta d'odori, presti facile, & amichevole strada alli nostri spiriti di salir nelle parti soprane per contemplar Iddio, come è parere d'alcuni [2].

Here it is obvious that the Telesian mind is dangerously confused with, perhaps even identified with, the spirit, the same corporeal spirit that is of a like nature to odours. It is perhaps this same spirit which in saints and prophets is said to have been purified of all stains and become "celestial" [3]. But to what degree is the following outburst metaphorical?

Potrem noi dunque divenir celesti? Mai si che potremo, & si come sì degni spiriti sono chiamati stelle, sole, luna, cielo, cosi potremo anchor noi, anzi angioli soprani, & del primo ordine, non che del secondo, & terzo, come pel fuogo della carita Seraphimi, per lo splendor della' ntelligenza, Cherubini, per la fermezza del giudicio Throni. Et se non veggo male, sommi delle fiate abbattuto in persone che con la loro convenevolezza di corpo armata di celeste spirito mi son parute di figurar le figure celesti, & i giri delle sfere, quasi a buon hora cominciando a deificarsi, & a farsi celesti [4].

If we remember Donio's immortal spirit uniting itself with the aether of the heavens, we must at least suspect that Persio means quite literally that, after death, our corporeal spirit will be united with the fabric of the sky and become something like a planetary angel [5], and that this process sometimes even begins before death. Since in this work he is combining Telesian philo-

---

[1]   Ibid., p. 100.

[2]   Ibid., p. 101.

[3]   Ibid., p. 120. The fact that Persio does occasionally distinguish the God-given mind from the spirit (e.g. p. 38) shows that he is not just loosely using the latter term in its present-day sense; if the Telesian spirit takes over religious activities, the Telesian mind is left with nothing whatever to do.

[4]   Persio, *Trattato*, pp. 120-1.

[5]   Bodin, not only in the *Heptaplomeres* (ed. Noack, 1587, pp. 93-4), but also in his last published work, *Universae Naturae Theatrum* (Lugduni, 1596, pp. 771-784), asserts that human souls are corporeal, naturally spherical and made of the same substance as the sky, and that after death good souls will become angels; he quotes *Daniel*, XII, 3: "And they that be wise shall shine as the brightness of the firmament: and they that turn many to righteousness as the stars for ever and ever."

sophy with Platonic themes, it seems to me likely that, as I suggested for Ficino[1], Persio also has in mind the Neoplatonic astral body, which comes from the heavens, is made of the substance of the stars, and returns whence it came[2].

Persio's treatise ends with a long, lyrical prayer to the sun, or rather to "quel vero, unico, & trino Sole, il quale per sua immagine ha dato il sole, che ci illumina visibilmente"[3]. In this Ficino-like passage[4], the soul does seem to be distinguished from the spirit. God illuminates the former; the Sun the latter. But it is through the sun's action on the spirit that man's *ingegno* acquires true wisdom, an acquisition that is only perfected by God[5]; those who acquire wisdom shall shine like the firmament, and those who teach it like the stars[6]. The prayer ends by asking that, as the eagle fixes the sun with its eyes, so may we, with our *ingegno*, always look to the true Sun, which is God, who will illuminate us as He once hid His Light (the Son) in the pure and beautiful Virgin, whose garment is the sun and whose crown is the stars[7].

Here, I think, is the missing hymn we were looking for—the crowning, most efficacious part of Persio's solarian operations on the spirit. But the fusion with ordinary religion has become complete; the distinction between the spirit and the mind is blurred, if it is there at all, and the distinction between the Sun and God is, to say the least, shaky. Persio is not describing a religious kind of magic, but a magical religion, a highly unorthodox kind of Christianity.

[1] V. supra p. 38.

[2] Persio may well have read Patrizi's *Discorso della Diversità de i Furori Poetici* (in his *La Citta felice*, Venetia, 1553, fo 44), where differences in poetic genius are explained by a detailed account of the descent of the astral body through the spheres.

[3] Persio, *Trattato*, p. 124.   [4] Cf. supra p. 18.

[5] Persio, ibid., p. 128.   [6] Quoted from *Daniel*, v. supra 197 note (5).

[7] Persio, ibid.: "Siaci per te dunque conceduto, o Sole, che noi conosciam bene il primo sole, e per conseguente l'amiamo: e tu Vero e primo Sole concedine che queste luci delle nostre anime, per poco lucenti stelle divenute, a guisa de quelle celesti, che maggior lume dal celeste Sole si beono, da te divin Sole per divino stile sieno illuminate, & a simiglianza della pura, e bella Vergine che di Sol vestita, coronata di stelle, a te sommo Sole piacque sì, che in lei tua luce nascondesti, sollevati, & alzati da questi corporali soli, imagini di te Sol vero, in te sempre collo ngegno donatoci, com'aquile gli occhi fissi tegniamo a te . . ."

(4) FRANCIS BACON

Francis Bacon's *Historia Vitae et Mortis* (1623) deals with the prolongation of life and youth by a proper treatment of the spirits [1]. His conception of the human spirit comes from Telesio and Donio [2], particularly the latter [3], though he is too orthodox to identify mind and spirit. The way to postpone senility and death is to see to it that the spirits are dense and consequently have a gentle heat that will not dry up and eventually destroy the body. Ways of condensing the spirit are: to take opium, breathe cold air, smell fresh earth [4]. Ways of keeping it gently warm are: to eat garlic, "Venus saepe excitata, raro peracta" [5]. Violent emotions must be avoided, since they attenuate the spirits; moderate emotions, including sadness, are good because they strengthen and condense them [6].

Like Ficino, Bacon was trying to achieve a healthy and stable condition of the spirits, and he had read the *De Triplici Vita*, to which he refers three or four times [7]. But one can see from the small sample just given that his methods of producing this condition are totally different from Ficino's, perhaps carefully and deliberately so. The reason for this is that he disliked magical or astrological practices; he mentions and contemptuously dismisses astrologically prepared medicines and talismans in a

---

[1] Bacon, *Historia Vitae et Mortis*, London, 1623, *Works*, ed. Spedding, Ellis, etc., London, 1857-1901, II, 102 seq.

[2] In the *De Augmentis Scientiarum* (IV, iii, *Works*, ed. cit., I, 606) Telesio and Donio are the only two modern authors Bacon cites on the human spirit.

[3] Bacon's theory that the spirit gradually dries up and shrinks the solid parts of the body, thus eventually causing old-age and death, plainly derives from Donio; cf. e.g., Bacon, *Works*, II, 119-120, and Donio, *De Nat. Hom.*, II, xiv, p. 95.

[4] Bacon, *Works*, II, 162 seq..

[5] Ibid., II, 169.

[6] Ibid., II, 171-2.

[7] Ibid., II, 158, 174, 199, 201.

list of "superstitious and fabulous" means of prolonging life and preserving health [1]. But this dislike itself needs some explaining; for Bacon believed in most of the theoretical premises on which Ficino's magic is based.

Like so many apparently fierce critics of astrology, Bacon approved of "good" astrology. His "astrologia sana" excludes horoscopes and exact predictions of particular events, but asserts the reality of celestial influences, consisting not only of heat and light, and accepts the traditional characteristics ascribed to the various planets [2]. He emphasizes that the human spirit is particularly subject to these influences [3]. He also believed in at least some of the effects of the power of the imagination, and explained them by transformations and emanations of the spirit. Indeed, he suggested the most interesting experiments in telepathy and faith-healing to test the influence of confidence and credulity on the efficacy of the imagination and spirits [4]. If, for example, you wish to cure a sick gentleman by faith, first pick out one of his servants who is naturally very credulous; while the gentleman is asleep, hand the servant some harmless concoction and tell him that it will cure his master within a certain space of time. The spirits of the servant, made receptive by his complete faith in your medical powers, will be powerfully stamped with the image of this future cure; they will flow out and similarly stamp the spirits of his master, also in a state of receptivity because he is asleep. Thus the cure will be effected. This is even less like a scientific experiment than most of those in the *Sylva Sylvarum*, and shows clearly, I think, that Bacon still believed in the traditional doctrine of the magical power of imagination fortified by credulity. Another ingredient of Ficinian magic which Bacon

[1] Ibid., II, 158: ". . . et de horis fortunatis secundum schemata coeli, in quibus medicinae ad vitam producendam colligi et componi debent; atque de sigillis planetarum, per quae virtutes coelitus ad prolongationem vitae haurire et deducere possimus; et hujusmodi fabulosis et superstitiosis; prorsus miramur homines ita mente captos, ut iis hujusmodi res imponi possit."

[2] Bacon, *De Augm. Scient.*, III, iv, *Works*, I, 554-9.

[3] But he rejected the Platonic *spiritus mundi*, precisely because it was a basis of non-demonic magic (Bacon, *Sylv. Sylv.*, Century X, *Works*, II, 640 seq..)

[4] Bacon, *Sylv. Sylv.*, X, 939-959, *Works*, II, 652-660.

accepted was the powerful effect of music on the spirit, explained by the peculiarly moving, dynamic nature of sound [1]. But Bacon, like Campanella [2], did not apparently believe in the mathematical theory of musical intervals [3], perhaps because of his general distaste for mathematics [4], and in consequence has no grounds for connecting celestial and musical harmonies.

The only explicit reason Bacon gives for his dislike of magic is that it is too easy a way of reaching one's goal. In the *Advancement of Learning*, when discussing the power of the imagination, he dismisses the excessive claims of the Paracelsans and their "miracle-working faith", but accepts as "nearer to probability" "transmissions and operations from spirit to spirit without the mediation of the senses", aided by "the force of confidence". But, he goes on,

if the imagination fortified have power, then it is material to know how to fortify and exalt it. And herein comes in crookedly and dangerously, a palliation of a great part of ceremonial magic. For it may be pretended, that ceremonies, characters, and charms, do work, not by any tacit or sacramental contract with evil spirits, but serve only to strengthen the imagination of him that useth it; as images are said by the Roman church to fix the cogitations, and raise the devotions of them that pray before them. But for mine own judgment, if it be admitted that imagination hath power, and that ceremonies fortify imagination, and that they be used sincerely and intentionally for that purpose; yet I should hold them unlawful, as opposing to that first edict which God gave unto man, "In sudore vultûs comedes panem tuum". For they propound those noble effects, which God hath set forth unto man to be bought at the price of labour, to be attained by a few easy and slothful observances [5].

---

[1]   Ibid., II, 114-5, *Works*, II, 389-391.

[2]   V. infra p. 231.

[3]   Bacon (*Sylv.*, II, 184-7, *Works*, II, 409-410) suggests experiments with different lengths of strings and pipes which would lead to the discovery of the proportions of musical consonances; but he nowhere mentions these proportions, which had been common knowledge since the time of Pythagoras.

[4]   E.g., *De Augm. Scient.*, III, vi (*Works*, I, 577): "Nescio enim quo fato fiat, ut mathematica et logica, quae ancillarum loco erga physicam se gerere debeant, nihilominus certitudinem suam prae ea jactantes, dominatum contra exercere praesumant."

[5]   Bacon, *Advancement of Learning*, Book II, *Works*, III, 381; same passage in *De Augm. Scient.*, IV, iii, *Works*, I, 609.

The particular kinds of magic Bacon is thinking of are: alchemical gold-making and the preservation of youth by operations on the spirit. A little earlier in the same work [1] he states that it may be possible, by prolonged and arduous investigation and experiment, to make gold or rejuvenate the spirit; but that false magicians wickedly try to do these things without sweat and toil. That is to say, anything like Ficino's spiritual magic in the *De Triplici Vita* is impiously easy, whether it works or not, and Bacon's *Historia Vitae et Mortis* shows us the right, hard, empirical way to the same end. Magic, then, is wrong because it makes experiments unnecessary, and Bacon liked doing and planning experiments.

He may also have thought, not without some reason, that Ficinian magic might be contaminated with pagan religion. After a passage about the beneficial effect on the spirits of the odour of newly-turned earth [2], he adds:

I commend also, sometimes, in digging of new earth, to pour in some Malmsey or Greek wine, that the vapour of the earth and wine together may comfort the spirits the more; provided always it be not taken for a heathen sacrifice, or libation to the earth.

[1] Bacon, *De Augm. Scient.*, III, v, *Works*, I, 574-5 ("Attamen tanta exercet humanum genus impotentia et intemperies, ut non solum, quae fieri non possunt, sibi spondeant, sed etiam maxime ardua, sine molestia aut sudore, tanquam feriantes, se adipisci posse confidunt.")

[2] Bacon, *Sylv.*, X, 928, *Works*, II, 649.

CHAPTER VII. CAMPANELLA

INTRODUCTION

In Campanella's life and works we find a practical revival of Ficino's magic. Ficino's original ideas and purposes are powerfully refracted by Campanella's extraordinary personality and mental outlook; this is my justification for treating them so fully. This revival was also conditioned by certain events in his life. It is with this biographical background that I shall deal first [1].

Campanella had a spirit-dominated philosophy [2], which he had taken over from Telesio and Persio and, independently of Ficino, he was interested in, and practised, astrological magic. His astrological system too was centred on the sun. For a fundamental theme of his thought and motive for his actions, throughout his life, was the belief that the millenium was imminent, and that this was being heralded by (amongst other portents) the sun's gradually approaching the earth, which it would finally consume—the sun, the centre of love, would absorb the earth, the centre of hate [3]. At the age of about fifty-eight, that is in 1626 or shortly afterwards, he had urgent practical need of some kind of especially powerful, yet apparently respectable, astrological magic, and he found just what he was looking for in Ficino's

---

[1] My account will be founded largely on Luigi Amabile's monumental work, *Fra Tommaso Campanella ne' Castelli di Napoli in Roma ed in Parigi Narrazione ...*, Napoli, 1887, where nearly all the relevant documents will be found.

[2] For a full and competent exposition of the whole of Campanella's philosophy see Léon Blanchet, *Campanella*, Paris, 1920. For the sake of simplicity I shall avoid, as far as possible, discussing the evolution of Campanella's metaphysics (see Blanchet, op. cit., pp. 263 seq.). In any case, by the period that concerns us (from the 1620's on), the decisive stage in this evolution was already passed.

[3] Campanella, *Universalis Philosophiae seu Metaphysicarum rerum, juxta propria dogmata, partes tres, Libri 18 ...*, Paris, 1638, Pars III, pp. 71 seq.; *Astrologicorum Libri VI ...*, Lugduni, 1629, pp. 69 seq.; cf. Blanchet, op. cit., pp. 250 seq..

De Vita coelitùs comparanda; he may well have been led to Ficinian magic by the *Trattato dell'ingegno* of Persio, who had been a close friend of his [1]. The reason he needed it was as follows.

[1] See L. Firpo, "Appunti Campanelliani III", *Giom. crit. della filos. ital.*, 1940, pp. 435 seq..

(1) CAMPANELLA'S MAGIC AND URBAN VIII

In 1599 Campanella was put in prison at Naples after the failure of his Calabrian revolt, which was to have established his Utopian and highly unorthodox City of the Sun [1]. In 1603, after abominable tortures, he was condemned to perpetual imprisonment, as a heretic; he had escaped being put to death by simulating madness. He remained at Naples, writing copiously, until 1626, when he was released by the Spaniards; but after a few months he was rearrested and put in prison at Rome [2]. Campanella's eschatalogical hopes were by now largely centred on the Pope, as they once had been on the king of Spain and later were to be on the king of France. If he could convince the Pope of the sun's slow approach and the events this portended, then missionaries, trained by Campanella, would go forth from Rome to convert the whole world to a reformed, "natural" Catholicism, which would introduce the millenium, the universal City of the Sun [3]. The Pope's favour was also now his main hope of personal freedom.

Now Pope Urban VIII was a firm believer in astrology, although Sixtus V's Bull of 1586 ("Coeli et Terrae") had condemned judiciary astrology and although he himself was to publish a Bull ("Inscrutabilis") against it in 1631. He had horoscopes cast of the Cardinals resident in Rome and was in the habit of openly predicting the dates of their deaths [4]. He was, however, paid back in his own coin. From 1626 onwards astrologers began to

---

[1] See Campanella, *Città del Sole*, ed. Edmondo Solmi, Modena, 1904, and Blanchet, op. cit., pp. 70 seq..

[2] See Blanchet, op. cit., pp. 54-5.

[3] V. ibid., pp. 56-7.

[4] See Amabile, *Fra Tommaso Campanella ne' Castelli di Napoli* ..., Napoli, 1887, I, 280 seq..

predict his own imminent death, and by 1628 rumours of it became loud and widespread [1]. There seems little doubt that these rumours and predictions were actively encouraged by the Spanish, who also made noisy preparations for the next conclave [2]. Annoyed at his persistently pro-French policy, they hoped to frighten the Pope to death; and but for Campanella's magic they might have succeeded. How seriously worried Urban VIII was by these predictions can be seen from his Bull against astrology [3]. Though this confirms in general terms the condemnations of Sixtus V's Bull, the only practices it specifically condemns are predictions of the deaths of princes and especially of Popes, including members of their families up to the third degree of consanguinity inclusive; these are to be considered as crimes of lèse-majesté, punishable by death and confiscation of goods [4]. The two dangerous years were 1628, when there was an eclipse of the moon in January and of the sun in December, and 1630, with a solar eclipse in June.

In diplomatic reports from Rome of 1628 there are several mentions of the Pope and Campanella being frequently closeted together [5]. They are said to be engaged on some astrological activity connected with the predictions of the Pope's death, to be doing "necromancy", and, in one document, to be celebrating nocturnal rites with lighted candles [6]. What they were doing, as

[1]   Amabile, op. cit., I, 298, 311-2, 324 seq..
[2]   V. ibid., I, 347.
[3]   And cf. Amabile, op. cit., I, 347 seq..
[4]   See *D. Urbani divina providentia Papae VIII. Constitutio Contra Astrologos Iudiciarios, qui de statu Reipublicae Christianae, vel Sedis Apostolicae, seu vita Romani Pontificis, aut ejus consanguineorum Iudicia facere, necnon eos qui illos desuper consulere praesumpserint,* Romae, 1631. That this Bull seemed oddly personal at the time appears from Campanella's defence of it; one of the objections to it which he refutes is: "Bulla haec magis insectatur Astrologos, quàm haereticos, & schismaticos. Etenim excommunicat, aufert bona omnia, applicatque fisco, poenaque capitali etiam in prima vice punit Astrologos: quod haereticis non fit; unde videtur magis suae tranquillitati, & consanguineorum consulere, & sub majori cautela, poenaque quàm Fidei divinoque cultui" (Campanella, *Disputatio Contra Murmurantes . . . in Bullas SS. Pontificum Sixti V. & URB. VIII. adversus Iudiciarios editas,* in his *Atheismus Triumphatus,* Parisiis, 1636, p. 256); cf. infra pp. 218-9.
[5]   See Amabile, *Castelli,* I, 271, II 153-5.
[6]   Ibid., I, 281 (Teodoro Ameyden, *Elogia Summorum Pontificum,* ms.: "Pontifex fidem praestigiis adhibebat, sacra nocturna accensis cereis una cum Campanella Monaco Praedicatore, temeritate satis noto, celebravit").

Amabile and after him Blanchet[1] have, in my opinion, rightly conjectured, was to take proper measures against the disease-bearing eclipses and the evil influences of Mars and Saturn.

First they sealed the room against the outside air, sprinkled it with rose-vinegar and other aromatic substances, and burnt laurel, myrtle, rosemary and cypress. They hung the room with white silken cloths and decorated it with branches. Then two candles and five torches were lit, representing the seven planets; since the heavens, owing to the eclipse, were defective, these were to provide an undefective substitute, as one lights a lamp when the sun sets. The signs of the Zodiac were perhaps also represented in the same way; for this is a philosophical procedure, not a superstitious one, as common people think. The other persons present had horoscopes immune to the evil eclipse. There was Jovial and Venereal music, which was to disperse the pernicious qualities of the eclipse-infected air and, by symbolizing good planets, to expel the influences of bad ones. For the same purpose they used stones, plants, colours and odours, belonging to good planets (that is, Jupiter and Venus). They drank astrologically distilled liquors.

These goings-on are described in a chapter on eclipses in Campanella's *De Fato siderali vitando*, which appeared as the 7th Book of his *Astrologica*, published at Lyons in 1629[2]; it has

---

[1] Amabile, *Castelli*, pp. 324 seq.; Blanchet, op. cit., p. 56.

[2] Campanella, *Astrologicorum Libri VI. In quibus Astrologia, omni superstitione Arabum, & Iudaeorum eliminata, physiologicè tractatur, secundùm S. Scripturas, & doctrinam S. Thomae, & Alberti, & summorum Theologorum; Ita ut absque suspicione mala in Ecclesia Dei multa cum utilitate legi possint*, Lugduni, 1629, Lib. VII, *De siderali Fato vitando*, iv, 1, pp. 11-13, *De vitandis malis ab eclipsi imminentibus*; if the lunar or solar eclipse threatens the whole region where you are, then go away; if, from your horoscope, you know that it threatens only you, then take the following measures against the "semina tibi pestifera" it is diffusing in the air:

"Satage ergo primum, ut temperatè, secundum rationem, & quàm proximus Deo vivas, per orationes & sacra illi te dedicando. Secundò domum clausam undique, ne aër alterius subeat, asperges aceto rosaceo, & aromatum odoribus: ignem adhibebis in lauro, myrto, rosmarino, cupresso, aliisque aromaticis lignis accensum. Hoc enim nihil validius ad opera coeli, etiam si à diabolo ministrantur, venefica dissipanda.

Tertiò pannis albis, sericeis, & foelicibus ramis aedem adornabis.

Quartò accendes luminaria duo, & faces quinque, qui coeli planetas repraesentent, & cum deficiant in coelo, non desint, qui tibi vices eorum gerant in terra. sicuti in nocte abeunte Sole lucerna eius vices supplet, ut non desit ablatus dies. Sint autem

separate pagination, and is preceded by a publisher's note saying it came into his hands after the first six Books had already been printed. According to Campanella, and there is no reason to doubt him, he did not mean to publish this treatise. It was sent to the printer by two highly placed Dominicans [1], who wished to prevent Campanella gaining the post of "Consultor" in the Holy Office [2]; this post would have enabled him to exercise considerable control over the censorship of theological publications. This act of malice was successful; for Urban was extremely angry at the publication and Campanella never obtained his post, though he managed quite soon to regain the Pope's favour and to have an official examination of the treatise, which cleared it of heresy and superstition [3]. He was freed from his imprisonment in April 1629. By the next year he had obtained the Pope's permission to found a college at Rome ("Collegio Barberino") for the training of missionaries in accordance with the principles set forth in his book *Quod reminiscentur* [4], that is to say, missionaries who would

aërei ex aromatica confecti mixtura. Sique duodecim signa etiam imitatus fueris, philosophicè, non superstitiosè, ut vulgus arbitratur, incedes.

Quintò adhibe socios amicos, quorum genesis eclipsis malo juxta aphetas subjecta non sit. Multum enim prodest conversatio contraria, aut consimilis eventui. Illa fugat, ista accersit eventum.

Sextò musicam jovialem & veneream apud te habebis, ut aëris malitia frangatur, & beneficarum symbola excludant maleficarum stellarum vires.

Septimò quoniam reperiuntur cujusque sideris symbola in lapidibus, & plantis, & coloribus, & odoribus, & musica, & motionibus, sicuti in 5. lib. medicinalium docuimus: eos adhibebis allicies, qui beneficarum alliciunt vires, maleficarum fugant. Plurimum valent stillatitij liquores, astralitates extractae adhibitaeque secundum rationem, ut dictum est, & in 3. parte metaphysicae.

Haec facies tribus horis ante principium eclipsis, ac tribus post finem, & donec beneficae pervenerint ad angulos, & robur assumpserint." For dangerous comets (ibid., p. 14) "Non modo quidem simulabis coelum cum planetis signisque intra cubiculum, sed insuper addes cometae simulacrum ex aëreis medicatis, utiliter quod tibi fulgeat eo in situ & motu proficua fulsione noxiam temperante. Caetera ut supra."

[1]　See Luigi Firpo, *Ricerche Campanelliane*, Firenze, 1947, pp. 155 seq.

[2]　See Amabile, *Castelli*, I, 342-3.

[3]　Ibid., I, 360-1; cf. Campanella's *Apologia*, for this treatise, infra p. 220.

[4]　See Amabile, *Castelli*, I, 362, where he quotes a letter of 1630 from Campanella to Cardinal Barberini, in which Campanella says he intends to train Calabrian Dominicans and "far'un Collegio Barberino de Propaganda Fide fondato nel libro del reminiscentur" (this book has been edited by R. Amerio, *Quod Reminiscentur ...*, Patavii, 1939, Lib. I & II; *Per la Conversione degli Ebrei*, Firenze, 1955 (Lib. III of same work)).

convert the whole world to Campanella's kind of Catholicism [1].

These incidents confirm the conjecture that Campanella and the Pope did actually practise this magic together [2]; it seems also highly probable that Campanella made it up especially for this purpose and occasion. That he had not evolved this magic before he came to Rome in 1626 is indicated by the fact that it is not mentioned in the first two versions of the *Città del Sole* (1602, and 1612 published in 1623), whereas in the final version, published in 1637, there is a description of the Solarians practising it, followed by a discussion of the Bulls against astrology [3]; nor is it mentioned in his *De Sensu Rerum et Magia* [4], where one might expect to find it, nor in any other of his works earlier than the *Astrologica* (1629).

Another time when Campanella used his magic was in 1630— the little son of Don Taddeo Barberini, one of the Pope's nephews, was threatened by a bad "influx"; hence the mention of the third degree of consanguinity in Urban's Bull of the following year [5]. One of the "Avvisi di Roma", preserved in the *Collezione Estense* at Modena [6], reads:

21 Dec. 1630. Il P. Campanella, ch'è il maggior Astrologo de nostri tempi ha cura di fare la bolla contra gli Astrologhi tutti, et egli è quello che la ravvede hora diligentissimamente ... Nel suo libro stampato

[1] This college never came into being, and his situation at Rome, from about 1631 until his departure for Paris in 1634, became steadily worse (see Blanchet, op. cit., pp. 57-9).

[2] Cf. Campanella, *Discorso Politico*, in Amabile, *Castelli*, II, 320: "E li Spagnoli dissero ch'il Papa si salvò da quelli influssi per haver usato il remedio ch'il Campanella pose nel Libro de Fato Siderali Vitando" (and similar statement, ibid., II, 335; as Amabile (I, 327) remarks, in neither case does Campanella deny this); Firpo, *Ricerche*, p. 156, passage quoted from Gaspard Schopp's memoirs: "Urbanus tamen, paucis post annis, cum Campanellam Inquisitio ab Hispanis sibi permissum Roman misisset, eum quot hebdomadis ad se arcessere, horasque plures cum eo solus agere solebat; a quo cum quadam die fuisset monitus caeli siderumque affectione non nisi infaustum aliquid ac dirum sibi portendi, de consilio eius parietes conclavium atro panno velasse, clausisque de die fenestris ac multis facibus ardentibus ex ordine collocatis, astra illa horribili adspectu capiti suo illucentia plena thuris acerra suppliciter veneratus esse fertur".

[3] Campanella, *La Città del Sole*, ed. Edmondo Solmi, Modena, 1904, p. 44.

[4] Campanella, *De Sensu Rerum et Magia Libri Quatuor*, Francofurti, 1620.

[5] V. supra p. 206.

[6] Amabile, *Castelli*, II, 150.

di Astrologia ha insegnato quomodo fata vitentur; e dicono ch'ulti-
mamente in casa di questi signori Padroni sia stato praticato un certo
suo documento di candele e di torcie, che significano li pianeti, per
schivare un influsso, che soprastava al figliuolo di D. Thadeo.

This confirms that Campanella did practise the rite described in
his *De siderali Fato vitando*, and that the seven lights symbolizing
the planets were an essential feature of it. The statement that
he helped to draft Urban's anti-astrological Bull may well be
correct [1].

There is one other occasion on which we know that Campanella
used this magic: for his own benefit, on his death-bed, as a
prophylactic against the eclipse of the sun on June 1st 1639. He
died on May 21st of that year [2].

There is no doubt at all that this magic practised at Rome by
Campanella derives directly from Ficino. At the end of the chapter
on eclipses in the *De siderali Fato vitando*, when dealing with the
capture of good influences from favourable eclipses, Campanella
refers the reader to what is said in his *Metaphysica* on "instituting
one's life celestially", i.e. "de vita coelitùs comparanda" [3]. If we
look at this, we find not a discussion of Ficino's treatise, but a
full and very competent summary of it, presented as such [4].
Campanella does not here explicitly accept all Ficino's views; but
it is evident that he does approve of his magic [5], since he frequently

---

[1] Cf. Amabile, *Castelli*, I, 398-9.

[2] See Quétif & Echard, *Scriptores Ordinis Praedicatorum . . .*, Paris, 1721, II, 508:
"Audivi a nostris senioribus tum viventibus Campanellam Fatum siderale sibi
semper metuisse & praedixisse ab eclypsi solis prima junii MCDXXXIX ventura,
nihilque propterea in antecessum omisisse eorum, quae ad illud vitandum ipse
praescribit Astrolog. lib. 7 cap. 4 art. 1, spectantibus & mirantibus qui tum aderant
Fratribus: sed ad diem illum non pervenit . . ."

[3] Campanella, *Astrol.*, VII, 13: "Cum verò bonum pollicetur eclipsis, captandum
est, adhibendique illices, vel joviales, vel venerei, vel martiales, quemadmodum de
his, quae de vita coelitus comparanda disputavimus. & in secundo medicinalium
docebamus"; a few lines before there is another reference to *Pars* III of his *Metaphysica*.

[4] Campanella, *Universalis Philosophiae seu Metaphysicarum rerum . . .*, Paris, 1638,
Pars III, XV, vii, ii-viii, pp. 179-183; the first mention of the *De Vita Coelitùs
comparanda* is on p. 154.

[5] Campanella does devote two later chapters of his *Metaphysica* (III, xv, viii, iii;
III, xv, ix, i; pp. 186-190) to a criticism of Ficino's (and Proclus') theory of astrological magic; but the criticism boils down to Ficino's failure to use Campanella's
terminology.

completes Ficino's theories and directions by references to his own works, particularly to the *De Fato siderali vitando* and his *Medicinalia*. In one section, for example, after having shortly described one of Ficino's talismans, he writes [1]:

But how things are to be used which generate much spirit, preserve it and perfect it; that is, make it lucid, fine, pure, subtle, ... we have written in the 5th Book of the *Medicinalia* and in the 4th Book of the *De Sensu Rerum*. And what odours, tastes, colours, temperature, air, water, wine, clothes, conversations, music, sky and stars are to be used for breathing in the Spirit of the World, which is implanted and inserted in its individual parts and is diffused through the whole of it, and under what constellations, you will find in the same books. There is, therefore, no need to spend any more time on Ficino's less full account. Just consider of which star you wish the favour and through what things.

Campanella's summary, which includes Ficino's music-spirit theory and his rules for planetary music [2], is immediately preceded by a full exposition of those Neoplatonic astrological and magical writings which were, as we have seen, Ficino's main source: Iamblichus, Proclus, Porphyry, *Hermetica* [3]—among them the passage from the *Asclepius* on attracting celestial demons into idols by means of rites and music [4]. When introducing the sections on Ficino, he refers back to this passage, remarking that "all this doctrine" seems to derive from Hermes Trismegistus [5]; that is

---

[1] Campanella, *Metaph.*, Pars III, XV, vii, iv (title: "Ex Fic. Plat. qua ratione nobis applicantur res illices spiritus, & animę Mundi, & cęlestium, & Angelorum"), p. 181: "Quomodo autem applicandae sint res, quę spiritum multum generant, servant, perficiantque: id est quae lucidum, tenuem, purum, stabilem, providum, primalitatibus vigentem, scripsimus in lib. 5. Med. & in 4. de Sensu rerum. Et qui odores, qui sapores, qui colores, quis tepor, quis aër, quae aquae, quod vinum, quae vestes, quae conversatio, quae Musica, quod Coelum, quae stellae ad hauriendum spiritum Mundi singulis in partibus ejus implantatum insertumque, & in toto vagantem, ibidem habes: & sub quibus constellationibus: quare non est, cur immoremur in Ficini commento longè exiliori. Tantum cogita, cujus stellae vis favorem, & per quas res." The 4th Book of the *De Sensu Rerum* deals with magic, but does not contain anything specifically Ficinian; on the *Medicinalia*, cf. infra p. 230-3.

[2] Campanella, *Metaph.*, III, XV, vii, vii, pp. 182-3.

[3] Ibid., III, XV, v, i, p. 171 (Iamblichus); III, XV, vii, i, p. 179. (Proclus); III XV, vi, ii, p. 177 (Porphyry); III, XV, iii, i-iv, pp. 167-170 (*Hermetica*).

[4] Ibid., III, XV, iii, i, p. 168; cf. supra p. 40.

[5] Ibid., III, XV, vii, ii, p. 179: Ficino, "Procli, Plotinique sectator", showed how, "per res ordinis solaris, virtutem solis nobis conciliamus: per res Veneri dicatas, Venerem ... scripsimus autem in lib. 5. medicinalium, quaenam sint solaris

to say, Ficino's astrological magic consists of the same kind of operation as that described in the *Asclepius*, the "idol" becoming either a talisman or a human being (the operator) [1].

Campanella, then, not only adopted Ficino's magic, but was also fully aware of its sources [2], including the most dangerous. He must have realized that behind the spiritual magic of the *De V.C.C.* were prayers and rites addressed to planetary angels [3]. But, as we shall see, Campanella would not have had very strong fears or scruples about that. He was looking for a magic that could be defended as natural, and this the *De V.C.C.* provided; he was not looking for magic that was really non-demonic.

ordinis, & quae jovialis, & quae aliarum Planetarum, tam de stellis fixis, quam de Daemonibus: quam de lapidibus, & de Plantis, & animalibus . . ., non ineptè. Tota autem haec doctrina à Mercurio videtur propagata, quemadmodum suo in loco anterius memoravimus."

[1]   Ibid., III, XV, vii, vii, p. 182: "Ex Fic. Plat. Antiquiores putabant, quemadmodum alliciuntur in corpora humana ignei Daemones per humores, spiritusque igneos . . . sic etiam per radios stellarum spiritus earundem stellarum, & per suffumigia & odores, & sonos, & colores, illis stellis congruentes. & hoc in statuis, & in humanis corporibus."

[2]   He also cites Peter of Abano when dealing with Ficino's talismans (ibid., p. 181).

[3]   Cf. ibid., III, XV, viii, iii, p. 186, on Ficino's methods of attracting demons and angels; and the mention of demons in passage quoted above, p. 211 note (5).

(2) Campanella's Defences and Theory of Astrological Magic

We now have some picture of the operations in which Campanella's magic at Rome consisted, and know that it was based on Ficino's *De V.C.C.*. From his defences of it, and from his more general writings on Astrology and magic, we can learn more about the theories behind it, and hence about its real nature. We are faced here with difficulties of interpretation with regard to Campanella's religious beliefs. It was essential for the realization of his millenial projects that he should be able to use the power of the church, and therefore that he should remain within it; but there is little doubt that the religion to which he was going to convert the world was far from orthodox [1]. In consequence, Campanella, in all his works that touch on religion, is trying simultaneously to prove that he is a good Catholic and to propagate his own new kind of religion. This inevitably makes it very difficult to determine quite how unorthodox, and in what way, his own religious views were—to decide, for example, whether the repentance and renunciation of earlier errors, expressed with such eloquent remorse in the *Quod Reminiscentur* [2], is merely an expedient fiction, or refers to some real rejection of diabolic magic, such as his spiritualistic experiments [3]. With regard to his defences of Ficinian magic, I doubt whether he truly believed that it was free from commerce with demons or angels; and even after he adopted it, he continued to have at least strong leanings towards magical practices involving good demons, especially planetary angels [4]. We must, then, read all his defences bearing

---

[1]   Cf. Blanchet, op. cit., pp. 66 seq.

[2]   Campanella, *Quod Reminiscentur* . . ., ed. R. Amerio, Tomus Prior, Patavii, 1939, pp. 23 seq.; cf. Blanchet, op. cit., pp. 90 seq.

[3]   V. infra p. 228.

[4]   V. infra p. 224.

in mind that they were written primarily from motives of practical expediency, which are, however, frequently counteracted by his natural indiscretion and audacity. He was an odd mixture of politic cunning and ingenuous rashness.

Campanella makes even greater use than did Ficino of the authority of Thomas Aquinas in defending his astrological magic; for Campanella, living in a post-tridentine world, this authority was still more important. He had, moreover, the additional support of Cardinal Caietano's commentaries on Thomas' *Summa Theologica*, which boldly defend the legitimacy of astrological predictions and talismans against Thomas' condemnation of both [1]. Thus Campanella in his defence is able to use at the same time both Thomas and the commentator who contradicts him. This use of Thomas to defend practices which he explicitly condemns is perhaps not so odd as it appears at first sight.

Thomas, in the *Contra Gentiles* and in the two *Opuscula* which deal with astrology [2], gives strong support for a moderate astrological determinism, from which only man's free-will is exempt; everything else God rules through the stars [3]. Even human free-will is not wholly exempt; for the soul may be disposed, though not determined, in a certain way through its connexion with the body, which is subject to astral influence. In one of the *Opuscula* he concludes that the heavenly bodies are moved by angels [4], and that these angels should not be worshipped with *latria* as the authors of the benefits received from them, but reverenced with *dulia* as servants of God who transmit His gifts; that is to say, the cult of planetary angels is put into the same class as that of saints [5]. Then there is the treatise *De Fato*, where, in addition to an astrological determinism which even

---

[1]   The crucial place is: *Summ. Th.*, 2da 2dae, q. 96, art. ii; for Caietano's commentary on this see Thomas Aquinas, *Opera Omnia*, Romae, 1570, T. XI, Pars Altera, fos 241 ro-242 ro.

[2]   Thomas, *Opusculum* IX (*Responsio ad Magistrum Joannem de Vercellis de Articulis xlii*), XXII (*De judiciis astrorum ad fratrem Reginaldum*).

[3]   Thomas, *Summa contra Gentiles*, III, lxxxii-lxxxvi, civ-cvi.

[4]   Thomas, *Opusculum* IX.

[5]   Cf. supra p. 137, and infra p. 226.

includes the human mind, we find the approval of talismans [1]. Now this treatise is not usually considered genuine. It flatly contradicts the rest of Thomas' utterances on astrology. It is not in the list of his works drawn up for his canonization by Bartholomew of Capua; and it appears often with the title *De Fato Secundum Albertum*—indeed it is almost certainly by Albertus Magnus [2], whose *Speculum Astronomiae* was a trump-card which Campanella, like Ficino, often played. Nevertheless, it is understandable that Campanella should still be able to make great use of the *De Fato* in his defences of astrology; for it appears, without the "secundum Albertum" in the title, or any word of doubt about its genuineness, in the official edition of Thomas' works, the great Roman edition of 1570, dedicated to Pius V and edited with express regard to the decrees of the Council of Trent [3]. This edition also contains the pro-astrological commentaries of Cardinal Caietano on the *Summa*, and no others. It is not surprising that Campanella, with this ammunition in his bag, was forbidden, towards the end of his stay at Rome, to teach Thomism [4].

How valuable, as a protective shield, Campanella considered the authority of the two great Dominican theologians, Thomas and Albert, can be clearly seen from the presentation of his *Astrologica*, of which the full title reads [5]:

Six Books of Astrological matters, in which Astrology, purged of all the superstitions of the Arabs and Jews, is treated physiologically, in accordance with the Holy Scriptures and the doctrine of St. Thomas, Albert, and the greatest theologians; so that they may, without suspicion of evil, be read with profit in the Church of God.

The preface, in which Campanella outlines his own views on astrology, is full of references to Thomas, who is even used to combat Augustine [6], whose competence in these matters is

---

[1] Thomas, *Op. Omn.*, 1570, T. XVII, fo 203 *Opusc.* XXVIII.

[2] See Martin Grabmann, *Die Werke des Hl. Thomas von Aquin*, Münster i. W., 1931, p. 348.

[3] Thomas, *Opera Omnia*, Rome, 1570, T. I, *Pio Lectori*.

[4] See Amabile, *Castelli*, I, 408 seq.

[5] V. supra p. 207 note (2).

[6] Campanella, *Astr.*, p. 5, citing Ps. Thomas, *De Fato*, on Augustine, *Civ. Dei.*, V, iv (dissimilarities of Esau and Jacob).

anyway doubtful, since he was ignorant of mathematics, as is shown by his denial of the existence of the Antipodes [1]. Campanella's own position is summed up in the following statement [2]:

> We therefore say, with the support of the doctrine of Thomas, Albertus Magnus and the most subtle theologians, that man's free-will is not directly subject to the stars, but accidentally (*per accidens*), in so far as the body is affected by the heavens and stars, likewise the animal spirit, which is rarefied and corporeal, and the humours.

This appears to safeguard free-will by allowing astrological influences to reach no higher than the spirit. But we must remember that Campanella's spirit, like Telesio's, performs the functions of perceiving, knowing and desiring, and is really a slightly inferior double of the soul or mind, from which it differs almost solely by being corporeal [3]. Thus planetary influences on the spirit may to a high degree determine the character of the mind:

> As when God wishes to make a perfect Holy Man He may use the stars and elements for tempering the body rightly for the reception of the soul, and thus make the animal spirits subtle and pure [4].

Indeed the astrologically determined state of the spirits is of such importance that it is reasonable to decide irrevocably the course of your whole life on the basis of your horoscope. If, for example, this indicates that your spirits are crass, dull and smoky, you will be irremediably stupid and ignorant, and had better subject yourself entirely to the will of others. A good way of achieving this is to enter a monastery; if the "family of the wise", that is, the Franciscans or the Dominicans, will not take you, try the Jesuits. If you are only moderately stupid, try to become

---

[1] Campanella, *Astr.*, p. 1.

[2] Ibid., p. 4: "Nos igitur, D. Thomae & Alberti Magni & subtilissimorum Theologorum doctrina suffragante, dicimus hominis arbitrium astris non esse subditum directè, sed per accidens, quatenus corpus afficitur à coelo & sideribus, similiter spiritus animalis, tenuis, corporeus, & humores ipsi".

[3] Campanella does also share Telesio's (v. supra p. 191) belief that the soul elevates the spirit to divine activities, e.g. Campanella, *Realis Philosophiae Epilogisticae Partes Quatuor, Hoc est de Rerum Natura* . . ., Francofurti, 1623, pp. 165, 175.

[4] Campanella, *Astr.*, p. 5: "Ut cum Deus vult Religiosum optimum facere, potest uti stellis & elementis ad temperandum corpus probè ad susceptionem animae, & spiritus animales inde tenues & puros conficere."

a Thomist or a Platonist. If your horoscope indicates likelihood of imprisonment, become a Carthusian—and so forth[1].

The truth of the traditional names and characters of the stars, on which the reliability of horoscopes depends, is guaranteed in the most absolute way possible by a tradition which is a kind of *prisca astrologia*:

They must have been divine, or taught by God, those men who have handed down to us these sympathies and antipathies, and names, of the stars.

In fact, the Egyptians learnt them from Abraham, Abraham from Noah, Noah from his ancestors, and so back to Adam and God[2].

The Sun is of course immensely more influential than the other planets, who receive all their power from It.[3] Since Campanella's new religion was both portended and caused by the Sun's movements, it is natural that he should approve of the theory that the rise and fall of all religions, including Christianity, is astrologically determined[4].

The main factor in these religious changes is the approach of the sun towards the earth. When it was at its most distant point, the seat of religion was with peoples living near the equator, the sun being far enough away to rarefy and purify their spirits without burning them. As it approached nearer it made their spirits smoky, and religion passed to Egypt, where the same thing happened, the smoky period producing the worship of beasts. Thence, as the temperate region crept northwards and westwards, religion went successively to the Babylonians, Jews, Persians, Greeks, Romans, French, Germans, Spanish, and now to the New World[5].

If religions themselves are astrologically determined, it is

[1] Campanella, *Astr.*, VII, v, i, pp. 15-6.
[2] *Astr.*, p. 7: "Divinos autem fuisse oportet, vel à Deo edoctos homines illos, qui tales sympathias, & antipathias, & nomina syderum cum rebus inferioribus nobis tradiderunt . . ."
[3] Ibid., I, ii, i, pp. 12-3.
[4] Ibid., pp. 66-74; cf. *Quod reminiscentur*, ed. cit., pp. 15 seq.
[5] Campanella, *Astr.*, II, iii, 2, pp. 70-1; VI, vi, p. 229.

perhaps reasonable to order the details of religious devotions in accordance with the planets. Campanella discusses at length the question: should prayers be said at astrologically favourable times? In favour of the answer yes we have these points: first, Solomon's recommendation in the Book of *Wisdom*[1] to pray at sunrise, which is supported by the facts that the sun, rising always with Mercury and Venus, disposes the soul to contemplation, as Ficino noted in the *De Tr. V.*[2], and that altars are at the East end of churches. Secondly, David said: "Seven times a day do I praise thee"[3], and there are seven canonical hours; these, the Astrologers think, are allotted to the seven planets, like the days of the week, the seven ages of the world, etc.. Campanella accepts the first of these arguments with the qualifications that the action of the planets is on the body and spirit, rather than the soul, and that a good man may successfully pray at any time. The second he rejects on the grounds that the hours of prayer are seven, not because of the planets, but because of the seven stations of the Cross and the Seven Last Words, and the seven gifts of the Holy Ghost, or because God has harmoniously arranged everything in sevens[4]. This rejection is certainly dishonest; for, as we shall see, Campanella did not believe in a harmonically or numerologically constructed universe, in the manner of Giorgi, and he did believe that the days of the week and the ages of the world corresponded with, and were dominated by, the planets[5].

Since Campanella's *Astrologica* contained these none too orthodox theories, it is understandable that he should have been anxious to protect himself with the authority of Thomas, Albert, and Caietano, especially as, unlike the other magicians we have met, he was writing after Sixtus V's Bull against astrology and just before Urban VIII's. Campanella later dealt with these two

---

[1] *Wisdom*, XVI, 28.
[2] Ficino, *Op. Omn.*, pp. 499-500 (*De Tr. V.*, I, vii).
[3] *Psalm* 119, v. 164.
[4] Campanella, *Astr.*, VI, ii, 2, pp. 214-6.
[5] Ibid., VI, vi, p. 227; II, iii, 2, p. 74.

Bulls in an ingenious way: at the end of the 1636 edition of his *Atheismus Triumphatus* he published a defence of them [1] which makes so many concessions to the imaginary astrologers who are supposed to have attacked them, that the Bulls end up by appearing to recommend "good" astrology and condemn only a few "bad" astrologers who claim to predict particular events with absolute certainty. He makes as much as he can of the approval, given by the Council of Trent and confirmed by Sixtus V's Bull, of astrology employed in the useful arts of agriculture, navigation and medicine [2]. The Council of Trent had condemned only those books on divinatory astrology which claimed a certainty and precision of prediction infringing free-will; whereas Sixtus V condemned every kind of divination [3], not however, says Campanella, because general, uncertain predictions are false, but because they may be dangerous—and of course "the Holy Father does not deny that we are inclined by the heavens to certain actions and choices", but merely wants to assert that we can resist these inclinations and therefore cannot make certain predictions about them [4]. Thomas and Caietano are again brought in to establish that the heavens, though indirectly and not irresistably, influence our minds and characters [5]. The most important kind of prediction from Campanella's point of view was that of

---

[1] Campanella, *Atheismus Tr.*, Parisiis, 1636, pp. 253 seq.: *Disputatio Contra Murmurantes citrà & ultra montes, in Bullas SS. Pontificum Sixti V. & URB. VIII. adversus Iudiciarios editas* . . . .

[2] *Constitutio S.D.N.D. Sixti Papae Quinti Contra Exercentes Astrolgiae Iudiciariae Artem*, in *D. Urbani . . . Papae VIII. Constitutio Contra Astrologos Iudiciarios . . .*, Romae, 1631, condemns all "Astrologos, Mathematicos, & alios quoscunque dictae judiciariae Astrologiae artem, praeterquam circa agriculturam, navigationem, & rem medicam in posterum exercentes . . ."

[3] Ibid.: the Council had condemned all book of judiciary astrology which "de futuris contingentibus . . . aut ijs actionibus, quae ab humana voluntate pendent certo aliquid eventurum affirmare audent, permissis tamen judicijs, & naturalibus observationibus, quae navigationis, agriculturae, sive medicae artis juvandae gratia conscripta fuissent"; since this ban has not been observed, Sixtus now condemns "omne genus divinationum".

[4] Campanella, *Disput.*, p. 270: "Nec negat S. Pontifex quod inclinamur ad operandum, & eligendum à caelo: cum enim aestuat eligimus umbras: cum pluit tectum: cum vernat venerem homo, & plantae, & animalia appetunt: At particulares inclinationes, vel ignoramus, vel cum moventur non sectamur."

[5] Campanella, *Disp.*, p. 263.

large-scale supernatural events from celestial portents, since all his eschatalogical hopes were deduced from the peculiar behaviour of the sun. Though such predictions quite plainly cannot be included in any of the permitted classes, agriculture, navigation, medicine, he firmly asserts their legitimacy, supporting himself with the Star in the East [1]. He does not discuss the condemnation in Sixtus V's Bull of those who revive pagan idolatry by "saying prayers to demons, with fumigations of frankincense and other things, or offer other sacrifices, light candles, or misuse sacred things" [2]; which must have made awkward reading both for him and for Urban VIII [3]. Campanella ends his defence of the Bulls by referring his readers, for fuller information, to his *Metaphysica*, where they would have found, amongst other curious things, the full and favourable exposition of Ficino's magic and its Neoplatonic sources [4].

Campanella's *Apologia* for his *De Fato siderali vitando*, that is to say, for his eclipse-magic, was never published [5]; it was composed in 1629, when this treatise was officially examined for heresy and superstition [6], and probably gives us the arguments with which he defended himself on this occasion. He begins by resuming this magical operation, but omits, significantly, the music, thereby avoiding the charge of using incantations or invocations. We are then told, with the usual battery of references to Thomas, including the *De Fato*, that remedies against astrologically caused evils must be pious, because, if there were no such remedies, then fate would be unavoidable—there would be

---

[1] Ibid., pp. 252, 262; cf. *Astr.*, p. 1 (using Luke, XXI, 25), *Quod remin.*, pp. 15-6.

[2] "Alij verò aliquas pristinae, & antiquatae, ac per Crucis victoriam prostratę Idololatriae reliquias retinentes, . . . ad futurorum divinationem intendunt. Alij . . . nefarias magicae artis incantationes, instrumenta, & venefica adhibent, circulos, & diabolicos characteres describunt, Daemones invocant . . . eis preces, & thuris, aut aliarum rerum suffimenta, seu fumicationes, aliave sacrificia offerunt, candelas accendunt, aut rebus sacris . . . abutuntur . . ."

[3] Campanella here (*Disp.*, p. 269) denies that he believed the predictions of Urban's death; he must of course have disbelieved their certainty, or there would have been no point in doing the magic.

[4] Campanella, *Disp.*, p. 273. Cf. supra p. 210.

[5] It is given in Amabile, *Castelli*, II, 172 seq.

[6] See Amabile, ibid., I, 360-1.

no free-will, and hence no just rewards and punishments [1]. These remedies could be condemned as superstitious, again according to Thomas, only if they involved a tacit or express pact with the Devil or his demons [2]; as for the latter

That there is no express pact is evident, since it is a remedy, carried out with an invocation to God, of that secret philosophy which the Persians called magic [3].

Then we have the familiar distinction between bad, demonic magic and good, natural magic, which applies "active to passive, and celestial to terrestrial" [4]. There is no tacit pact with the Devil, because the remedies proposed all have a natural action against the effects of the eclipse. "That clean, white garments have a force contrary to the black eclipse is obvious" [5]; that aromatic odours purge the air of the noxious seeds of pestilence is admitted by "all doctors, in particular by Marsilio Ficino, Florentine Canon, Great Theologian and philosopher, in his treatise on the plague". The second of these two is one of the few honest and valid statements in the whole *apologia*; cleansing the air in this manner was in fact a normal remedy against the plague [6]. Campanella can also claim that his remedies are free from "characters or letters", which, according to Thomas and Caietano, are the marks of demonic magic, since they can only act as signs and must therefore be addressed to an intelligent being [7].

But what about the seven lights? These were the most dangerous feature of the whole operation; for they seemed plainly

[1] Ibid., II, 172.

[2] Cf. supra p. 43.

[3] Campanella apud Amabile, *Castelli*, II, 172: "Quod non expressum [sc. pactum], patet, quoniam remedium secretae philosophiae cum invocatione Dei: quam philosophiam vocant Persae magiam".

[4] Ibid.: "alia [sc. magia] vera, qua utuntur philosophi, et Reges, et Principes applicando activa passivis, et coelestia terrestribus".

[5] Ibid.: "Quod enim vestes mundae et albae contrarientur Eclipsi nigrae palam est. Quod acetum, aquae stillatitiae, odoriferae, et odores aromatici, et ignes, corrigant malitiam aeris, et dissolvant, aut arceant semina pestilentiae, et noxiorum influxuum, probant omnes medici: precipue Marsilius Ficinus canonicus florentinus Magnus Theologus atque philosophus in libello de peste."

[6] V. e.g. Fracastoro, *De Contagionibus*, III, ii, vii (*Opera Omnia*, Venetiis, 1555, fos 133, 141).

[7] Cf. supra p. 43.

to be a sign or a symbol, and Campanella himself had said that they "represented the planets" [1]. He therefore devotes the greater part of his *Apologia* to arguing that these seven lights could have a natural, physical effect. He begins by asserting that numbers alone can be physical causes, for "God has made everything in number, weight and measure", and gives a formidable list of patristic authorities for the powers and virtues of numbers [2]. As I have already said, Campanella did not believe in a Pythagorean or Platonic harmony of the universe, and could not honestly use such arguments.

We come a little nearer the truth when Campanella abandons numerology and tacitly admits that the point about the lights is not their sevenness, but their representation of the planets. He cites Thomas, yet again, to show that the terrestrial world is governed and ordered by means of astral influxes, and Ficino, not as the Great Theologian and medical writer, but as the author of *De V.C.C.*, to support the view that these influxes are more effectively captured "by imitating the heavens, than by not imitating them" [3]. Then comes a general defence of the opinion that natural, celestially derived power can be given to artefacts by making them of a suitable shape or figure; that is to say, the arguments normally used to show that talismans can act naturally, but which are now applied to Campanella's candles. Thomas, in the *Contra Gentiles*, admits that artefacts can acquire occult, celestial virtues; this he contradicts, but does not expressly retract, in the *Summa Theologica*, as Caietano points out [4]. Campanella then summarizes some of Caietano's subtle arguments in favour of the natural action of talismans, for which, as Campanella says, "he fought valiantly" [5]. These arguments, mostly drawn from

---

[1] V. supra p. 207.
[2] Campanella, ibid., pp. 174 seq.
[3] Campanella apud Amabile, *Castelli*, II, 175: "Magis autem captatur influxus coeli imitando coelum, quam non imitando, ut testatur Ficinus in lib. de vita coelitus comparanda ..."
[4] Campanella, ibid., p. 177; Thomas, *Contra Gent.*, III, cv; Caietano, *Comm. in Summ. Th.*, 2da 2dae, q. 96, ii.
[5] Campanella, ibid., p. 178: "fortiter pugnat pro eis".

the behaviour of magnets and variously shaped floating metal bodies, have only a rather tenuous relevance to talismans, and none at all to candles.

We come still nearer the truth when Campanella tells us that his lights imitate the planets not only in their number, but also in their substance; for both of them are fiery [1]. The lights in the sealed room are, I think, quite simply a substitute for the defective, eclipsed celestial world outside; the real heavens have gone wrong, so we make ourselves another little normal, undisturbed, favourable heaven. This is indeed quite clear from Campanella's directions for dealing with dangerous comets:

You will not only simulate, within the room, the heavens, with the planets and signs of the zodiac, but you will also add a simulacrum of the comet, made out of aërial, medicated material, so that this may usefully shine for you in such a position, and with such motion, as will, by shining there, temper the harmful [influences] [2].

This is a form of natural magic which is radically different from any others we have met. It is no longer a kind of psychological technique centred on the imagination, but, at least apparently, a quite simple, physical operation. It was only conceivable with a Telesian cosmology, in which the substance of the heavens was not any sort of quintessence, but just ordinary fire. It was thus possible to make, quite literally, a miniature heaven out of ordinary lights, arranged in the most favourable conjunctions, and sit and absorb its beneficial influence, rather as people now use sun-ray lamps. This was certainly one way in which Campanella thought his magic worked; but there may have been other ways too, just as Ficino's magic could be either spiritual and natural, or demonic.

[1] Ibid.
[2] V. supra p. 207 note (2).

(3) Campanella and the angels

In his *Atheismus Triumphatus* Campanella discusses various pagan religions, among them the worship of the stars, the sky and the Sun. This, he thinks, is less reprehensible than other kinds of non-Christian religion:

for these portions of the world are seen to be far from corruption, and endowed with a vivid and simple beauty; and they are the nobler causes of lower things, and live in a sublime region, continually bene-fitting us by pouring out light, heat and influences, generating, changing, producing all things; on account of all this the pagans could easily be led to think that they were gods [2].

But, on examining this subject more closely, Campanella found that after all one should not worship the stars as divine; but his regret and hesitation are so evident, that, from this passage alone, one would strongly suspect that he himself did practice this kind of worship. The crucial question for Campanella is whether the stars are the living bodies of souls, or, according to the Aristotelian and Thomist view, they are merely inanimate bodies moved by Intelligences; he takes it for granted that in the latter case no one would consider worshipping them, nor, apparently the moving Intelligences. If the former view, which is held by the Platonists and many Fathers, and which Thomas allows to be compatible with Christian dogma [1], is correct, then

---

[1] Campanella, *Atheismus Triumphatus*, Romae, 1631, p. 111: "Minore tandem reprehensione dignos deprehendi eos, qui adorant Sidera, Coelum, & Solem: quoniam hae portiones Mundi se ostendunt, à corruptione distantes, & pulchritudine vivida, simplicique donatae: suntque nobiliores rerum inferiorum causae, & in sublimi regione degunt, continuò beneficientes nobis, lucem effundendo, calorem, & influentias: generando, alterando, omniaque producendo: quas ob res magis movere possunt Gentes ad credendum quòd sint Dii."

[2] Ibid., pp. 111-2: "... quanquam vera esset sententia Philonis & Origenis, Platonicorumque (quam Divus Thomas non includi, nec excludi à doctrina fidei docet, licet Sanctus Hieronymus, & Divus Augustinus dubitent, & Patres multi ita sentire videntur) videlicet Solem & Sidera viva esse corpora, & sentire prorsus longe magisque, quàm Animalia ..."

the stars have intellectual souls and living bodies made entirely
of very subtle spirit (which is perhaps why the Sun is called
"spirit" in *Ecclesiastes*), with which they can sense and communicate[1]. But even so, they are unfortunately, like angels, only
creatures and should not therefore be worshipped. But then
again, Caietano thinks that the animation of the stars is the
official opinion of the church and should not be doubted. For
in the Preface of the Mass one sings: "Deum laudant Angeli,
adorant Dominationes, tremunt Potestates: Coeli, Coelorumque
Virtutes, ac beata Seraphim &c. incessabili voce proclamant",
and this shows that the Church holds that not only the orders
of angels, but the heavens themselves, and the Virtues of the
heavens, praise God, as animate bodies and souls; which is also
implied by God's words in *Job*: "When the morning stars sang
together, and all the sons of God shouted for joy"[2].

"When I thought on these things", says Campanella, "I was
in doubt whether the stars should be worshipped". He finally
concludes that they should not, since it is not known for certain
that they are animated. They probably are, but this dogma,

on account of the inconstant foolishness of the people, and its uncertainty, for it has not been expressly revealed by God, is not much
mentioned. And indeed, God is worshipped with no less wisdom and
magnanimity in Himself, than in these living statues and images of Him[3].

The implication of this passage is certainly that, if we could
be absolutely sure that the stars are the spiritual bodies of intellectual souls, then of course we would worship them. In Campanella's *Metaphysica*, published in the same year, 1636, as the last
edition of the *Atheismus Triumphatus*, after a recapitulation of the

---

[1] Ibid.: ". . . stellas esse totas spiritum tenuem (nam propterea putant Solem
vocari Spiritum, Ecclesiast. 1.) . . . et se radiis tangere, et motus audire mutuos, et
harmoniam edere . . ."
[2] *Job*, XXXVIII, 7.
[3] Campanella, ibid., pp. 112-3: "Haec cum cogitassem dubitabam, an Coelestia
sint colenda: & tamen conclusi, quoniam haec sunt incerta . . . non esse colenda,
nec quippiam sciri certe, an sint animata . . . Nihilominus propetr populi inconstantem
stultitiam, & dogmatis incertitudinem, cum à Deo non sit revelatum expressè,
subticetur. Quin non minori sapientia, ac magnanimitate adoratur Deus in se ipso,
quàm in his statuis, imaginibusque ejus vivis."

reasons and authorities in favour of astrology that he had given in the *Astrologica*, we find, as an argument against the plurality of worlds [1]:

I believe most firmly—and it seems believable to all peoples, as Philo and Origen witness—that the stars are a Republic of supernal spirits (*spirituum*), who have come out of the mental into the bodily world.

The fiery heavens are a fit abode for them, "for fire is a most active, lucid, sensitive thing, and hence most perfectly suited to spirits (*spiritus*) endowed with power and wisdom".

In this republic, which seems to me more like a monarchy, all the stars are strictly subordinated to the Sun, from whom they receive their heat and light. Later we learn that "One of the Dominations rules everything in the world, as the Vicar of God"; this angel's body is the visible sun and his soul is the same as the *anima mundi*. The angels who are the other stars are of the order of Virtues [2].

Campanella, then, did firmly believe that the stars were animated. But they were, nevertheless, only creatures, and, according to Thomas Aquinas, their cult should therefore not go beyond the bounds of *dulia* [3]. Campanella apparently accepted this limitation; for we are told of the citizens of the *Città del Sole* [4]:

Niuna creatura adorano di latria altro che Dio, et però a lui solo servono sotto l'insegna del Sole, che è imagine e volto di Dio, da cui viene salute e calore, et ogni altra cosa. Però l'altaro è come un Sole fatto, et li sacerdoti pregano Dio nel Sole, et nelle stelle, come in altari et nel Cielo come Tempio, e chiamano gli Angeli buoni per intercessori, che stanno nelle stelle, vive case loro . . .

In what manner should one worship these star-angels? A few pages further on in the *Metaphysica* Campanella begins his expo-

---

[1] Campanella, *Metaph.*, III, XI, ix, i, p. 52: "firmissimè credo, quod & gentibus omnibus credibile videtur, teste Philone & Origene, sydera esse Respub. spirituum supernorum, cum in mundum corporeum ex mentali egrediantur . . . Nam activissima res est ignis lucidissima, sensitivissima, idcircò maximè conveniens spiritibus potestate & sapientia decoratis . . ."

[2] Ibid., III, XV, ii, iii, p. 162: "Unum ex Dominationibus mundalia omnia regere, tanquam Dei Vicarium . . ."

[3] V. supra p. 137.

[4] Campanella, *Città del Sole*, ed. Solmi, p. 39.

sition of Neoplatonic magical texts, which leads to his summary of the *De V.C.C.*, and in Porphyry, or rather in Ficino's version of the *De Abstinentia*, we find what is perhaps the answer: to God Himself we offer the silent elevation of our mind; to good incorporeal angels, vocal praise, numbers and mathematical characters; "to the embodied celestial gods, that is, the Sun, moon and other stars, it is proper to sacrifice fire and lamps, since from them we have fire and light" [1].

This, then, was another way in which Campanella's version of Ficinian magic perhaps worked: as an act of worship, or at least reverence, addressed to the living stars, identified with angels. The theoretical reconciliation of the spiritual with demonic magic is more feasible for Campanella than for Ficino. The bodies of Campanella's planetary angels are the visible planets, and these are wholly spirit, which they continually pour forth; there is therefore no conflict between a theory of planetary influence transmitted by an impersonal *spiritus mundi* and a theory of one transmitted by multiple personal demons. The *spiritus mundi*, for Campanella, *is* the visible Sun, the body of the *anima mundi*, who dominates all the other planets. Moreover, the distinction between effects on the human spirit produced by the *spiritus mundi*, as opposed to effects on the soul or mind, produced by angels or demons, is very blurred in Campanella, since his human spirit is so near to being a second soul. It does, however, still matter for him whether planetary influence stops short at the spirit or not, because in the former case man still has one free soul, whereas in the latter both are subjected to the heavens.

I think it, then, quite likely that Campanella's magic was meant to work in two ways at once: as a miniature model of the heavens, and as a religious ceremony directed toward planetary angels, primarily the Sun-angel. Campanella would not have been afraid of such magic, although he was quite aware from his own experience that there were bad demons as well as good angels.

[1] Ibid., III, XV, vi, ii, p. 177: "Diis vero coelestibus corporatis, hoc est, soli, & lunae, & astris caeteris, sacrificare convenit ignem & lucernas: quoniam ab eis lucem & ignem habemus ..."; cf. Ficino, *Op. Omn.*, p. 1934.

Much earlier in his life he had practised a different kind of astrological magic, as we know from the evidence of a fellow-prisoner of his at Naples, and from thinly disguised accounts by Campanella himself in his *Atheismus Triumphatus* and in a letter of 1606 [1]. If we look at these accounts, we can see, especially in the light of the Thomist reason for condemning magic, namely that it must involve demons, why Campanella, when he saw his chance of giving astrological aid to Urban, did not use his own earlier magic, but had recourse to practices based on Ficino's spiritual magic, which was at least apparently more respectable.

In 1603 Campanella noticed that this fellow-prisoner, whom he calls an "idiota adolescens", had a horoscope indicating the power of communicating with demons and angels. He taught him to address prayers to the sun and other planetary deities; and, after unspecified ceremonies, put him into a state "between sleeping and waking", in which he transmitted the angels' replies to Campanella's questions on important matters—that is to say, he was a medium in a trance. The spirits which appeared claimed to be the angel of the sun, of the moon, and sometimes God Himself. The answers began by being satisfactory, and included truthful prophecies; the controls were evidently angels. But soon this became more doubtful, when the control denied the existence of hell and asserted the transmigration of souls. Then, when Campanella asked for an unequivocal sign of their angelic nature to be given to the youth, they arranged, with great cunning, for his removal from the prison and eventual death. Campanella carried on alone, and finally the control said that Campanella had written well on free-will, but that Calvin had written better; when asked its opinion of Augustine and Chrysostom on the same subject, it prudently remained silent. For Campanella, who was always a fanatical anti-protestant, this was conclusive proof

---

[1] Campanella, *Ath. Tr.*, 1631, pp. 113-4; edition of 1636 (which contains a slightly different version), p. 161; Amabile, *Fra Tommaso Campanella La sua Congiura, i suoi Processi e la sua Pazzia*, Napoli, 1882, I, 21-2, II, 349-354, III, 588, 601; cf. Campanella, *Opusculi Inediti*, ed. L. Firpo, Firenze, 1951, pp. 42-4.

that the control was now a bad demon, and that, as he had suspected, Calvin was directly inspired by the Devil.

Campanella did not conclude from this, as any orthodox
Catholic would have done, that the controls had been diabolic
all the time and were merely luring him on at the start with
satisfactory answers, but that he now knew by experience that
"there existed devils of evil will, as also good angels" [1]. This
experience did not, then, teach him the lesson that attempts to
get into contact with angels by magical means will always result
in deception by bad demons [2]; and it must also be remembered
that Campanella was a very courageous man indeed. He did
realize, I think, that this particular spiritualistic magic was rather
perilous and uncertain, and there is no evidence that he ever
tried it again. But he was left with his faith in good planetary
angels unimpaired; and this, together with his belief in the
supreme eschatalogical significance of the sun and his practical
requirements with regard to the Pope, led him to his revival and
transformation of the magic of the *De V.C.C.*, which he probably
knew to be demonic, but which was defendable as natural and
spiritual.

[1] Campanella, *Ath*. *Tr.*, 1631, p. 114: "hinc certus ergo experimentis omninò
sum extare Diabolos, perversae voluntatis: sic etiam bonos Angelos."

[2] For polemical purposes Campanella sometimes took the more orthodox line,
as in his defence of the anti-astrological Bulls (*Ath*. *Tr.*, 1636, pp. 262-3): "Nam
etsi dicat divinaculus, se nolle à Diabolo responsum, sed ab Angelo, & protestatur:
cum tamen procedit ex non causis pro causis, & ex non signis pro signis, nugaciter
operatur, & à Nugatore illudi interpretativè saltem vult. Nemo enim fornicans,
vult facere contra legem Dei, & si signo crucis se muniat; facit tamen, peccatque."

(4) Music and Words in Campanella's Magic

There are several differences, both general and particular, between Ficino's magic and Campanella's version of it; one of the most evident is that in the latter music and words appear to play a much less important part. Although Campanella does in the *Metaphysica* resume Ficino's rules for planetary music, and though the description of the magical operation in the *Astrologica* mentions Jovial and Venereal music[1], we are told nothing more about this music, nor whether it had words, nor if so, what they were. Campanella's theoretical views on music and words can perhaps throw some light on these omissions.

Like Ficino, Campanella lays great stress on the movement of sound, in the air that conveys it and in the human spirit, as opposed to the static nature of sight[2]. But, according to Campanella, there is no direct contact between the musically moved air and the human spirit; the two are not substantially united, but the air transmits its movement to the spirit by striking the eardrum[3]. There is also this general difference between Campanella's and Ficino's music-spirit theory. For Ficino the spirit is a substance used as a medium of transmission by sentient and cognitive souls—it is not itself sentient, appetitive or cognitive. Campanella's spirit does feel, think and desire. Thus, whereas Ficino's theory attempts a real explanation of psychological facts, that is, correlates them with facts of a different order—hearing, for example, with movements in the air and in the spirit; Campanella's theory, strictly speaking, explains nothing at all. He cannot correlate two

---

[1] Campanella does also in his *Medicinalium juxta propria principia, Libri septem*, Lugduni, 1635, p. 320, advise the use of solarian music (*Musica apollinea*) for improving the spirit of melancholics; cf. ibid., pp. 309, 348.

[2] E.g. Campanella, *Metaph.*, I, II, v, xi, p. 167 (sight), p. 171 (hearing).

[3] Campanella, *Real Phil. Epil.*, I, xii, vi, pp. 153-4.

distinct orders of facts, for his spirit has broken down the body-mind barrier. It is idle to explain the fact of a man's hearing by positing a vapour inside him which hears.

The marvellous effects of music are due to this transmission of movement from the air to the spirit. But, unlike Ficino and most later musical humanists, Campanella does not think of these effects as primarily ethical or emotional, but as therapeutic or producing sheer pleasure or pain. The human spirit has a natural rhythmic movement, indicated by the pulse, which is essential to its preservation; music which produces in the air movements similar to, but a little stronger than this, will confirm and encourage this natural movement of the spirit. Low sounds bruise, condense and thicken the spirit; high ones rarify and lacerate it; what is required, then, is a combination of the two which is "consonant" to the spirit's natural movement. The spirit, being thereby preserved and strengthened, is delighted—hence the pleasure caused by "consonant" music [1]. For Campanella, as for Bacon [2], musical consonance is not determined by the simple mathematical ratios of two or more soundwaves or vibrating strings, but is an entirely relative quality determined by the conformity of musical sounds to any given kind of spirit [3]. This accounts for differences between the musical styles of various nations, and for the fact that different animals like different kinds of music.

This theory leads Campanella to a refutation of Paolini's

---

[1] Campanella, *Medic.*, II, iv, ii, pp. 60-1, IV, iii, iii, i, p. 161; *Metaph.*, I, II, v, xi, pp. 171-2; *Real. Phil. Ep.*, I, xii, vi, pp. 154-5; *Poetica*, ed. L. Firpo, Roma, 1944, pp. 229-230.

[2] V. supra p. 201.

[3] Campanella, *Metaph.*, I, II, v, xi, p. 171: "asper [sonus] diversitatem mobilis seu moventis [annunciat]; sonorus aequalitatem moventis, aut motionis: Consonans consimilitudinem motionis cum innata motione spiritus: dissonans, discrepantiam; tollit enim spiritum à sui motus symmetria. Quapropter non rectè Musici consonantias omnes in Mundo esse eas, quae in nostra Musica habentur, qualis est inter primam & tertiam, vel septimam, vel octavam graduationem vocis. Asinis enim & serpentibus, & leonibus aliae sunt consonantiae, quia aliter temperatùm habent spiritum: immò in genere hominum alia nationum aliarum alia est Musica; Hispana enim sapit asperum, Gallicana blandum, Italica medium tenet locum, Turcica luctuosum quid refert, Scytica obstreperum, & dissonans. Similiter & hominibus ejusdem nationis alia aliis placet melodia pro cujusque temperie."

explanations of Orpheus' musical effects [1], but of a very different kind from Del Rio's [2]. Orpheus' music could not have attracted all the wild animals, but only those having an affinity to our temperament and spirit, such as nightingales, deer, horses and dolphins—not flies, snakes, eels and octopuses [3]. This relativity of consonance also applies to the harmony of the spheres. Orpheus' lyre cannot have had such power from being tuned to the music of the heavens. Different parts of the heavens are favourable or unfavourable to different things in the terrestrial world; there is therefore no one celestial harmony which is in consonance with all earthly things [4].

In vain do Plato and Pythagoras make up a Music of the World out of our music; indeed they are talking nonsense . . . If there is a harmony in the heavens and in the angels, it is of a different order and has consonances other than the fifth, fourth and octave . . . Our voice is to theirs as an ant's voice is to ours, and the smallest of their voices exceeds the greatest possible thunder-clap, and is not music for us, but quite excessive . . . [5].

Campanella, however, appears to accept the reality of these multiple harmonies of the heavens, and looks forward to the time when, just as the telescope has made perceptible hitherto invisible stars, so some new instrument will make these harmonies audible [6].

---

[1]   V. supra p. 130.

[2]   V. supra p. 183.

[3]   Campanella, *Metaph.*, III, XV, viii, iv, p. 193: "possibile non est, ut Orphei musica traxerit omnes feras, sed illas tantum, quae nostro temperamento sunt affines, ut carduos, luscinios, cervos, equos, delphinos: & hujusmodi: non autem muscas, colubros, & anguillas, & polypos."

[4]   Campanella, *Metaph.*, loc. cit.: "Ratio autem illa, quoniam Coelum harmonicè movetur, & omnia subsunt Coelo: igitur & Orphei ad Coeli modulamen concinnatae lyrae: vanissima est. Omnes enim res habent proprias à Coelo formationes & dotes, quibus aliae Coeli partes favent, aliae obsunt. Igitur non potest inveniri harmonia omnibus inferioribus consona, & perceptibilis simul. Nec vocalis (inquam) harmonia, neque realis."

[5]   Campanella, *Poetica*, pp. 229-230: "Frustra Plato, Pythagoras ex nostra musica mundi musicam componunt: delirant quidem . . . Si ergo est harmonia in coelo et in angelis, alterius est rationis et alias habet consonantias, quam diapente et diatesseron et diapason. Utrum autem analogas istis alibi dictum est [e.i. passage just quoted from *Metaph.*]. Item vox nostra illis est sicut nobis vox formicae, et vox ipsorum minima excedit omne permagnum tonitruum, neque nobis est musica, sed excedens valde . . ."

[6]   Campanella, *Astr.*, VII, iii, p. 11.

Campanella is interested in the effects of sound not only on the human and animal spirit, but also on the air. An instance of this is to be found in his directions for dealing with a plague-infected city; these also show that, having abandoned the mathematical basis of consonance, he no longer could make any absolute distinction between musical sound and noise. After normal instructions about burning infected clothing, purifying wells, and so forth, we come to this [1]:

Bells, incrusted with aromatic fluids and incense, should be rung seven times a day; and three times a day, at stated times, men, women and children are to come out on the roof-tops, and, when the signal is given, shout at the top of their voices: Have mercy upon us, O God, and send us help against the devils, Thy enemies. For thus the air will be purged and thinned, and these religious words will inspire confidence and drive out the diabolic powers in the air ... The noise of cannon and brass vases being struck will also help, if produced at the same time as the shouting.

Campanella's light-hearted dismissal of the mathematical basis of musical consonance indicates that, unlike Ficino, he knew very little about the theory of music—perhaps Mersenne was right when he said that Campanella did not even know what an octave was [2]. Like most of his thought, Campanella's views on music are original and interesting, but lacking in any empirical foundation and, in the last analysis, silly.

Music and musical effects conceived from this point of view could evidently not play an important part in astrological magic. The identity of proportion between musical sound and the heavens is explicitly denied, and with this denial disappears the possibility of using sympathetic vibration, of attuning the move-

---

[1] Campanella, *Medic.*, VI, ii, i, v, p. 326: "campanae fluoribus thuris, & aromatum incrustatę, semper sonent septies in die, & homines super tecta, & pueri, & mulieres statutis horis egredientes, dato signo simul conclament altissimis vocibus. *Misericordia, ô Deus, tua super nos, & auxilium contra diabolos hostes tuos*: sic enim purgatur, & attenuatur aër, & vocibus religiosis animi captent fiduciam, & potestates aëreae diabolicae depelluntur ... Confert etiam rumor bombardarum, & archibugiorum, & percussorum vasorum aeneorum. Quae omnia simul cum vociferatione fiant ter in die."

[2] Mersenne, letter to Peiresc of 1635, cited by Blanchet, op. cit., p. 261.

ments of our spirit to those of a planet. The effects of music are
no longer delicately shaded states of emotion, produced by the
precise and universally valid use of consonances, intervals and
modes, but are broad classes of mainly physical reactions produced
by high or low music or noises that, for the same effect, must
vary with time, place and individual; and the proper use of these
sounds could only be discovered by Baconian experiments. In
Campanella's magic, then, music could do no more than, very
broadly and uncertainly, put one in a suitable "spiritual" and
physical state to receive a planetary influence, and perhaps purify
the air, as in the public magical operation against the plague,
just described. The effects of this music would be far less exact
and powerful than those of the seven lights, which precisely
imitate the heavens and their influences. For invoking demons
or angels music would be of still less use; for their spiritual
bodies are of a different nature from ours and our music would
have no effect at all on them. All these remarks also apply to the
metre of verse [1].

Of what use might words be in Campanella's magic? Campanella held a "natural" theory of language, such as provides the
usual basis for the magical use of words (*vis verborum* B). But
his theory is of a more rational kind than that of most magicians.
It rests on the assumption, not that words receive their connexion
with things and hence their power over them from the divinely
inspired naming carried out by Adam, but that words are representational or imitative symbols. Words imitate the things they
designate either onomatapoeically:

from the sound Tup. Tup. which is made by one piece of wood
striking another the Greeks have the verb typto, and we in the vernacul-
ar Batto [2].

or by gestures of the speech-organs—*altum*, for example, means
high because the tongue is raised to the highest point of the palate.

---

[1] Campanella, *Poetica*, pp. 228 seq.
[2] Campanella, *Real. Ph. Ep.*, I, xii, vii, p. 159: "ex sonitu Tup. Tup. quem
lignum efficit alterum percutiendo lignum, Graeci habent verbum Typto, nos vero
vulgariter Batto".

The differences between various languages are due mainly to climatic conditions. The Germans, for example, have constricted spirits owing to the cold of the North, and strike the air frequently to keep warm; in consequence their language has many consonants and few vowels, whereas Italian has the opposite characteristics owing to the warm, relaxing climate [1].

This theory of language, though it is compatible with a belief in the magical power of words, does not necessarily lead to it, and did not, I think, do so in Campanella's case. Although he calls poetry a kind of magic [1], he is thinking of an A use of the power of words. These, since they are for him representational symbols, have a more immediate effect than would purely conventional symbols; but, apart from this, his explanation of the effects of poetry, of the transmission by it of meaning and emotion, is ordinary and rational [1]. Campanella's poetry is, nevertheless, much more closely connected with his magic than is his music. One can use the A power of words, it will be remembered for magical purposes, and it is, I think, probable that Campanella did so—for demonic, not natural magic.

In his *Poetica* he discusses the questions: "whether poems (*carmina*) are effective in the invocation of angels and demons, and for drawing down the moon from the sky". The answers are: no, for the second operation; yes, for the invocations [1]:

An invocation of a demon or angel consists not in the metre of the poem, but in its meaning and emotional content; for to pious men angels appear when invoked, to impious men, devils.

The demons or angels, whose spiritual bodies would remain quite unaffected by human music or poetic metre, would under-

---

[1] Ibid., pp. 159-160.

[1] Campanella, *Poetica*, p. 267: "perfectissima pars vocalis magiae est poëtica"; a poem is an "instrumentum magicum".

[1] Campanella did believe in telepathic communication by means of spirit transmitted in air (*Metaph.*, I, II, v, xi, p. 172, cf. *De Sensu Rerum*, IV, xviii, p. 340); but he does not apply this to the effects of poetry.

[1] Campanella, *Poetica*, pp. 242-3: "Utrum autem carmina valeant ad angelorum et daemonum invocationem et ad lunam de caelo deducendam"; "Invocatio autem daemonis et angeli non in numero carminiis consistit, sed in sensu et affectu: piis enim angeli apparent invocati, impiis diaboli." But the words of the eucharist are effective "ex institutione Dei" (cf. Del Rio, supra p. 181).

stand and be affected by Campanella's poetry, just as any human being might be, since they could understand the representational symbols of which it was composed.

Several differences between Ficino's magic and Campanella's version of it have already been pointed out; I conclude by indicating a few more, of a general kind.

Campanella's astrology was centred on the sun, as Ficino's was; but his eschatalogical obsession gave his magic a different direction. He was not, like Ficino, so much concerned with a positive strengthening and brightening of the spirit by capturing the influences of the sun, and of Jupiter and Venus, as with warding off the pernicious effects of eclipses, comets, and the bad planets, Mars and Saturn. The end of the world was being announced not only by the approach of the sun towards the earth, but also by all sorts of heavenly and earthly anomalies and catastrophes: the Protestant heresies, the Nova Cassiopeiae (1572), the discovery of America, etc [1].. The main purpose of his magic, therefore, was prophylactic; in the sealed room the torches and candles represented an undisturbed, normal celestial world, which was to counteract the effects of the dislocated reality outside.

Another difference is that Campanella's religious and magical aims were both more practical than Ficino's and more public. Ficino's magic, both spiritual and demonic, aimed at subjective effects; practised within a small, aristocratic circle, it was meant to purify and elevate the spirit and soul. Campanella's attention was directed primarily to practical ends of the vastest scope. By his religious writings he hoped to transform Catholicism, and to convert and unite all the religions and nations of the world. By his magic he hoped to gain the power to enforce this conversion, by gaining the confidence and support of those who then possessed this power—the Pope, the King of France or Richelieu. And with Urban VIII he came very near to success.

---

[1] See, e.g., Campanella, *Quod Remin.*, pp. 17 seq.

INDEX

References in italics are to pages containing bibliographical indications.